PUBLIC SECTOR EFFICIENCY MEASUREMENT

*Applications of
Data Envelopment Analysis*

PUBLIC SECTOR EFFICIENCY MEASUREMENT

Applications of
Data Envelopment Analysis

By

J.A. Ganley
Queen Mary and Westfield College
University of London
UK

and

J.S. Cubbin
NERA and Queen Mary and Westfield College
University of London
UK

1992
NORTH-HOLLAND
AMSTERDAM • LONDON • NEW YORK • TOKYO

ELSEVIER SCIENCE PUBLISHERS B.V.
Sara Burgerhartstraat 25
P.O. Box 211, 1000 AE Amsterdam, The Netherlands

Library of Congress Cataloging-in-Publication Data

Ganley, J. A. (Joseph Augustine), 1963–
    Public sector efficiency measurement : applications of data
envelopment analysis / by J.A. Ganley and J.S. Cubbin.
        p.   cm.
    Includes bibliographical references.
    ISBN 0-444-89047-5 (alk. paper)
    1. Government productivity--Measurement. 2. Government
productivity--Great Britain--Measurement. I. Cubbin, John.
II. Title.
JF1525.P67G35 1992
350.1'47--dc20   92-27224
                                                      CIP

ISBN: 0 444 89047 5

This book is printed on acid-free paper.

Printed in The Netherlands

To

May May

PREFACE

The core problem tackled in this book is the measurement of public-sector efficiency with Data Envelopment Analysis (DEA). The academic literature is diverse and thus far there is no critical, book-length exploration of DEA. It is hoped that the book represents a contribution in its own right, injecting some new ideas—not always fully explored— into the literature.

Considerable effort has been invested in making the treatment readable and intuitive. Formalism for its own sake has been avoided. This should broaden the audience to include policy-makers and civil servants working on the control of public expenditure, privatisation, etc. Graduates and advanced undergraduates should also find the book a valuable introduction to the nature and implementation of DEA. These will include students on economics, management science and accounting degrees. Some, notably operational researchers, may find the book provocative in places. This will reflect the differing educational traditions on economics and management science faculties. In addition, however, the existing literature has perhaps been over-enthusiastic in its reception of DEA. The fundamental output measurement and variable selection problems are rarely recognised in applied studies. This book acknowledges the limitations these and other problems may bring. We hope this more cautious attitude to DEA will actually encourage its use.

This book has been hard work in the making, with both authors on their own personal frontiers for almost two years trying to complete it! The research originated in 1985/86 at Queen Mary and Westfield College through Maurice Peston's interest in the public sector and our own desire to bring DEA to bear on new and unusual problems like prison productivity. John Cubbin now continues his research at NERA, London. All of the programming results are based on John Cubbin's DEA software which has allowed us to implement some of the latest developments in the field—such as the Banker/Thrall conjecture on multiple most productive scale sizes. The book was written by Joe Ganley drawing on his (1989) Ph.D. thesis. Readers should note that the contents of the book do not necessarily reflect the views of our current or previous employers.

Many "thank-you's" are appropriate. At QMW, Dick Allard, Danny Beeton and Maurice Peston all made useful comments at one stage or another. Elsewhere Mick Hudson, Peter Jackson and an anonymous referee made valuable suggestions; while Brian Henry overcame possible organisational difficulties. None of course bear any responsibility for what remains. Financial support was provided by the ESRC and for this we are grateful. The difficult job of typing tables and parts of the manuscript was expertly accomplished by Karen Hunt, Sarah Phillips, Lisa McDonald and Sarah Friend. The greatest burden was shouldered by Kim Pompilii who, in the context of many other demands, set the book to camera-ready standards in Ventura. We are both extremely grateful to Kim for her unstinting generosity during this time. Last, but not least, Joe Ganley must thank his family, particularly his wife May May to whom the book is dedicated, for enduring his long absences and soulless appearance over the past year.

CONTENTS

LIST OF TABLES

LIST OF FIGURES

CHAPTER 1

INTRODUCTION AND OVERVIEW

1.1. Motivation: Why DEA?

This book investigates the measurement of public-sector efficiency using the Farrell frontier methodology—or Data Envelopment Analysis (DEA) as it is now more commonly known. It is the first comprehensive study of public-sector efficiency in the UK using the frontier methodology. Despite special emphasis on the difficulties encountered in the public sector, the analysis remains of relevance to productivity measurement more generally. Applications of DEA in the private sector, to banking services for example, are becoming increasingly familiar (see Field (1990), Frain (1990) and Vassiloglou and Giokas (1990)). In what follows, section 1.1 outlines the criteria which motivate the use of a frontier approach and DEA in particular. The discussion is deliberately brief to avoid repetition of material covered in depth in later Chapters. Section 1.2 provides a concise overview of the book, guiding the reader through, Chapter by Chapter.

For some time, the Farrell approach was largely ignored in the mainstream economics literature because it imposed restrictive scale and disposability assumptions on the production technology. Modern developments are now forcing a reassessment. More flexible scale and disposability assumptions are possible, incorporating a broader range of more realistic technologies.

Nonetheless, DEA is only one of several approaches to frontier estimation. Each of these is superior to a least squares approach and is consistent with the definition of the production or cost function as a boundary function (cf Dmitruk and Koshevoy (1991), Russell (1989)). Several studies have sought to compare the various frontier methodologies.[1] Ferrier and Lovell (1990) concluded that DEA and stochastic frontier estimates "are in substantial agreement on several important issues". A more recent study, Lovell and Wood (1992), also found broad agreement between econometric and DEA frontiers. This should not, however, obscure the advantages which a Farrell frontier may have over its stochastic counterpart.

Varian (1990), for example, argues that empirical specifications of parametric production functions involve an overly restrictive sense of "significance". A model developed from classical significance tests is not necessarily consistent with an *economically* significant alternative. In practice there is little need to impose a parametric structure on the data when weaker non-parametric assumptions are available. Furthermore, an econometric frontier is based on a single optimisation over the whole data set. The fitted technology that results is an "average" or sample-wide estimate, which may not replicate behaviour at individual decision-making units (DMUs). In employing a series of optimisations, one for each

---

(1) Bjurek *et al* (1990) compare DEA with the less common parametric programming approach.

DMU, DEA provides a better fit to each observation.   As a consequence the revealed technology is a closer estimate of the true, unknown technology underlying the data.

The nature of public sector activity provides additional impetus to the use of DEA. Government departments typically produce many outputs, denominated in non-homogeneous units.   Historically this has resulted in the definition of multiple, single-factor productivity ratios.   *A priori*, there is little guarantee these will give a consistent overview of performance; and in the absence of market prices there is no valuation system to allow their aggregation.   DEA embodies the principle of total-factor productivity and provides a system of weights allowing the reduction of multiple ratios into a scalar overview of performance.   Several studies have shown that the DEA ratio is preferable to traditional single-factor ratios (Ahn *et al* (1989), Charnes *et al* (1989)). Indeed, in embodying all inputs and outputs simultaneously, DEA can be interpreted as a generalisation of traditional ratio analysis.

The need for the application of improved productivity measurement in the public sector appears indisputable.   For decades national accounts statisticians have used input measures (employment and pay, etc) as crude proxies for outcomes (Beeton (1988), Levitt and Joyce (1986)).   Efficiency evaluation breaks down in these circumstances since the data imply constant productivity growth—irrespective of actual performance.   Policy-makers' interest in public outcomes has grown nonetheless.   This reflects the scale of the resources involved and research linking slow private sector productivity growth to public-sector spending (Ford and Poret (1991), Aschauer (1989)).

These considerations have led to new policy initiatives in many countries in the 1980s. In the UK, the Financial Management Initiative has sought to devolve budgets and objectives down the line management chain to achieve greater accountability.   The increased responsibility of line managers obviously creates a need for improved performance assessment.   In principle, this could take any form.   But targets based on best practice have a particular appeal since they are both demanding and observable (at least indirectly).   These can be derived from DEA and may be aggregated to a level appropriate to broader public expenditure control.

In the UK the scope for an annual DEA review of public-sector activities is perhaps enhanced through development of the Agency initiative.   Potentially this scheme involves tens of thousands of staff.   It aims to remove non-policy-making, executive functions from the major spending departments, allowing them to run on an independent, quasi-commercial footing.[1] Further afield, the privatisation of the former Communist economies of eastern Europe offers similar, though substantially greater, opportunities for the application of DEA.   The regular application of DEA by policy-makers could shed some light of the famous Averch-Johnson result that efficiency rises as the degree of government regulation falls—in addition to improving the control of public expenditure.

---

(1)   See *Improving management of government: The Next Steps Agencies, Review 1990.*   Cm 1261, London: HMSO.

Before proceeding further it is worth adding a final word. DEA is not a panacea. While the range of potential applications is large, many weaknesses and ambiguities will become evident in subsequent Chapters. The literature has tended to overlook the fundamental problem of output measurement. This is particularly important in the public sector and to a methodology which lacks formal variable selection criteria. In the implementation of targets DEA does not explain *why* a DMU departs x% from frontier performance. Lacking in behavioural content, and with only peer DMUs as guidance, there is little post-DEA which actually demonstrates *how* targets may be achieved.

1.2. Overview and Plan of the Book

Much of the book is built around the application of DEA to public-sector production. Chapter 2 sets the scene for these results, laying out the underlying theoretical framework in which they can be interpreted. Before introducing DEA explicitly, it takes a look at the problems facing public sector efficiency measurement, particularly the selection of weights in a multi-factor environment. The efficiency measure is developed in terms of the relevant cost or production boundary. DEA is then motivated as a total-factor efficiency ratio since it embraces all inputs and outputs simultaneously. The total-factor interpretation is not recognised in the literature, perhaps because empirical research has tended to focus on *current* costs. There is nothing in principle, however, which excludes inclusion of (appropriately discounted) capital inputs.

Having outlined its total-factor interpretation, Chapter 2 goes on to derive the operational linear programs (L.P.s) from the stylised fractional program. The dual technology is given the usual diagrammatic interpretation as a Farrell isoquant. More general L.P.s, prompted by Banker (1984), are added to allow the discussion of returns to scale. It is not intended to provide a comprehensive survey of the literature and the coverage is limited to those DEA models implemented later in the book. Several excellent survey papers provide a more exhaustive treatment (Seiford and Thrall (1990), Banker *et al* (1989)); some interesting non-standard programs can be found in Petersen (1990) and Bessent *et al* (1988).

DEA is applied to the measurement of educational efficiency in Chapter 3, based on a varying returns program with strong disposability of inputs and outputs. The results in this Chapter, and indeed throughout the book, are defined in terms of input efficiency. This reflects an initial emphasis in UK government efficiency policy and the relatively greater measurability of inputs *vis-à-vis* outputs. Although the literature on educational production is already vast, estimation traditionally uses an econometric approach (cf Hanushek (1986)). Given that the selection of variables is inextricably *ad hoc*, careful justification is provided for the DEA model. Output is defined in terms of exam pass rates. This is satisfactory in as far as the final outputs of the educational process (general cognitive ability, self-esteem, etc) are reflected in intermediate outputs. (Goetz and Debertin (1991) discuss the use of exam scores as a proxy for educational attainment.) Fortunately the new national curriculum in the UK opens up the possibility of standardised testing of pupil cohorts and hence measurement of net, rather than gross, outputs. A range of controllable and non-controllable inputs are also included in the model. The non-controllables are designed to capture the family background of pupils, incorporating the educational impact of family income, occupational status and ethnic origin.   In the interests of replication, the full data set is added in an Appendix.

A theme taken up in Chapter 3 and continued throughout is the information content of the peer group.   Charnes *et al* (1990), among others, have suggested that the number of citations in DEA peer groups can be interpreted as a measure of the "robustness" of best practice.   It is simple to demonstrate that this provides an indicator of the comparability, rather than the intrinsic quality, of best-practice efficiency.

A second case study follows in Chapter 4 using data on UK local prisons.   With the exception of Ganley and Cubbin (1987), the application of DEA to prisons is unique in the literature.   The model underlying the results is chosen to be consistent with the principal objectives of penal policy, namely secure containment and efficient use of resources.   An important distinction is made in the model to reflect the additional costs associated with remand prisoners.   The results suggest that dominance or sub-dominance on a single variable provides little secure evidence on the efficiency status of a DMU.   This may be explained in terms of the encompassing nature of a total-factor comparison, which is essentially a weighted average of performance on *all* variables.   Again for purposes of replication, the full data set is added in an Appendix.

Chapter 4 returns to the evaluation of the peer group.   It is unclear from an inspection of inefficient performance (at Canterbury) in what measure, and indeed in which direction, the target variables might be adjusted to achieve best practice.   This runs counter to the suggestion in the literature that the peer group offers an operational blueprint to improve performance.   Lastly, Chapter 4 explores the writings of Leibenstein on X-efficiency.   It is argued that under certain circumstances, DEA efficiency may be interpreted as a quantitative guide to the scale of X-efficiency. This may be of considerable significance to the X-efficiency hypothesis which, historically, has lacked credibility owing to the absence of formal quantification.   This interpretation of DEA is now beginning to win support in the literature—see Leibenstein and Maital (1992).

Traditional applications of DEA have been to branch-level operations.   Chapter 5 acknowledges that, for funding purposes at least, branch performance must usually be considered collectively.   This creates a need for aggregate efficiency information which simplifies and generalises branch performance.   Using the cost targets from the prison model, Chapter 5 sums branch-level performance to give an overview of efficiency in the prison spending programme.   The procedure is generally more tractable to input targets defined in homogeneous (monetary) units.   However, as Charnes *et al* (1989) have pointed out, it is possible to "dollarise" targets in non-homogeneous units—notably those for outputs—using unit prices from the linear program.   Potentially this makes all variables additive and tractable to aggregation.

As alternative technology assumptions have become available, empirical applications of DEA have tended to incorporate either constant (CRS), or varying (VRS), returns to scale.   However, why one assumption should be preferred over the other is generally unclear.   Chapter 5 implements both assumptions at the branch and programme levels for the prison model. This allows the separation of technical and scale efficiencies. Identification of scale allows reallocation of the workload among branches—from units with decreasing, to those with increasing, returns. The constant returns technology is therefore valuable in making these additional (scale) adjustments possible. However in general, adjustment to a CRS frontier can be thought of as a long-run target, whilst its VRS counterpart can be regarded as a short-run goal. In this sense, the VRS frontier is nested, or encompassed, by the CRS technology. This suggests, by analogy, a Venn characterisation of efficiency, since full efficiency is built out of a hierarchy of more narrowly-defined components (Fare, Grosskopf and Lovell (1985)). At the lowest level, the set of all purely technical efficiencies is contained in a broader set eliminating both purely technical efficiencies and congestion. This latter set is (fully) technically efficient and contained in a more general set eliminating allocative inefficiencies. Note that one set contains another in the sense that it is more general; this need not imply in some more literal sense that it is larger.

Lastly, Chapter 5 considers the possibility of multiple most productive scale sizes—a concept advanced by Banker and Thrall (BT) (1989). BT suggest there may be an infinity of points of maximal average productivity in a particular facet of the frontier. In principle, these can be identified as bounds on the slopes of line segments in the production frontier. This suggestion is evaluated alongside our own solution to the problem based on identification of the maximum and minimum values of the original Banker (1984) scale indicator.

DEA is essentially an empirical calculus deriving from the implementation of relatively straightforward linear programs. The underlying theoretical justification for its use is the concept of a boundary production function. Coupled with this, however, has been the concept of Pareto efficiency. This has been equated with best practice and underlies the recommendation of DEA targets. Chapter 6 disputes the Pareto interpretation of DEA targets arguing that best practice will usually include welfare inferior states (input-output combinations). This should not be read as an intrinsic rejection of the Pareto Criterion or of best-practice targets. Rather it seeks to make clear that the requirements for Pareto efficiency are much stronger than the literature has generally acknowledged. The DEA target contains greater justification if is restyled as a Pareto Improvement. This admits that best practice is a second best, but nonetheless an outcome which yields a net welfare improvement over existing inefficient production plans.

Chapter 6 goes on to discuss some further difficulties in the DEA-efficiency comparison, including the problems of noise, inflation and quality adjustment. Most of these problems are now beginning to receive some attention in the literature. In a study of the performance of nursing homes, Kleinsorge and Karney (1992) found the inclusion of a quality variable has a significant impact on the numbers of best-practice DMUs (cf Smith *et al* (1991)). Various strategies have been suggested to deal with noise, most promisingly in the work of Sengupta (1990a) and Banker (1988). Others have made more *ad hoc* proposals. Berger and Humphrey (1990), for example, develop a (non-DEA) "thick frontier" approach. The efficiency comparison is of the "efficient" data—approximated by those observations in the lowest cost quartile—and the inefficient data in the highest cost quartile.

Chapter 7 replicates the educational efficiency results from Chapter 3, separating the data set into three recognised administrative clusters. This is prompted by the need to maximise the internal homogeneity of the cross section and hence to ensure that the efficiency comparison is of like-with-like. The results also constitute a form of sensitivity analysis. To date, the literature has examined the impact of altering the size of the variable set (Ahn and Seiford (1990)). However, there has been no investigation of the effects of altering the size of the comparison, for given numbers of variables. In a very large population, successive additions to the cross section allow an investigation of whether efficiencies converge (asymptotically) to some underlying, "structural" or equilibrium level. The results in Chapter 7 indicate that DEA efficiency is potentially highly sensitive to the size of the comparison, the numbers of best practice altering significantly in smaller, less discriminating comparisons. The substantial variations in the clustered results suggest that, in practice, the desirability of a restricted cross section must be traded off against the need to preserve the discriminating power of DEA. In principle, the results offer support for the arguments in Chapter 6 on the distinct definitions of Pareto and DEA efficiency—i.e. DEA best practice may be a welfare inferior form of dominance.

The benefits of a DEA approach to public-sector evaluation are recapitulated in Chapter 8. This is supplemented with a summary of the principal empirical findings on education and prison efficiency. Although DEA has advantages over other evaluation methodologies, Chapter 8 points out four areas where increased research activity is desirable. The problem of stochastic data has generally been treated in an *ad hoc* manner, ignoring the intrinsic weaknesses of a deterministic frontier. Variable selection for the DEA model remains essentially a subjective exercise, which at best is based on expert opinion. It would clearly be appropriate to develop more formal, less disputable, selection criteria. This should increase the credibility of the DEA model and make it more difficult for DMUs to manipulate their efficiency score. The total-factor interpretation of the DEA ratio is not complete without inclusion of capital inputs. These naturally have a multi-period dimension such that it would be appropriate to move towards some more general, dynamic DEA modelling. The normative side of DEA is embodied in the use of the peer group and the setting of targets. A host of problems suggest that in practice these concepts will be of limited use in improving performance. Additional (non-DEA) criteria may be required in the implementation of changes in performance.

The book concludes with an appeal for research on the definition of public outputs. Although this is beyond the scope of DEA as such, the quality of any DEA evaluation will depend in some measure on the veracity of the underlying data.

CHAPTER 2

AN INTRODUCTION TO FRONTIER EFFICIENCY CONCEPTS AND DATA ENVELOPMENT ANALYSIS

2.1. Introduction

Much of subsequent Chapters will be absorbed in the empirical application of Data Envelopment Analysis (DEA) to relative efficiency measurement in the public sector. This Chapter attempts to define the terms and concepts which will be required in the interpretation of these results. It can be considered a "survey" in the sense that it discusses important contributions to the basic Farrell/Charnes and Cooper methodology.

To remain within space constraints, the treatment does not cover the growing number of empirical applications of DEA unless these have had a notable impact on the development of the subject. Nevertheless, frequent reference is made to relevant empirical work in subsequent Chapters. Other survey-type material has also been covered in later Chapters. Some of the general problems encountered in public sector evaluation are discussed in Chapter 3 while Chapter 4 discusses some of the theory of the production correspondence underlying the efficiency comparison. Similarly, Chapter 6 covers material on the meaning of efficiency in DEA.

The discussion in Chapter 2 focuses on the measurement of input efficiency and thereby on the input minimisation dual program. Output efficiency and the output maximisation program have not been used in the empirical work in later Chapters and therefore they are discussed only cursorily in Chapter 2. Note however that the efficiency comparison, the target and the peer group are defined in an analogous way, *mutatis mutandis*, in the output dual.

Chapter 2 is laid out as follows. The next section, 2.2, takes a broad look at the need for weights for efficiency measurement in the public sector. Section 2.3 explores the fundamental notion of a *frontier* efficiency comparison in terms of the production function and of the cost function. Data Envelopment Analysis is introduced explicitly in section 2.4 which covers the basic constant returns program suggested by Farrell (1957) and Charnes, Cooper and Rhodes (1981, 1979, 1978). Revised programs *à la* Banker (1984) permitting more flexible scale assumptions are discussed in section 2.5. Section 2.5 also notes the effects of the disposability assumption on efficiency. Finally, section 2.5 provides a full taxonomy of efficiency scores based on the scale and disposability distinctions.

2.2. The need for weights in the public sector

The bulk of this book is concerned with the application of Data Envelopment Analysis to public sector production in the United Kingdom. This section does not discuss DEA directly. Rather, by way of introduction, it underlines the importance of weights in public productivity measurement.[1] It should be emphasised that weighting problems are not confined exclusively to the public sector.   For example large multi-plant or multi-national organisations operating in the private sector *transfer* rather than sell raw materials and semi-finished outputs between divisions.   Since these transactions do not take place on an open market, their value will have to be imputed (ie weighted) in some manner. Note however that the accounting values chosen in such circumstances may or may not correspond to the true opportunity costs.

For many years national accounts statisticians have avoided the use of measures of public output, preferring instead to use measures of input—usually spending or employment.[2] However, problems in the control of public expenditure have led to a growing emphasis on the output dimensions of public sector production (Hanusch (1982)).

A typical department like Health or Social Security has many functions and will be overseeing scores of distinct policies.   In principle, each policy has an output.   The measurement of these outputs is problematic for they are usually qualitative and lack the physical characteristic of "countability"; that is policy outputs do not usually accrue in discrete, physical lumps.   Service outputs generally involve a "client-change", such as the increments to knowledge and ability deriving from education (Marris (1985)).   These qualitative changes are difficult to quantify in both public and private sector services (see Kendrick (1987), Schroeder, Anderson and Scudder (1986) and Achabal, Heineke and McIntyre (1985), for example).

If service outputs can be defined, it is probable that they will be denominated in non-homogeneous units.   This will make it difficult to form a *summary* picture of departmental performance.   For example, it is not clear how the success of screening for cervical cancer could be satisfactorily added to the results of a programme designed to improve dental hygiene.   The combination of outputs to form *summary* measures of departmental performance is desirable from first principles.   Ruchlin (1977) has noted that output is the result of *all* inputs operating in combination.   A partial factor-ratio like output per head therefore gives a misleading indication of intrinsic labour productivity.

This reflects a lack of appropriate weights.   In general, traded outputs have market prices which can be used to form financial summaries of performance like profitability.   Public programmes such as health and education are currently non-traded.   To summarise the performance of these programmes requires some form of shadow pricing.   In principle, shadow prices can be attached to the various components (ie the outputs and inputs) of a programme to form a summary, total-factor productivity ratio.   There are several potential ways to generate these

(1)   The broader issues confronting output and performance measurement in the public sector are discussed in greater detail in Jackson (1987), Pliatzky (1986), Dunlop (1985), Fisk (1984), Haveman (ed.) (1984, 1982), Hjerppe (1982, 1980) and Carley (1980).

(2)   See *United Kingdom national accounts: Sources and methods.*   Studies in official statistics, no. 37. London: HMSO, 1985; and Levitt and Joyce (1986).

weights—from client or expert opinion of services for example.   An alternative, *non-subjective* approach to weight formation is Data Envelopment Analysis.

DEA can be used to form a summary picture of departmental operations by generating suitable weights on inputs and outputs.   The main prerequisites of this approach are satisfactory input and output measures and a "line" (or branch) structure within the department.   Since DEA is a *relative* efficiency measure, it computes weights through the *comparison* of performance.   That is, its implementation requires a line structure where each branch is producing the same set of outputs from the same set of inputs.   This sort of structure is common in many programmes administered by government departments.   Potential candidates for DEA evaluation include Job Centres (Department of Employment), hospitals (Health), prisons and remand centres (Home Office), welfare benefit offices (Social Security), schools (Education/Environment) and post offices.   Some departments, however, eg the Foreign and Commonwealth Office, do not have an appropriate branch structure for DEA evaluation.

2.3. The nature of a frontier efficiency comparison
This section outlines objections to average efficiency concepts and develops an alternative *frontier* approach.

Historically, production and cost functions have been estimated using Ordinary Least Squares regression (Hammond (1986), Tyler and Lee (1979), Lee and Tyler (1978)). For the purposes of efficiency measurement the resulting *average* function is a misleading indicator of efficient production possibilities in both theory and practice. In practice, an average performance standard will tend to institutionalise inefficiency. This can occur because in reducing what appears to be attainable, average standards act as a disincentive to further improvements in performance.   Furthermore, an average production function is inconsistent with the theoretical notion of a boundary function which reflects maximising behaviour.   Hammond (1986, page 971) for example has noted that "drawing on the theoretical underpinning of the cost curve it can be demonstrated that the classical least squares regression model is inappropriate. Under the assumption that factor prices are parametric, costs are subject to a technically determined lower bound.   Therefore in addressing issues such as the efficient scale for the provision of a public service . . .   it is the lower bound on costs, the cost *frontier*, which is of interest." It follows that an Ordinary Least Squares' cost curve implies a non-maximising assumption such as "satisficing" behaviour.

Nature of a frontier
Frontier performance comparisons flow directly from the definition of the production function itself.   Broadly speaking, production is a process of physical transformation in which inputs are combined to generate output.   The production function should be interpreted as the purely technical relationship which defines efficient transformation possibilities, given the set of feasible techniques (the technology).   Predicted rates of output corresponding to given rates of factor input may then be said to represent solutions to a technical maximisation problem.   Thus Johnston (1960, page 4) notes that "the production function can be stated simply as the relationship describing the *maximum* flow of output per unit of time achievable for any given rates of flow of

input services per unit of time" (emphasis added).   An equivalent interpretation holds for the cost function.   Duality theory establishes the relationship between production and costs.   For given factor prices, the cost function must be interpreted as a frontier function, because it is impossible to achieve costs lower than the minimum input requirements implied by the production frontier.

The word "frontier" is applied in either case because the function sets a bound on the range of possible observations.   Thus, production may take place below the frontier, but at no points above it; analogously, costs can be observed above the cost frontier but not below it.   The amounts by which an organisation lies below its production frontier or the amount by which it lies above its cost frontier, can be regarded as measures of *relative* efficiency.

The first empirical treatment of the production function as a *frontier* is in Farrell (1957) and Farrell and Fieldhouse (1962).   Consequently, frontier efficiency comparisons have become synonymous with "Farrell efficiency measurement".   The Farrell methodology has seen significant revisions in recent years.   Nevertheless this approach remains the foundation of modern frontier analysis.

Farrell began by dichotomising Overall (or Pareto) efficiency (OE) into 2 multiplicative components:

$$OE \equiv TE.AE$$

where *TE* is technical and *AE* is allocative efficiency.   Each of these can be defined in terms of a production frontier as the ratio of potential and actual performance.

Consider for example an organisation consuming two inputs, X_1 and X_2, producing an output y.   It has a production function $y = f(X_1, X_2)$ which Farrell assumed exhibits constant returns to scale.   Accordingly, the production function may be written $1 = f(X_1/y, X_2/y)$ so that the frontier technology can be characterised by the unit isoquant II' in Figure 2.3.1.   In this Figure, an organisation is producing unit-output at point C.   Its technical efficiency *(TE)* is the ratio of potential to actual input consumption.   This is the radial measure OB/OC, which in this case is less than unity.

Figure 2.3.1

Farrell efficiency measurement

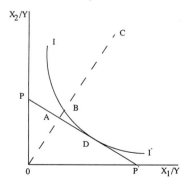

Potential or "maximal" performance is defined along the frontier.   As observed performance worsens, the distance of an observation from the frontier increases so that the technical efficiency ratio falls toward zero.   Likewise, as performance improves, the efficiency ratio rises in value to unity.   In general then:

$$0 \leq TE \leq 1$$

Farrell also included an allocative efficiency ratio within his frontier framework. Like technical efficiency, the allocative component is a radial measure which lies between zero and unity.   At a point such as B in Figure 2.3.1 $AE = OA/OB$ where PP' is the isocost line defined by the ratio of factor prices.   Allocative efficiency is significant in that it emphasises that boundary production *per se* is not sufficient to minimise costs.   Full efficiency (i.e. $OE = 1.0$) requires simultaneous technical and allocative efficiency, *viz.* $AE = TE = 1.0$ which obtains at D in Figure 2.3.1.

To fix ideas, it is useful to show how the technical efficiency ratio in Figure 2.3.1 can be defined directly in terms of the production or cost function.   If inefficiency is possible, the production function may be written as an inequality:

(2.3.1) $y_i \leq f(X_i ; \beta)$

where y_i is observed output at establishment i, and X_i is a vector of inputs and β a vector of parameters which describe the transformation process. $f(.)$ is the production function and has the interpretation of a frontier, or y_{max}.   At inefficient operations, potential output (y_{max}) will exceed observed performance (y_i).   Hence, technical inefficiency implies $(y_i - y_{max})$ is negative.   The difference between observed and potential performance can be treated as a residual in the production function which is equivalent to the technical efficiency ratio.   If these residuals are denoted ε_i then in terms of the production function in (2.3.1), the technical efficiency ratio can be written:

$$\varepsilon_i = y_i / f(X_i; \beta)$$

To preserve the frontier interpretation of $f(.)$ the ε_i are always non-positive.   This ensures that observed output cannot exceed potential and that the distribution of the residuals is one-sided.   The addition of the efficiency residuals "balances" the production function in (2.3.1):

$$y_i = f(X_i; \beta) - \varepsilon_i, \qquad \varepsilon_i \leq 0 \text{ for all } i.$$

The technical efficiency ratios, ε_i, can be estimated econometrically (see e.g. Richmond (1974)).   This requires the choice of a specific *one-sided* distribution for technical efficiency, negative half-normal or negative exponential distributions being the most common assumptions (Aigner, Lovell and Schmidt (1977)).   Unlike conventional OLS residuals, the efficiency distribution *must* be one-sided in order to ensure actual output cannot exceed potential, i.e. that $y_i > y_{max}$ is not possible.   Hence all the efficiency residuals in the production function are non-positive and truncated at zero such that deviations are only possible *below* the production frontier.

Figure 2.3.2
Inefficiency and the production frontier

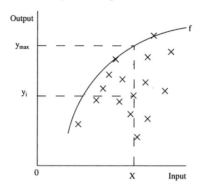

This should be clear from Figure 2.3.2.   Unit i is producing output y_i which for input OX is less than frontier output y_{max}.   The difference between actual and potential output, ε_i, is negative and hence production at unit i is relatively inefficient.   Notice that efficient production implies observed and frontier attainments coincide and that the efficiency residual equals zero.

An analogous interpretation can be given to inefficiency in the cost function (Hammond (1986)).   If excess costs are possible then the cost function may be written as an inequality:

(2.3.2) $c_i \geq g\,(z_i;\,\alpha)$

where c_i represents average cost at establishment i, z_i are determinants of costs and α a vector of parameters. $g(.)$ has a frontier interpretation denoting minimum costs, c_{min}. The efficiency ratio is defined by the residuals, θ_i, in the cost function.   That is:

$$\theta_i = g\,(z_i;\alpha)\,/\,c_i$$

which is the equivalent to the ratio of potential to observed costs.   Where there is inefficiency, costs are greater than potential and the efficiency ratio is less than unity. This means that the efficiency residual, θ_i, is positive.   This should be apparent from Figure 2.3.3 where observed costs at unit i, c_i, are greater than the minimum costs on the appropriate part of the boundary.   Since boundary costs are the minimum feasible, observed costs cannot fall below minimum costs, i.e. $c_i \geq c_{min}$.   This is essential to preserve the frontier interpretation of the cost function and implies that the residuals in the cost function are non-negative:

$$c_i = g\,(z_i;\,\alpha) + \theta_i, \qquad \theta_i \geq 0 \text{ for all } i.$$

The θ_i can be estimated by choosing an explicit distributional form for cost inefficiency and estimating a statistical frontier.   For reasons of statistical tractability, positive half-normal or positive exponential distributions are the most common distributional assumptions in statistical cost studies (see Schmidt (1986)).

Figure 2.3.3
Inefficiency and the cost function

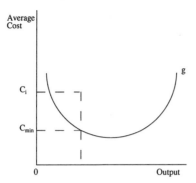

The details of the estimation of efficiency in statistical cost studies will not be pursued here.   Rather, the next section introduces the estimation of frontier efficiency ratios using Data Envelopment Analysis.   DEA does not explicitly identify the efficiency residual.   However, the concept of a ratio comparison of potential and actual performance remains at the heart of the analysis.

2.4. The measurement of efficiency in Data Envelopment Analysis

Introduction
Section 2.3 outlined the nature of frontier efficiency comparisons.   This section examines *estimation* of the frontier using Data Envelopment Analysis.   Initially, it is necessary to distinguish the terminology of alternative frontier methods.   However a full treatment of statistical and other approaches is not included.[1]   Following this, section 2.4 explores the interpretation of DEA as a fractional program.

Before proceeding it is important to notice that the word "program" will be used to describe a mathematical program for optimisation.   On the other hand, the alternative spelling "programme" denotes a government budget on health, education etc.   This distinction holds throughout the book and is especially relevant in Chapter 5.

A second important distinction is the meaning of the term parametric.   This can be used in *three* contexts in frontier estimation:

(1) Non-parametric programming
This is another term for Data Envelopmant Analysis as developed by Farrell (1957) and later Charnes, Cooper and Rhodes (1979, 1978).   DEA is a deterministic linear program used to construct a frontier technology.   It is non-parametric in the sense of Diewert and Parkan (1983, page 131).   That is, it does *not* assume that the underlying technology "belongs to a certain class of functions of a specific functional form which depend on a finite number of parameters, such as the well-known Cobb-Douglas

---

(1)   There are several excellent survey articles which cover alternative frontier procedures: Bauer (1990),
        Lovell and Schmidt (1988), Schmidt (1986), Fare, Grosskopf and Lovell (1985, Chapter 9), Kopp (1981)
        and Forsund, Lovell and Schmidt (1980).

functional form". Note that DEA is also "non-statistical" because it makes no explicit assumption on the probability distribution of "errors" (i.e. the efficiency residuals) in the production function (Sengupta (1987a)).

(2) Parametric programming

Like (1), this approach uses a deterministic linear program to estimate a frontier technology. Its main difference *vis-à-vis* (1) is that the parametric technology is *smooth* while its non-parametric counterpart is piecewise linear. Parametric programs have had a limited number of applications, for example in Forsund and Hjalmarsson (1979), Forsund and Jansen (1977) and Aigner and Chu (1968). A useful exposition of the parametric program is contained in Chapter 9 of Fare, Grosskopf and Lovell (1985).

(3) Parametric statistical estimation

In contrast to both of the programming approaches, statistical techniques may be used to estimate a parametric representation of technology. There are a large number of statistical frontier applications in the literature—see Ferrier and Lovell (1990), Hughes (1988), Dawson and Lingard (1988), Dawson (1987), Huang and Bagi (1984), Bagi and Huang (1983) and Aigner, Amemiya and Poirier (1976), for example. The statistical methodology involves the explicit identification of the underlying functional form *and* of the distribution of technical efficiency. Proponents of the programming approach have argued that estimation of an explicit functional form imposes unwarranted structure on the technology (Sengupta (1987a), Banker and Maindiratta (1986)). Similarly the choice of a distribution for the efficiency residuals is usually arbitrary, guided mainly by its computational tractability. Schmidt and Lin (1984) have shown that statistical efficiency comparisons are not invariant to the choice of distribution. Nevertheless the statistical approach has the advantage that deviations from the frontier can be separated into noise and efficiency components (Jondrow *et al* (1982)). The programming approaches, by contrast, attribute the *whole* of deviations from the frontier to differences in efficiency. Notably, however, some work is now being undertaken to limit the effects of noise in DEA, e.g. Banker (1988). Similarly, Sengupta (1990a,b, 1988, 1987a,c) is exploring ideas originally proposed by Timmer (1971) in the use of chance-constrained programs where the constraints hold probabilistically.

The fractional DEA program

Having distinguished the non-parametric approach from alternative methods, the remainder of section 2.4 is devoted to a more narrowly focused discussion of the program underlying DEA efficiency measurement. It should become clear that the literature on DEA is a collection of programs—both "fractional" and linear. The fractional program is the parent of the linear program and so it must be discussed first. Essentially, the fractional program can be thought of as the conceptual DEA model, while the linear program is that used in actual computation of the efficiency ratio.

Probably the best way to introduce the fractional program is to recall the idea of a total-factor productivity ratio. This is a means of summarising performance by weighting inputs and outputs in a single ratio. Assume that an organisation produces outputs Y_i, $i = 1, \ldots, t$ from inputs X_k, $k = 1, \ldots, m$. Then given a set of appropriate weights $(V_i, i = 1, \ldots, t; W_k = 1, \ldots, m)$ on these variables, it is possible to form the total factor productivity ratio:

(2.4.1)
$$\frac{\sum\limits_{i=1}^{t} V_i Y_i}{\sum\limits_{k=1}^{m} W_k X_k}$$

The numerator of the ratio can be thought of as a "virtual output" since the weights reduce the t output levels into a unique scalar number. Analogously, the denominator is a "virtual input" so that the whole ratio reduces to a scalar measure of total-factor productivity.

In the private sector, market prices may be used as weights on inputs and outputs. However in the non-trading sector, prices on outputs are absent and a total-factor view of efficiency requires an alternative source of weights. Under certain circumstances these can be generated in Data Envelopment Analysis. Specifically, DEA requires that outputs be delivered through a branch system where each branch uses the same set of inputs to produce the same set of outputs. A summary efficiency ratio like (2.4.1) can then be formed for each branch and weights computed for that branch *relative* to performance at other branches.[1]

Consider then the performance of a set of Z departmental branches each using the same set of inputs to produce the same set of outputs. The total-factor efficiency of each branch is the solution to a fractional program. Hence for any branch p, efficiency can be measured as the maximum of the ratio of weighted outputs to weighted inputs subject to constraints reflecting the performance of the other branches. DEA treats the observed inputs (X_k) and outputs (Y_i) in this ratio as constants and chooses values of the input and output weights to maximise the total-factor efficiency of p relative to the performance of its peers. That is:

(2.4.2)
$$\underset{V_i, W_k}{MAX} \frac{\sum\limits_{i=1}^{t} V_i Y_{ip}}{\sum\limits_{k=1}^{m} W_k X_{kp}}$$

subject to Z "less-than-unity" constraints

---

(1)   Charnes, Cooper and Rhodes (1979, 1978) introduced the term "decision-making unit" (or DMU) which is now widely used in the literature. This Chapter generally uses the term branch, but "establishment" and "organisation" are also used to denote a production unit. Terminology aside, the important point for DEA evaluation is that each unit is sufficiently similar to make efficiency comparisons meaningful.

$$0 \le \sum_{i=1}^{t} V_i \, Y_{ic} / \sum_{k=1}^{m} W_k \, X_{kc} \le 1,$$

$$c = 1, \ldots, p, \ldots, Z$$

and $V_i, W_k > 0$, for all i and k.

This formulation of the fractional program is due to Charnes, Cooper and Rhodes (1979, 1978). The program is computed separately for each branch, generating Z sets of optimal weights. The weights in the objective function are chosen to maximise the value of the branch's efficiency ratio subject to the "less-than-unity" constraints. These constraints ensure that the optimal weights for branch p in the objective function do not imply an efficiency score greater than unity either for itself or for any of the other branches.

The efficiency "score" generated by the program is consistent with a frontier interpretation of performance. A score of unity implies that observed and potential performance coincide. In this case a branch is said to be "best-practice". Where observed performance is lower than potential a branch receives less-than-unity efficiency. This implies that its performance is poorer than that of some of its peer organisations and so it is *relatively* inefficient.

The linear DEA program: primal formulation

The fractional program is not used for actual computation of the efficiency scores because it has intractable non-linear and non-convex properties (Charnes, Cooper and Rhodes (1978)). Rather, Charnes and Cooper have advocated the use of a transformation to convert the fractional program into an ordinary linear program. The transformation is quite simple and derives from Charnes and Cooper (1973, 1962). The resulting linear program may be constructed to allow either "output maximisation" or "input minimisation". The former computes the output efficiency ratio of a branch, and the latter its input efficiency ratio. In line with all linear programs, each has two components—a primal and a dual.

The linear program (L.P.) for the pth branch is obtained by setting the denominator in the objective function of the fractional program equal to unity and hence:

(2.4.3) $\qquad \qquad \underset{V_i, W_k}{MAX} \ \sum_{i=1}^{t} V_i \, Y_{ip}$

subject to

$$\sum_{i=1}^{t} V_i \, Y_{ic} \le \sum_{k=1}^{m} W_k \, X_{kc}, \ c = 1, \ldots, p, \ldots, Z$$

$$\sum_{k=1}^{m} W_k X_{kp} = 1$$

and V_i, $W_k > 0$, for all i and k.

The program (2.4.3) is linear.   It constrains the weighted sum of inputs to be unity and maximises the weighted sum of outputs at the pth branch choosing appropriate values of V_i and W_k.   The less-than-unity constraints of the fractional program are embodied in the constraints of the primal L.P. such that the efficiency score cannot exceed unity.

An analogous formulation of the L.P. is obtained by minimising the weighted inputs for branch p, setting its weighted outputs equal to unity, *viz*.:

(2.4.4) $$\underset{W_k, V_i}{MIN} \sum_{k=1}^{m} W_k X_{kp}$$

subject to

$$\sum_{k=1}^{m} W_k X_{kc} \geq \sum_{i=1}^{t} V_i Y_{ic}, \ c = 1,...,p,...,Z$$

$$\sum_{i=1}^{t} V_i Y_{ip} = 1$$

and V_i, $W_k > 0$, for all i and k.

Notice that the input and output weights (W_k and V_i respectively) in the primal are strictly positive when in conventional L.P.s they are non-negative.   The strict positivity requirement on the weights was introduced by Charnes, Cooper and Rhodes (1979) as a correction to their first presentation of the model with non-negative weights in (1978).   Thus Charnes, Cooper and Rhodes (1979) restricted the input and output weights such that:

$$W_k > \varepsilon \ , \quad k = 1,...,m$$

and

$$V_i > \varepsilon \ , \quad i = 1,...,t$$

Where ε is an infinitesimal or non-Archimedean constant usually of the order 10^{-5} or 10^{-6}.   Lewin and Morey (1981) termed the positivity restrictions on the weights "lower-bound constraints".   They were introduced into the primal because under certain circumstances the (1978) model implied unity-efficiency ratings in the fractional program for branches with non-zero slack variables such that further improvements in performance remained feasible.[1]

It is worth pointing out that the need for these positivity requirements cannot be doubted in principle.   However in actual empirical implementations (based on non-integer data) it will usually be the case that inclusion of the infinitesimal makes little significant difference to the results—see Bjurek, Hjalmarsson and Forsund (1990).

The DEA linear program: dual formulation

(2.4.3) and (2.4.4) are the primal linear programs.   Computation of the efficiency score is done on the "DEA-side" of the program (Charnes and Cooper (1984)); that is, computation uses the dual of (2.4.3) or (2.4.4).   The dual of (2.4.3) constructs a piecewise linear approximation to the true frontier by minimising the quantities of the m inputs required to meet stated levels of the t outputs.   That is:

(2.4.3*)
$$\underset{\lambda_c}{MIN}\ h_p - \varepsilon \left(\sum_{k=1}^{m} S_k + \sum_{i=1}^{t} S_i \right)$$

subject to

$$X_{kp} \cdot h_p - S_k = \sum_{c=1}^{z} X_{kc}\, \lambda_c, \ \ k = 1,...,m$$

$$Y_{ip} + S_i = \sum_{c=1}^{z} Y_{ic}\, \lambda_c, \ \ i = 1,...,t$$

and

$$\lambda_c \geq 0, \quad c = 1, \ldots ,p, \ldots, Z \quad \text{(weights on branches)}$$

$$S_k \geq 0, \quad k = 1, \ldots, m \qquad \text{(input slacks)}$$

$$S_i \geq 0, \quad i = 1, \ldots, t \qquad \text{(output slacks)}$$

with h_p unconstrained; and ε is an infinestimal (or non-Archimedean) constant analogous to that used in the primal (Charnes and Cooper (1984)).   Although the dual program is not as tidy as the primal its interpretation remains simple.   The pth branch is relatively efficient if and only if the efficiency ratio, h_p^*, equals unity and the slack variables are all zero.   That is, if and only if:

(2.4.5)
$$h_p^* = 1 \text{ with } S_k^* = S_i^* = 0, \text{ for all } k \text{ and } i$$

---

(1)   The importance of strictly positive weights in the primal problem is discussed at greater length in Boyd and Fare (1984) and Charnes and Cooper (1984).

where the asterisk denotes optimal values of the variables in the dual program. Where the efficiency conditions in (2.4.5) are fulfilled, the branch in question must be operating at the end-point of a negatively-sloped facet of the frontier isoquant. Branches in these circumstances are said to be "dominant" or "best-practice" *vis-à-vis* inefficient producers. Consequently the efficiency conditions (2.4.5) can be thought of as a definition of "best-practice" performance.

Notice that the shadow price interpretation of the choice variables is confined to the primal since the dual calculates weights *(λ_c)* on branches rather than on inputs and outputs. Additionally, the dual weights are non-negative.

In computation, the dual program is more tractable than the primal. In the primal the constraints are indexed on all Z branches. By contrast, in the dual the constraints are indexed on inputs and outputs and sum over branches. The number of inputs and outputs is never likely to exceed the number of branches. Phillips, Ravindran and Solberg (1976) have shown that the computational efficiency of the simplex method falls with increases in the size of the constraint set. Hence the dual program with only *(m + t)* constraints on inputs and outputs is computed in preference to its (equivalent) primal with Z constraints.

For completeness, note that the output maximisation dual of (2.4.4) is:

(2.4.4*)
$$MAX_{\lambda_c} \; f_p + \varepsilon \left(\sum_{k=1}^{m} S_k + \sum_{i=1}^{t} S_i \right)$$

subject to

$$f_p . Y_{ip} + S_i = \sum_{c=1}^{z} \lambda_c \, Y_{ic}, \; i = 1,...,t$$

$$X_{kp} - S_k = \sum_{c=1}^{z} \lambda_c \, X_{kc}, \; k = 1,...,m$$

and

$$\lambda_c \geq 0, \quad c = 1, \ldots, p, \ldots, Z$$

$$S_k \geq 0, \quad k = 1, \ldots, m$$

$$S_i \geq 0, \quad i = 1, \ldots, t$$

with f_p unconstrained.

Again the dual is the program used in the computation of the efficiency ratio, although in this case it determines the output efficiency of a branch p for a given set of inputs.

Diagrammatic interpretation of the dual program

Subject to minor adjustments for returns to scale (which will be discussed in the next section) the dual program (2.4.3*) for input minimisation is that used in the local education authority and prison case studies later in the book.   It is appropriate therefore to offer at this point a diagrammatic interpretation of the dual.

The estimated dual technology is not smooth but constructed out of a series of intersecting linear facets.   Each of these facets represents a constraint in the optimal solution to the dual.   Collectively they intersect to form a convex production set which is closed and bounded from above.   The frontier for efficiency comparisons is the lower convex hull of the possibility set, illustrated in Figure 2.4.1.

Before explaining Figure 2.4.1 it is useful to note the following definition of technical efficiency in terms of which the dual technology can be interpreted:

Input technical efficiency [1]
A branch is technically efficient in its use of inputs if no other branch, or linear combination of branches, is producing equal amounts of outputs for less of at least one input.

This definition is equivalent to the formal efficiency conditions (2.4.5) from the dual; to recap, a branch p is efficient if and only if the efficiency ratio is unity and all of the slack variables are zero:

$$h_p^* = 1$$

and

$$S_k^* = S_i^* = 0, \quad \text{for all } k \text{ and } i.$$

where (*) denotes optimal values of the variables.

Figure 2.4.1

The dual technology

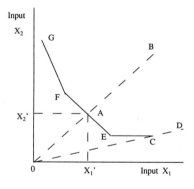

---

(1)   The meaning and definition of efficiency in DEA will be discussed in greater detail in Chapter 6.

Figure 2.4.1 illustrates a hypothetical frontier technology based on 5 branches producing a single output, Y, from 2 inputs, X_1 and X_2. Branches G, F and E, lying on the frontier, are "best-practice"; this implies that no other branch or linear combination of branches can be identified which is producing the same level of output for less of either or both inputs. These branches have unity efficiency ratios and zero slacks in the solution to the dual. Consider for example, the solution of the dual for branch F:

$$h_F^* = 1$$

and the constraints are:

input 1 $\qquad\qquad\qquad X_{1F}.h_F^* - 0 = X_{1F}.\lambda_F^*$

input 2 $\qquad\qquad\qquad X_{2F}.h_F^* - 0 = X_{2F}.\lambda_F^*$

and on output: $\qquad\qquad Y_{1F} + 0 \;\; = Y_{1F}$

The left-hand side of the constraints defines the "target", which in this case is clearly equal to actual performance on the right-hand side of the constraints because best-practice implies $\lambda_F^* = 1$. The peer group drops out of the RHS of the constraints and for an efficient branch is none other than that branch itself since $\lambda_F^* = 1$ and $\lambda_c^* = 0$, $c \neq F$.

Branches B and D are inefficient relative to frontier performance. That is, for the same level of output it is possible to find a branch, or a linear combination of branches, which are using less of at least one of the inputs. Consider branch B, for example, with an efficiency ratio OA/OB which is less than unity. This reflects the fact that a linear combination of branches E and F is producing at least as much output as B with less of X_1 and X_2. The efficiency ratio can be used to suggest a target on the frontier for branch B which will improve its current performance such that it is not dominated by best-practice, *viz.*:

$$(OA/OB).OB = OA$$

In principle, existing consumption of inputs defined at the vector OB can be adjusted by the efficiency scalar to give a target vector OA. The target implies that input consumption at branch B can be cut to X_1' and X_2' in Figure 2.4.1 while maintaining its current level of output. It is widely recommended in the literature (e.g. Bowlin (1987, 1986), Lewin and Morey (1981)) that the attainment of these targets is assisted by examination of peer performance. In terms of Figure 2.4.1 the peer group for branch B is branches E and F. Since these branches are producing at least the same output for less input they are felt to represent examples of better managerial and operational procedures which may be borrowed by the inefficient branch to improve its performance. The peers are defined by those branches that have non-zero weights in the optimal solution in the dual. For unit B the solution is:

$$h_B^* = OA/OB < 1$$

and the constraints are:

input 1 $X_{1B}.h_B^* - 0 = X_{1E}.\lambda_E^* + X_{1F}.\lambda_F^*$

input 2 $X_{2B}.h_B^* - 0 = X_{2E}.\lambda_E^* + X_{2F}.\lambda_F^*$

and on output: $Y_{1B} + 0 \quad = Y_{1E}.\lambda_E^* + Y_{1F}.\lambda_F^*$

Target performance for B, $X_{iB}.h_B^*$, $i = 1,2$, is clearly equal to a linear combination of performance at branches E and F where λ_E^*, $\lambda_F^* > 0$ and the weights on the other branches are all zero: $\lambda_c^* = 0$, $c \neq E,F$.

Notice that there are constraints on inputs *and* outputs in the dual.   The input constraints define a radial (or equi-proportionate) contraction in inputs given by the efficiency ratio, h_p^*, with additional reductions given by non-zero input slack variables, S_k^*, $k = 1,...,m$.   In the input minimisation dual, the output constraints do not include a radial adjustment to outputs and are only of importance in so far as any of the optimal output slacks S_i^*, $i = 1,...,t$, are non-zero.   The solution for branch B has all input and output slacks equal to zero.   However branch D has a non-zero slack on input X_1.   The efficiency ratio for D is OC/OD which defines an initial radial contraction in both inputs.   However at point C, branch E is producing the same output for less of X_1 and the same amount of X_2.   Hence D is not fully efficient until it reduces its consumption of X_1 by the horizontal distance C to E.   This distance is given by a non-zero slack S_1^* in the final solution of the dual for branch D, *viz.*:

$$h_D^* = OC/OD$$

and the input constraints are:

input 1 $X_{1D}.h_D^* - S_1^* = X_{1E}.\lambda_E^*$

input 2 $X_{2D}.h_D^* - 0 = X_{2E}.\lambda_E^*$

and on outputs:

$$Y_{1D} + 0 \quad = Y_{1E}.\lambda_E^*$$

The target for branch D is a radial contraction in both inputs given by h_D^* plus the additional reduction in X_1, given by S_1^*.   Its peer group is branch D alone since its target coincides exactly with performance observed at this best-practice branch. Thus $\lambda_E^* = 1$ and $\lambda_c^* = 0$ for $c \neq E$.

In some circumstances the input minimisation program may also suggest adjustments to output where the optimal values of the output slack variables are non-zero.   These adjustments occur at the equivalent of horizontal or vertical facets of the output surface.   In Figure 2.4.1 the output surface would be a vertical extension of the input space.   However it is only with a minimum of 2 outputs that non-zero output slacks are possible.   Thus consider the output surface in Figure 2.4.2.   Like its input counterpart, it is piecewise linear, each facet reflecting the presence of an output constraint in the dual.   Assume that the solution to the dual for branch A is identical to that given above other than that there are now two constraints on outputs, *viz.*:

Figure 2.4.2
Output surface in the dual program

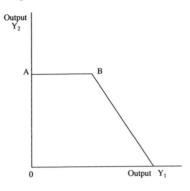

output 1 $Y_{1A} + S_1^* = Y_{1B}.\lambda_B^*$

output 2 $Y_{2A} + 0 = Y_{2B}.\lambda_B^*$

The slack value on output Y_2 is zero, i.e. $S_2^* = 0$. But that on Y_1 is positive, $S_1^* > 0$. This can be identified in terms of the output frontier in Figure 2.4.2. Branch A is producing the same amount of Y_2 as branch B but less of Y_1. The slack on Y_1 therefore represents the amount by which A must increase Y_1 to come up to the standards set by B; this is the horizontal distance $AB = S_1^*$.

It is apparent that there are two aspects to the target in the (input minimisation) dual program. The constraints define a radial (= equi-proportionate) reduction in inputs plus any further reductions in inputs suggested by non-zero input slacks. In addition however the presence of non-zero output slacks may require adjustments to outputs.

Throughout this book performance is evaluated using the input minimisation program because it was felt that the output maximisation version is inappropriate. This is because Government efficiency policy in the Financial Management Initiative was initially couched in terms of input rather than output improvements. Furthermore several authors have argued that in the face of output measurement problems in the public sector, evaluation should focus on the measurable aspects of production (Mersha (1989), Fare, Grosskopf and Lovell (1988), Kumbhakar (1988) and Mellander and Ysander (1987)). In practice this has meant efficiency studies have emphasised the input dimensions of efficiency. Sengupta (1987a, b and c) has argued that in education, for example, measurement errors on outputs are larger than on inputs. That is costs in financial terms are more tractable to measurement than increments to knowledge and ability through test scores, etc. Complementary arguments have also been proposed suggesting outputs are in general more prone to stochastic influences than inputs (Sengupta (*ibid.*)).

In many circumstances, outputs are exogenous. Take the example of prisons. Output in terms of prisoner days is not chosen by the prison governor. Rather, it reflects court sentencing policy, statute and the propensity to crime in the population at large. It may therefore be meaningless to suggest that output be raised to increase efficiency because, *inter alia*, this would necessitate a change to a harsher sentencing policy—something quite beyond the control of prison management.   In environments where output is controllable, the same reasoning may apply.   For it is fair to ask how much inefficient producers can reasonably be expected to achieve—at least in the short run. Since simultaneous input and output adjustments may be over-exacting, the targets defined for prisons and for local education authorities in later Chapters are for adjustments to inputs alone.   Additional changes to outputs which might be suggested in the slack variables are ignored.   The targeting criterion adopted is therefore of adjustment to inputs for *given* output.[1]

2.5.   Returns to scale

Section 2.5 examines some recent extensions to the original DEA program of Charnes, Cooper and Rhodes (1979, 1978).   These concern the addition of constraints to the program to permit a greater diversity of scale possiblities in the estimated production surface.[2]

Despite the revival of the programming approach by Charnes and Cooper in the late seventies, most economists continued to use statistical procedures for frontier estimation.   Grosskopf (1986) has argued that this was to be expected because the original Farrell/Charnes-Cooper program made over-restrictive scale (and disposablity) assumptions.   *Viz.*   Forsund *et al* (1980) stated that: "While his [Farrell's] measures are valid for the restrictive technologies he considered, they do not generalise easily to technologies that are not linearly homogenous or to technologies in which strong disposability and strict quasiconvexity are inappropriate".   However subsequent developments, particularly in Banker and Thrall (1989), Fare, Grosskopf and Lovell (1985, 1983), Banker (1984), Banker, Charnes and Cooper (1984) and Banker, Charnes, Cooper and Schinnar (1981), have extended the original Farrell program to allow for a wide range of more general reference technologies.   It is these revisions that are the subject of section 2.5.

The analysis of returns to scale in DEA

It is now appropriate to examine the analysis of scale in DEA.   Early uses of the non-parametric approach were based on a linear program which embodied constant returns to scale and strong disposability—these included Farrell (1957), Seitz (1971, 1970) and the first papers by Charnes, Cooper and Rhodes (1981, 1979, 1978). Many economists viewed these assumptions as over-restrictive so that alternative statistical procedures were generally adopted in place of DEA.   However, more recent work has enabled the relaxation of the constant returns assumption giving the programming approach wider applicability.   At the same time, Rolf Fare and his colleagues have developed programs which permit weak rather than strong disposability of inputs and outputs—see especially Fare, Grosskopf and Lovell (1985, Chapter 2).   These revised programs, with alternative scale and disposability implications, have generated new interest in DEA and have been used extensively in later Chapters.

---

(1)   There is further discussion of the feasibility and implementation of targets in Chapters 4, 5 and 7.
(2)   An extended empirical analysis of scale efficiency based on the approach in Banker (1984) and in Banker and Thrall (1989) will be found in Chapter 5.

The most important revisions to the original Farrell/Charnes-Cooper program can be found in Banker and Thrall (1989), Fare, Grosskopf and Lovell (1985, 1983), Banker (1984), Banker, Charnes and Cooper (1984) and Banker, Charnes, Cooper and Schinnar (1981). It is probably fair to say that the most important name among these is Banker who has made a consistently significant contribution to the development to the subject. Accordingly, the analysis of scale now to be developed broadly follows that in Banker (1984).

Construction of a constant returns to scale (CRS) frontier
As is so often the case, it is easiest to proceed via a stylised example of production. Assume that output is the result of a single input, as in Figure 2.5.1. Marked points in this diagram represent observed input-output combinations. The original Farrell/Charnes-Cooper program constructs a constant returns frontier by identifying that branch which *maximises* the ratio of output to input. This ratio can be interpreted as the maximum average productivity and denotes the scale efficient branch since it is consistent with a position of constant returns to scale (CRS).

Figure 2.5.1
Average productivity and returns to scale

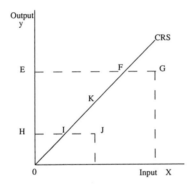

In Figure 2.5.1 branch K (on the frontier) maximises average productivity. A ray drawn from the origin to any of the remaining branches (J or G) would have a lower slope and would not maximise average productivity, i.e. $(Y_K/X_K) > (Y_c/X_c)$, $c \neq K$. A constant returns frontier is therefore an unbounded ray beginning at the origin and passing through a point of maximum average productivity such as at branch K. This is the frontier constructed by Farrell (1957), Charnes, Cooper and Rhodes (1979, 1978) and in the dual programs (2.4.3*) and (2.4.4*) explored earlier in section 2.4.[1]

It is instructive to examine the solution to the CRS dual corresponding to the ray $OCRS$ in Figure 2.5.1. Dropping subscripts on inputs and outputs, the stylised solution to the dual (2.4.3*) for branch K would be:

$$h_K{}^* = 1$$

---

[1]   Where (2.4.3') calculates the input efficiency ratio and (2.4.4') the output efficiency ratio in terms of the constant returns boundary.

and the input and output constaints are:

$$X_K.h_K^* = X_K.\lambda_K^*$$

and

$$Y_K = Y_K.\lambda_K^*$$

where $\lambda_K^* = 1$ and $\lambda_c^* = 0$, $c \neq K$.

Since branch K maximises average productivity it is scale efficient and has a unit weight in the constraints, i.e. $\lambda_K^* = 1$. The remaining branches J and G have lower average productivity ratios. Hence they are dominated by branch K and cannot appear in its peer group. The input-efficiency ratios of these branches are calculated relative to a vector extension of performance at branch K using an assumption of "Ray Unboundness" (Banker, Charnes and Cooper (1984)). This generates the ray *OCRS* in Figure 2.5.1. Since branch K is scale efficient the ray has a constant returns interpretation. Computationally it is constructed by varying the weights on the scale efficient branch (on the RHS of the constraints) in the solution to the dual.

Consider a dual solution for branch G which is consistent with Figure 2.5.1 (where input and output subscripts have been suppressed):

$$h_G^* = EF/EG$$

and the input and output constraints are:

$$X_G.h_G^* = X_K.\lambda_K^*$$

$$Y_G = Y_K.\lambda_K^*$$

where $\lambda_K^* > 1$ and $\lambda_c^* = 0$, for $c \neq K$. That is, the target vector for branch G, $(X_K.\lambda_K^*, Y_K.\lambda_K^*)'$, is a re-scaling (or vector extension) of performance at the dominant branch by the factor λ_K^*.

Next consider the solution for a branch such as J with *lower* inputs and outputs than the scale efficient branch:

$$h_J^* = HI/HJ < 1$$

and the input and output constraints are:

$$X_J.h_J^* = X_K.\lambda_K^*$$

$$Y_J = Y_K.\lambda_K^*$$

where $\lambda_K^* < 1$ and $\lambda_c^* = 0$, for $c \neq K$.

The target vector for branch J on the RHS of the constraints is again a re-scaling of performance at the dominant branch.   However, for input-output levels lower than scale efficient levels the optimal weight $\lambda_K{}^*$ is less than unity.

It is apparent from these examples that by varying the value of the weight(s) on the scale efficient branch(es)—that is by varying $\lambda_K{}^*$ in Figure 2.5.1, it is possible to construct a frontier consistent with a constant returns to scale technology.   Notice that at the origin $\lambda_K{}^* = 0$ and that for higher levels of inputs and outputs $\lambda_K{}^* \rightarrow + \infty$.

Banker (1984) pointed out that a useful "test" for returns to scale can be derived from the CRS dual.   In particular, branches such as J with *lower* inputs and outputs than the reference branch will have a target which is a scaling down of best-practice performance.   Analogously with higher inputs and outputs than at the reference branch, targets are a scaling up of best-practice performance.   That is, the weight on best-practice (e.g. $\lambda_K{}^*$ in Figure 2.5.1) describes the returns to scale:

$$\lambda^*_{bp} < 1 \Rightarrow \text{IRS}\quad(\text{increasing returns to scale})$$

$$\lambda^*_{bp} = 1 \Rightarrow \text{CRS}\quad(\text{constant returns to scale})$$

$$\lambda^*_{bp} > 1 \Rightarrow \text{DRS}\quad(\text{decreasing returns to scale})$$

where bp denotes the scale efficient or best-practice branch.

Notice that in the simple 1 x 1 case in Figure 2.5.1 only one branch is scale efficient. However, for multiple inputs and outputs several branches may be scale efficient on at least one variable (cf Nunamaker (1985)) such that the Banker scale indicator would be the *sum* of the optimal weights on each of those branches:

$$\sum_{c=1}^{z} \lambda^*_c < 1 \Rightarrow \text{IRS}$$

$$\sum_{c=1}^{z} \lambda^*_c = 1 \Rightarrow \text{CRS}$$

and

$$\sum_{c=1}^{z} \lambda^*_c > 1 \Rightarrow \text{DRS}$$

where some of the $\lambda_c{}^* = 0$ for inefficient branches.   The Banker indicator is used to explore the scale characteristics of local prisons and remand centres in Chapter 5.

Construction of a non-constant returns technology

Having explored the construction of the constant returns technology it is now possible to examine the Banker (1984) adjustment to the dual which permits the estimation of technologies which allow returns to scale to vary over the production surface.

It has been shown that the position of the frontier is embodied in the weights $(\lambda_c^*, c = 1,...,Z)$ in the constraints from the dual program. An unbounded CRS ray can be generated by unlimited extension (or contraction) of the optimal weights λ_c^*. It should be clear that if the program restricts the values which the λ_c^* may acquire, this will have a significant effect on the shape and position of the frontier. In particular, the frontier will have a "varying returns to scale" (VRS) interpretation incorporating decreasing, constant and increasing returns if the weights are constrained to sum to unity. The addition of the constraint $\Sigma\lambda_c^* = 1$ immediately excludes construction of the unbounded CRS ray because the unlimited vector extension of scale efficient performance is no longer possible.

A stylised example of a varying returns frontier is contained in Figure 2.5.2. Since increasing and decreasing returns are feasible, the frontier may include scale *inefficient* operations; i.e. branches such as *B* (with Increasing Returns to Scale) and *D* and *E* (with Decreasing Returns to Scale) which nevertheless are technically efficient for *given* scale. The result is a piecewise linear frontier *ABCDE*. The returns to scale vary from facet to facet, each of which represents the solution to a constraint in the dual. For combinations of input and output lower than the scale efficient branch, e.g. along the facet *BC*, there are increasing returns; facets reflecting higher levels of production have decreasing returns to scale. Notice also that the scale efficient branch *(C)* is included in both the VRS and the CRS frontiers and indeed represents the point of intersection of the two.

Figure 2.5.2
The varying returns to scale technology

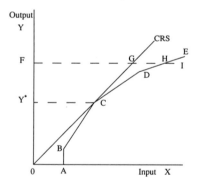

The full revised program of Banker (1984) is required to generate the VRS frontier. The full input minimisation program, permitting locally increasing, constant and decreasing returns to scale is then:

(2.5.1)
$$MIN \underset{\lambda_c}{h_p} - \varepsilon \left(\sum_{k=1}^{m} S_k + \sum_{i=1}^{t} S_i \right)$$

subject to

$$X_{kp}h_p - S_k = \sum_{c=1}^{z} X_{kc}\lambda_c, \ k = 1,...,m$$

$$Y_{ip} + S_i = \sum_{c=1}^{z} Y_{ic} \lambda_c, \ i = 1,...,t$$

$$1 = \sum_{c=1}^{z} \lambda_c$$

and

$$\lambda_c \geq 0, \ c = 1, \dots , p, \dots ,Z \quad \text{(weights on branches)}$$

$$S_k \geq 0, \ k = 1, \dots , m \qquad \text{(input slacks)}$$

$$S_i \geq 0, \ i = 1, \dots , t \qquad \text{(output slacks)}$$

The revised program is identical to that in section 2.4 other than for the addition of the constraint that the weights on branches sum to unity. This new constraint ensures that the frontier is composed of multiple convex linear combinations of best-practice where dominance is now more weakly defined to include regions of increasing and decreasing returns. Indeed any convex linear combinations of observed inputs and outputs is a feasible production plan.

Consider the solution of the dual for branch *I* in Figure 2.5.2 (and suppressing subscripts on inputs and outputs for convenience):

$$h_I^* = FH/FI < 1$$

and the input and output constraints are:

$$X_I.h_I^* = X_D.\lambda_D^* + X_E.\lambda_E^*$$

$$Y_I = Y_D.\lambda_D^* + Y_E.\lambda_E^*$$

and for varying returns to scale:

$$1 = \lambda_D^* + \lambda_E^*$$

(and $\lambda_B^* = \lambda_C^* = \lambda_I^* = 0$.)

Since $(X_D, Y_D)'$ and $(X_E, Y_E)'$ are observed input-output vectors, then by assumption the target vector is also feasible for any values of the weights which sum to unity; hence the target for branch I is a convex combination represented by point H on the facet DE in Figure 2.5.2.   Notice that branch I is neither technically or scale efficient compared to the extrapolation of average productivity from branch C.   If the CRS program were computed for branches D and E the optimal solution would suggest decreasing returns to scale because in each case $\Sigma\lambda_c^* > 1$.

Grosskopf (1986) and Fare, Grosskopf and Njinkeu (1988) have explored the effects on efficiency of altering the definition of the reference technology.   In general, a CRS efficiency comparison gives a poorer picture of performance since an organisation has to be both technically *and* scale efficient to qualify for a unity efficiency ratio.   Under a varying returns technology dominance is weaker in the sense that scale inefficient production may qualify as best-practice if it is technically efficient.   The effects of technological nesting will be fully discussed in Chapter 5.   For the time being, however, it is sufficient to note:

$$TE_{i,crs} \leq TE_{i,vrs};$$

i.e. for the same branch i, technical efficiency under constant returns is lower than under varying returns (other than where the two technologies coincide when the efficiency scores will be equal).   In general then the CRS efficiency can be thought of as a "lower bound" and the VRS as the "upper bound" measure of efficiency.   In some papers, (e.g. Rangan *et al* (1988)), VRS efficiency is termed pure technical efficiency to distinguish it from CRS efficiency which subsumes technical and scale components in performance.

However this does not exhaust the potential array of reference technologies which may be computed using DEA.   In addition to CRS and VRS there is a third non-increasing returns (NIRS) program.   The NIRS boundary is a composite of the CRS and VRS alternatives.   In Figure 2.5.2 it would be $OCDE$ where clearly the facet OC has constant returns, and those facets for output levels above branch C have decreasing returns.   It should be obvious that the inclusion of the constraint $\Sigma\lambda_c \leq 1$ in the dual (in place of $\Sigma\lambda_c = 1$) will be sufficient to generate the NIRS technology.   Hence for efficiency comparisons over the range OC, $\Sigma\lambda_c^* < 1$ in the NIRS program and for similar comparisons with the facets CD and DE $\Sigma\lambda_c^* = 1$.   Implementation of NIRS programs can be found in Jesson, Mayston and Smith (1987) and in Smith and Mayston (1987).   Notice that the NIRS technology could be constructed from the VRS program if an observation consisting entirely of zeroes is included in the data set.

Other uses of the piecewise reference technologies—a short digression

For nearly 20 years there has been a small number of contributions to a literature which seeks to establish whether real production data has been generated by well-behaved production or cost-functions.   In principle, there are circumstances under which it could be proved that the input set is consistent with cost-minimising behaviour.   Afriat (1972) and Hanoch and Rothschild (1972) showed that from the construction of appropriately defined linear programs it is possible to "test" for a behavioural assumption of cost minimisation.   These L.P.s compute bounds on the input set which are essentially identical to the frontier technology constructed using DEA.   More recent work has been done by Banker and Maindiratta (1988), Diewert and Parkan (1983) and also by Varian (1985, 1984) who has constructed L.P.s to test for utility maximisation in consumption data.

Disposability of inputs and outputs

A further important characteristic of the DEA possibility set is "disposability" which can refer to inputs or outputs and be either "weak" or "strong". Quite simply, disposability says that inefficiency is possible so that non-boundary production is possible. This is in contrast to traditional neoclassical analysis of production wherein all the relevant first and second order conditions are fulfilled ensuring frontier attainments.

Formally speaking, disposability can be defined in the manner of Banker, Charnes and Cooper (1984) who use the alternative term "Inefficiency Postulate". That is, given a production possibility set P:

(a) Disposability of inputs obtains if for $(X,Y) \varepsilon P$ and $X' \geq X$ then $(X',Y) \varepsilon P$;

and

(b) Disposability of outputs obtains if for $(X,Y) \varepsilon P$ and $Y' \leq Y$ then $(X,Y') \varepsilon P$.

That is, if a given input (output) vector is contained in P then a larger (smaller) input (output) vector is also contained in P. If the initial vector $(X,Y) \varepsilon P$ can be thought of as a frontier vector then this definition clearly permits inefficiency in the form of excess inputs or insufficient output. If the observed input-output combinations (X_c,Y_c), $c = 1,...,5$ for a set of five branches are feasible then so in principle are:

$$(X_1 + \rho_1 \; X_2 + \rho_2 \; ... \; X_5 + \rho_5 \; Y_1 - \sigma_1 \; Y_2 - \sigma_2 \; ... \; Y_5 - \sigma_5)'$$

where the quantities $\rho_c, \sigma_c \geq 0$, for all c. It follows that the whole of the feasible production set is generated by the twin assumptions of convexity and disposability. In Figure 2.5.2 (above) the vertical facet AB is feasible because there is output disposability, i.e. output lower than that produced at branch B is feasible since $Y_B - \sigma_B$ for $\sigma_B > 0$ is also feasible.

Disposability can be thought of in terms of marginal productivity. In particular, disposability of inputs is "strong" (or "free") if marginal productivity can be equal to zero. Figure 2.5.3 illustrates 2 stylised piecewise isoquants computed using DEA. The frontier $ABCD$ is said to exhibit strong disposability since marginal productivity remains non-negative throughout its length. Along the negatively-sloped facet BC both inputs have positive marginal products. However along horizontal or vertical facets e.g. AB or CD marginal productivity of the relevant input is zero. In a traditional neoclassical environment facets such as AB or CD are excluded by the ridge lines which demarcate positive from non-positive marginal productivity. However the disposability assumption permits extension of the isoquant to form horizontal or vertical facets.

Negative marginal productivity is called weak disposability or congestion (see Fare and Grosskopf (1983a)). It describes circumstances in which input levels are being

Figure 2.5.3
Weak & strong disposability of inputs

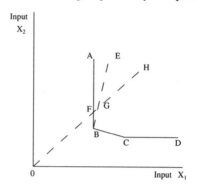

increased and output is actually falling.   Thus the technology *EBCD* is said to exhibit weak disposability since in at least one facet (*EB* in this case) marginal productivity is negative.

The disposability assumption is important because it will affect the magnitude of the efficiency score.   For production at *H* in Figure 2.5.3 the technical efficiency ratio *(WTE)* for the weakly disposable technology is:

$$WTE = OG/OH;$$

its strongly disposable counterpart being:

$$STE = OF/OH$$

where in general (Grosskopf (1986)):

$$WTE \geq STE.$$

Clearly, the efficiency score depends on the disposability assumption and in general efficiency under a weakly disposable technology will be higher.   The same holds for disposability of outputs and is illustrated in Figure 2.5.4.

The weakly disposable technology is *ABCE*.   For production at a point such as *G* the output efficiency ratio is *OG/OH*.   The strongly disposable technology, *ABCD*, defines a lower efficiency ratio *OG/OJ*.   The same efficiency relationship as under input disposability is evident.   Hence, a weakly disposable output frontier defines a higher efficiency score than its strongly disposable counterpart.

Further discussion of the effects of disposability is beyond the scope of this Chapter, but see Fare, Grosskopf and Lovell (1987) and Fare and Grosskopf (1983b).   It is important to make clear, however, that *all* of the estimated technologies reported in this book exhibit *strong* disposal of inputs and outputs.

Figure 2.5.4
Weak & strong disposability of outputs

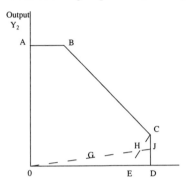

A final taxonomy of efficiency scores based on scale and disposability distinctions

Having discussed both scale and disposability it is worth summarising their combined effect on the efficiency score. Such a taxonomy was first presented in Grossskopf (1986).[1]

Recall Figure 2.5.2 which combined CRS and VRS technologies. It should be immediately obvious that the CRS technology dominates the varying returns technology. That is, for given levels of inefficient performance the CRS technology defines a *lower* efficiency score. The technical efficiency of unit *I* under VRS is *(FH/FI)* while the CRS efficiency score is *(FG/FI)* where the distance $d(F,G) < d(F,H)$; d being the distance function. In general then the following relationship holds between the two technologies:

$$TE_{i,crs} \leq TE_{i,vrs}$$

TE_i denoting the technical efficiency of the same branch i.

The non-increasing returns (NIRS) technology may also be included in the taxonomy by noting that *above* scale-efficient output:

$$TE_{i,nirs} = TE_{i,vrs}$$

and below scale-efficient output:

$$TE_{i,nirs} = TE_{i,crs}.$$

In Figure 2.5.2 this means that for outputs above Y^* the NIRS technology overlaps the VRS technology along facets *CD* and *DE*; while below Y^* the NIRS technology coincides with the CRS ray over the distance *OC*.

---

(1) Chapter 5 makes use of the Grosskopf taxonomy in interpreting the differences between prison efficiency under alternative CRS and VRS technologies.

In general this implies that the 3 possible DEA reference technologies, CRS, VRS and NIRS, have efficiency scores which can be ordered:

$$TE_{i,crs} \leq TE_{i,nirs} \leq TE_{i,vrs}$$

Other things equal, the VRS technology gives the highest efficiency score while its CRS counterpart gives the most exacting measure of performance.

The efficiency score can be further classified if the disposability assumption is made explicit.   It was noted earlier that a strongly disposable technology dominates the weakly disposable alternative in at least one facet and so the efficiency scores have the relationship:

$$STE_i \leq WTE_i$$

S denoting the strong and W the weak disposal technical efficiency for branch i.

Grosskopf (1986) noted that a full taxonomy   of technical efficiency scores incorporating scale and disposability assumptions is, using familiar notation:

(2.5.2a) $$TE_{vrs,w} \geq TE_{nirs,w} \geq TE_{crs,w}$$

and
(2.5.2b) $$TE_{vrs,s} \geq TE_{nirs,s} \geq TE_{crs,s}$$

where

$$(2.5.2a) \geq (2.5.2b)$$

For given performance the highest feasible efficiency score in DEA would result from a varying returns technology with a weak disposability of inputs and outputs, i.e. $TE_{vrs,w}$.   Analogously the lowest efficiency score in this context would be defined by $TE_{crs,s}$; that is, a constant returns technology with strong disposability of inputs and outputs.   The relationships between other possibilities for the efficiency score follow trivially from the discussion of scale and disposability.   It may simply be added however that dominance among various efficiency scores has been expressed with weak inequalities.   This is because the technologies may overlap in at least one facet and in this region the efficiency scores will be equal.   On other facets however dominance may be strong.

Before closing, it is appropriate to add which of the efficiency scores in the full taxonomy in (2.5.2a and b) apply in later chapters.   Chapters 3 and 7 compute a varying returns technology with strong disposability on a local education authority data set.   Likewise, Chapter 4 uses data on local prisons and remand centres assuming that the reference technology has VRS and strong disposability.   To compare the effects of an alternative reference technology on efficiency levels, Chapter 5 computes a constant returns technology with strong disposability.

CHAPTER 3

TOTAL FACTOR PRODUCTIVITY MEASUREMENT IN ENGLISH LOCAL EDUCATION AUTHORITIES: A NON-PARAMETRIC APPROACH

3.1. Introduction

"There are few practical problems in which the economist has a more direct interest than those relating to the principles [of] the expense of the education of children." (Marshall (1920).)

As much as in the private sector, the public sector decision-maker requires a methodology to identify the efficient set of choices in production. Typically, this choice is to be made without the assistance of market prices for outputs in a multiple input/multiple output environment. In this connection, Chapter 3 presents summary efficiency measures for maintained secondary school education using Data Envelopment Analysis (DEA). The results are a contribution to the educational production function literature which, to date, is econometrically oriented (see e.g. DES (1984, 1983), and Hanushek (1986) for a survey).

DEA uses non-parametric linear programming techniques deriving originally from Farrell (1957). The standard alternative approach to Farrell is parametric, and either deterministic or stochastic, where efficiency is measured relative to a production frontier estimated statistically. In general, the parametric approach to production behaviour[1] has been adopted because of a belief that DEA makes over-restrictive assumptions on the production technology. For example Forsund, Lovell and Schmidt (1980) have argued that "While his [Farrell's] measures are valid for the restrictive technologies he considered, they do not generalise easily to technologies that are not linearly homogenous or to technologies in which strong disposability and strict quasiconvexity are inappropriate." This claim is true of the linear program used in the early empirical DEA literature (e.g. Lewin and Morey (1981)) which typically imposed constant returns to scale and strong disposability of inputs. But subsequent analytical developments, the most important of which are Banker and Thrall (1989), Banker (1984) and Fare, Grosskopf and Lovell (1985), have generalised the linear programming model underlying the non-parametric approach allowing for a wide range of very general reference technologies.

Using the revised DEA program of Banker (1984), this Chapter provides new estimates of productive efficiency in British education. The use of the non-parametric approach has been most common on US data (e.g. Sengupta and Sfeir (1986), Bessent, Bessent, Kennington and Reagan (1984), Bessent and Bessent (1980)). More recent applications of DEA to UK education data using non-increasing returns (NIRS) programs can be found in Jesson and Mayston (1989) and Smith and Mayston (1987). Chapter 3 builds on this work using the full varying returns (VRS) program suggested

---

(1)   See examples in Kopp and Diewert (1982), Berndt and Khaled (1979), Schmidt and Lovell (1979).

by Banker (1984) to provide an illustrative set of performance statistics for public sector evaluation. It should be noted that the treatment in this Chapter is introductory, especially in reference to the Pareto interpretation of DEA and in the role of the peer group. These topics will be dealt with more critically and at greater length in later Chapters—see Chapters 4 and 7 on the peer group and Chapter 6 on Pareto efficiency in DEA.

In outline Chapter 3 develops as follows. Section 3.2 summarises the main difficulties encountered in attempting to measure productivity in the public sector. It recapitulates on the various alternatives which are available and redefines the basic fractional model of Data Envelopment Analysis. The bulk of the Chapter is contained in section 3.3 which develops a model of educational production in the local education authority (LEA). Technical efficiency measures are reported for all 96 English LEAs. Section 3.4 investigates a suggestion in Smith and Mayston (1987) that the number of citations for best-practice can be interpreted as a form of robustness statistic. Some conclusions are drawn together in section 3.5. In the interests of replication the data set is included in an Appendix.

3.2. Measurement in the public sector

Production in the public sector is difficult to evaluate, both in terms of its simple level and its efficiency. A large spending department or programme will typically produce multiple outputs. It is very often the case that these will be qualitative and will not have the physical characteristic of "countability". That is, unlike the production of palpable outputs such as motor cars, it may not be possible to observe distinct units of output in many public programmes. Service outputs in general typically involve an alteration in human abilities or satisfaction—a "client-change", like increments to knowledge or changes in appearance which are difficult to measure meaningfully on ordinary cardinal number scales (Jarratt (1985), Marris (1985)).

Where sensible measures of output can be defined, these will most probably be denominated in non-homogenous units. The combination of outputs for aggregate indicators then requires the selection of weights. Private sector organisations will use prices observed in product markets to calculate measures such as total revenue. In addition, through their access to the stock market, private organisations are endowed with capital market indicators of performance like the share price. Non-traded public production therefore precludes access to two of the most common sources of performance indicator.

The lack of market-price weights leaves a number of possibilities for the choice of weights to calculate aggregate indicators:

1. expert opinion;
2. client opinion;
3. ordinary least squares regression analysis;
4. econometric frontier analysis;
5. linear programming/data envelopment analysis.

(1) through (5) represent different methodologies for choosing a valuation system for non-marketed outputs. In some circumstances, the subjective weights of experts (such as policymakers and practitioners) or of clients themselves should be chosen (Macrae (1985)). However it is very often the case that policymakers are unwilling or unable to reveal policy-output priorities (Smith and Mayston (1987)). Systematic and robust surveys of client opinion on the level, quality and distribution of public output are not readily available in the UK context. For example, in an investigation of competitive tendering by local authorities, Ganley and Grahl (1988) found that indicators of service quality such as complaints were monitored irregularly and with questionable accuracy.

In the absence of client or expert weights, the modeller or decision-maker may attempt to specify an *a priori* model of the relevant production process and choose an appropriate estimator of its technological coefficients.

Ordinary Least Squares (OLS) regression analysis is simple to implement on a variety of software such as TSP or LIMDEP and is frequently used in the education evaluation literature (e.g. DES (1984, 1983)). Proponents of the programming approach like Banker and Maindiratta (1986) have argued that in choosing a functional form (e.g. Cobb-Douglas, C.E.S., translog, etc.) strong *a priori* assumptions are imposed on the production technology. Moreover, the average production function which results from OLS is not a boundary function. Therefore it is inconsistent with the economic theory of production, which is an important weakness when making efficiency comparisons. Forsund and Hjalmarsson (1979) argued that "estimates of the best-practice *frontier* . . . [are] a natural reference or basis for efficiency measures" (emphasis added). That is, Ordinary Least Squares is an inappropriate basis for efficiency comparisons because the *average* production function sets a performance norm which tends to institutionalise inefficiency (Hammond (1986)).

In recognition of the defects of OLS, a group of US econometricians, namely Dennis Aigner, Knox Lovell and Peter Schmidt, began the development of true *frontier* comparisons, precursors of which can be found in Richmond (1974) and Aigner and Chu (1968). Early work relied on the existence of one-sided residuals in the production or cost function which could be treated as measures of technical efficiency. However these early models were, like DEA, determinstic and did not permit conventional hypothesis testing for variable selection. Later models were able to account for noise by the incorporation of a composite residual. This had two parts: A one-sided residual to measure efficiency and a conventional symmetrical residual to account for noise (see Aigner, Lovell and Schmidt (1977) and Meeusen and Broek (1977)). Unfortunately, the composite residual confounded noise and efficiency because there was no known procedure to separate its noise and efficiency components *ex post*. Subsequently however Jondrow *et al* (1982) devised a transformation to extract the efficiency component of the composite residual. The transformation decomposes the residual into a symmetrical (normal) component and a one-sided efficiency component. Jondrow *et al* derive explicit formulae for the decomposition in the case of half-normal and exponential distributions. This represents a significant step forward for the econometric approach since it is able to measure efficiency and at the same time to account for noise.

Nevertheless important methodological problems remain in econometric efficiency comparisons. Among the most pressing of these is the choice of distribution for the one-sided efficiency residual. A whole host of distributional forms are feasible— half-normal, exponential, gamma and beta being the most commonly used. *A fortiori* the resulting efficiency measures are not invariant to the choice of efficiency distribution. A study of the effects of some alternative assumptions can be found in Schmidt and Lin (1984); while more complete coverage of the econometric approach than space permits here is available in Bauer (1990), Banker (1989), Schmidt (1986), and Forsund, Lovell and Schmidt (1980).

Historically, traditional ratio analysis has been devalued by the partial and equivocal picture of productive performance it can give (Smith (1990), Smith and Mayston (1987), Todd (1985)). Specifically, for a single-output production process $Y = f(X_1,...,X_m)$ there will be (Y/X_k), $k = 1,...,m$ partial factor productivity ratios. For a decision-making unit (DMU) jointly producing t outputs $Y_i = f_i(X_1,...X_m)$ $i = 1,...,t$ there are (Y_i/X_k), that is, $t \times m$, partial factor productivity indicators. Taken as a whole, there are no *a priori* arguments which could guarantee that these will form a *consistent* summary of performance for the DMU.

Note in passing that a DMU may be thought of in microeconomic or macroeconomic terms (Charnes and Cooper (1985)). In particular, efficiency comparisons are meaningful wherever a production function relationship is evident: In an organisation (as in this Chapter) or in an entire economy—witness the many studies on large sectors like manufacturing or agriculture (Fare *et al* (1990), Grabowski *et al* (1990), Dawson (1987), Fare, Grabowski and Grosskopf (1985), Rawlins (1985), Todd (1985) and Burley (1980)).

Building on the work of Farrell (1957), Charnes, Cooper and Rhodes (CCR) (1979, 1978) extended traditional ratio analysis to the case of multiple inputs and multiple outputs. This is the non-parametric approach to efficiency comparisons. CCR postulated a summary productivity ratio which can be written in the form of a fractional program. The total-factor efficiency of a DMU p in a larger cross section of Z units is:

$$(3.2.1) \qquad \underset{V_i, W_k}{MAX} \quad \frac{\sum_{i=1}^{t} V_i\, Y_{ip}}{\sum_{k=1}^{m} W_k\, X_{kp}}$$

subject to Z "less-than-unity" constraints

$$0 \leq \sum_{i=1}^{t} V_i\, Y_{ic} \Big/ \sum_{k=1}^{m} W_k\, X_{kc} \leq 1,$$
$$c = 1, \ldots, p, \ldots, Z$$

and $V_i,\ W_k > 0$, for all i and k.

Data Envelopment Analysis (DEA) treats the observed inputs *(X_k)* and outputs *(Y_i)* in this ratio as constants and chooses optimal values of the variable weights to maximise the efficiency of DMU *p* relative to the performance of the others in the cross section. The optimal weights chosen for each DMU therefore represent a value-system which provides the most optimistic possible rating of that DMU's performance relative to peer organisations (Nunamaker (1985), Lewin and Morey (1981)).

For a cross section of Z DMUs, DEA generates Z sets of weights such that the ratio in (3.2.1) collapses into a summary, scalar measure of productive efficiency for each DMU. The constraints in the program ensure that the efficiency index has an intuitive interpretation in the closed interval [0,1]. If the index is unity, a DMU is relatively efficient or best-practice. A value less than unity indicates a DMU is inefficient relative to peer organisations.

The DEA ratio in (3.2.1) is tractable given suitable measures of outputs and inputs. These themselves will depend to some extent on correct specification of the underlying production process. In the case of econometric boundary estimates like Richmond (1974) and of traditional ratio analysis (as in Packer (1983)), there is no test of significance of the resulting efficiency estimates. This is also true of the variable selection in the DEA ratio in (3.2.1).

Nonetheless, given suitable output measures, the non-parametric approach is commendable. In a great many situations, outcomes will be politically and publicly sensitive. Non-subjective, "data-based" weights generated endogenously by DEA can be substituted where policymakers' own weights are undecided, unrevealed or disputed (Banker and Morey (1989)).[1] Unlike the econometric approach DEA does not impose an arbitrary functional form on the production technology. Rather the technique makes weaker assumptions on the production possibility set. This is important because, as Bowlin (1986) has argued, the functional relationships underlying public production may be unusually complex and difficult to specify. DEA, whilst not imposing functional relationships, interpolates variables into a convex possibility set whose boundary is piecewise linear.

Burley (1980) has indicated in addition that DEA "does not require additive separability of factors in the production function, or the stability of own or cross price elasticities and avoids some statistical estimation problems arising from multicollinearity in *n* factor data". In addition, nearly all econometric efficiency comparisons have been limited to a single output or cost variable (Schmidt (1986)). This is especially inappropriate in a public sector context where programmes and organisations are usually of a very diverse character jointly producing many outputs. Assuming that appropriate measures of inputs and outputs exist, these are readily incorporated into the generalised DEA-efficiency ratio.

In contrast to DEA, traditional ratio methods like historical unit costs do not embody an optimising principle. This criticism also applies to the least squares approach

---

(1) In this respect DEA is clearly more flexible than an index number approach where the weights must be specified *a priori*.

which proceeds *via a single* optimisation across all DMUs, which amounts to averaging across all observations (Bowlin (1987)). An interesting study of efficiency in North Carolina hospitals by Banker, Conrad and Strauss (1986) has confronted non-parametric DEA estimates with a translog version of the production function. The translog results suggested that constant returns prevailed in the hospital sample, whereas the DEA procedure indicated that both increasing and decreasing returns to scale may be observed in different segments of the production correspondence, in turn suggesting that the translog model may be "averaging" diametrically opposed behaviour. In employing a series of optimisations, one for each DMU, DEA is consistent with orthodox neoclassical theory. Charnes and Cooper (1985) argue that, as a consequence, DEA provides a better fit to each observation and a better basis for identifying and estimating the sources of inefficiency in production.

3.3.   The efficiency of educational production in English local education authorities

The DEA extension to traditional ratio analysis outlined in section 3.2 is now developed in the context of cross-section data on the 96 English local education authorities (LEAs). The results are presented as a set of indicative public sector statistics which may be of value in informing efficiency policy.

Standard references containing educational performance data give an extremely weak and equivocal indication of LEA efficiency. The annual public expenditure White Paper, for example, contains aggregate partial-factor indicators such as the pupil/teacher ratio (PTR) and simple measures of pupil throughput.[1] The PTR is especially misleading as a measure of *contact* between children and staff because it is calculated on the total number of teachers employed, whether in schools, on secondment, or on training courses, etc. The resulting figures are not a measure of pupil/teacher ratios actually in effect in schools—and yet the PTR is probably the most widely quoted educational performance statistic. Other sources contain a confusing range of indicators. Audit Commission (1986a), for example, suggests about 60 indicators for secondary education but assigns no weights to these nor suggests any other means to forming an overall picture of schools' performance.

Specification of the model

The empirical model of LEA production developed in this Chapter contains three outcome variables and five input variables. Of the latter, four are socio-economic data which are uncontrollable from the LEA's point of view. It is very widely recognised that attainment at school reflects both school and non-school inputs (Armitage and Sabot (1987), DES (1984,1983), Perl (1973), Duncan, Featherman and Duncan (1972)).

The definitions of these variables are contained in Table 3.3.1. Each variable has been chosen to reflect important characteristics of educational production as indicated in government policy and the literature more generally. A public expenditure White Paper stated (in a manner very similar to its predecessors): "The Government's

---

(1)   See Chapter 3.12, Department of Education and Science, *The Government's Expenditure Plans*, Cm 56. London: HMSO.

principal aim for schools continues to be to improve standards of achievement for all pupils across the range of all school activities, securing the best possible return from the substantial investment of resources" and also "to improve the management of schools" (Cm 56, page 197).

Table 3.3.1 contains 3 outcome variables, (a) through (c), based on examination results in the former Ordinary-level/Certificate of Secondary Education syllabus from samples of maintained secondary schools.[1]   The results have been averaged from performance over three academic years (1980/81 to 1982/83) in an attempt to reduce the effect of once-off variations due to exceptional cohorts of pupils.   The use of examination results as an indicator of school output is pervasive in the literature—see for example Jesson and Mayston (1989) and Jesson, Mayston and Smith (1987) on UK data and Bessent, Bessent, Kennington and Reagan (1982) and Bessent and Bessent (1980) on US schools.   Their use has the implication that educational efficiency is couched in terms of intermediate rather than final outputs.[2]

Table 3.3.1
Variable set definitions for the LEA model
Outcomes
The percentage of maintained school-leavers in each LEA achieving:
(a)   At least 5 higher grade passes at "O" level/CSE;
(b)   6 or more graded results at "O" level/CSE;
(c)   100 less no graded results at "O" level/CSE.
Inputs
Discretionary:
(d)   Secondary school teaching expenditure per pupil;
Non-discretionary:
The percentage of children:
(e)   Living in households whose head is a non-manual worker, excluding junior non-manual workers and non-manual supervisors;
(f)   100 less percentage of children living in households lacking the exclusive use of one or more of the standard amenities or living in a household at a density of occupation greater than 1.5 persons per room;
(g)   100 less percentage of children born outside the UK, Ireland, USA and the Old Commonwealth or in households whose heads were born outside the UK, Ireland, USA and the Old Commonwealth;
(h)   Persons per hectare.
Notes: The outcome variables (a), (b) and (c) are the averages for the academic years 1980/81, 1981/82 and 1982/83.   (d) is an average of expenditure over the same period expressed in November 1982 prices.
Source: Department of Education and Science (1984).

Outcome (a) reflects an authority's success in the education of higher ability pupils. It is an indicator widely used by Her Majesty's Inspectorate, the Department of Education and Science, and others, e.g.   Gray and Jesson (1987) and Smith and Mayston (1987) in LEA comparisons.   Performance at "Advanced"-level (for 18 year-old pupils) has been excluded because of problems in the interpretation of data. Jesson, Mayston and Smith (1987 pages 263–264) argue that "differences in reported "A"-level pass rates between different authorities may at the moment simply reflect

---

(1)   The two-tier O-level/CSE examination system has recently been replaced by a single examination taken by all 16 year-olds: The General Certificate of Secondary Education (GCSE).
(2)   Bovaird (1981) contains a very useful discussion of the distinction between intermediate and final outputs.

differences in their institutional arrangements, whether sixth forms, tertiary colleges or technical colleges, under which "A"-level teaching takes place, rather than differences in . . . effectiveness". Analogously, outcome (b) is an indicator of the number of pupils reaching an average level of attainment in secondary schools. Finally, outcome (c) has been transformed to be the broadest indicator of *any* form of graded attainment, i.e. the output of *at least* one graded result at the "O"-level/CSE examination.

It is conventional (in the National Accounts for example) to think of output as value added—in this case the increment to knowledge and cognitive ability of the pupil whilst at school. Examination results at "O"-level and CSE measure the *gross* output of the LEA. Historically, the widespread standardised testing of cohorts on initial admission and then departure has not been undertaken in the UK (or overseas). Only pilot studies of this nature can be found, e.g. Mortimore and team (1985) on junior school education. However the reforms initiated by the 1980 Education Act allow for the standardised testing of pupils at different stages of their school career. As these data become available, assessment of value added in schooling may become a reality. This is consistent with the general thrust of the 1980 Act which sought to bring a shift from professional to public accountability in education. A necessity in so doing has been the generation of improved information on which the public (especially the tax payer and parent) can judge performance (Jesson, Mayston and Smith (1987)).

Five inputs have been incorporated into the model. The most commonly used of these in studies of LEA performance (e.g. Mayston and Smith (1987)) is secondary school teaching expenditure per pupil. (Where applicable the extra expenditure implied by the London weighting has been netted off.) It is a variable which is under the authority's control and reflects the quality of LEA management to some degree. Hence it is this variable for which targets may be set to improve performance in relatively inefficient authorities. Notice that to try and eliminate exceptional variations in costs, the teaching spend variable has been averaged over the three academic years 1980/81 to 1982/83.

The remaining input variables incorporated into the model are "non-discretionary"; that is, they reflect background factors in the LEA's catchment area which are beyond its own control. Variables (e), (f) and (g) summarise the family background of pupils and incorporate the educational impact of family income, occupational status and ethnic origin. More specifically, (e) is designed to reflect the numbers of pupils coming from families defined as belonging to higher socio-economic groups. (f) on the other hand is an indicator of children coming from poorer families and (g) from ethnic backgrounds. Variables like (f) and (g) are usually thought to have a negative impact on attainment in schools (Bessent, Bessent, Elam and Long (1984)). Consequently, (f) and (g) have been transformed such that increments to these variables can be thought of as educational benefits. The inversion of background variables such that increases in inputs are directly related to increases in outputs is common in the literature. This procedure has been followed in Smith and Mayston (1987), Charnes, Clark, Cooper and Golany (1985) and is recommended in Golany and Roll (1989). The treatment and effects of background variables in DEA models more generally are discussed in Ray (1988) and Banker and Morey (1986a,b).

One further variable, persons per hectare, is included in the model. This is an indicator of the demographic characteristics of the education authority. In principle, population density may have an influence on both attainment and costs. Up to some point there are likely to be economies of scale derived from locating larger schools in more densely populated areas: This would remove the need, for example, for larger numbers of small schools. Attainments, in addition to costs, may be influenced by population density. Broadly speaking, there should be a (weak) positive relationship between achievement at school and persons per hectare. Children who live further from their school and from their teachers (in remote areas) may be at a relative disadvantage. Other things equal, proximity to school and other children will raise the ability of pupils to interact with each other and with the learning resources provided by the school. Nevertheless it is acknowledged that after a point, high population density may produce negative interactions and lower attainment in children, although the model does not incorporate this effect.

Results on education authority efficiency using DEA

Results on the input efficiency of authorities based on these data are contained in Table 3.3.2. These have been estimated using the revised DEA program of Banker (1984). This program permits returns to scale to vary over the production surface. By contrast, earlier educational applications of DEA on US data imposed constant returns to scale—see for example Bessent, Bessent, Charnes, Cooper and Thorogood (1983) and Charnes, Cooper and Rhodes (1981). Existing applications on British data, *viz.* Jesson, Mayston and Smith (1987) and Smith and Mayston (1987) have used a non-increasing returns (NIRS) program. The approach taken here is more flexible in incorporating varying returns to scale; that is, the production surface may take on increasing, constant and decreasing returns as appropriate.

The input-minimisation version of the DEA program has been adopted in place of its output maximisation counterpart. This reflects an initial emphasis in Government efficiency policy in the UK on the input dimensions of policies and arguments in the literature suggesting that the input side of efficiency is more amenable to scrutiny in the public sector where outputs are often disputed (Mellander and Ysander (1987)). In addition those analyses of LEA performance which already exist have tended to focus on output efficiency (Gray and Jesson (1987) and Jesson, Mayston and Smith (1987)).

Table 3.3.2
Summary measures of LEA productivity with varying returns to scale

	LEA	Input efficiency	Peer group
1.	Barking	0.961	25,44,
3.	Bexley	0.971	50,59,86,95
5.	Bromley	0.911	48,78,95
6.	Croydon	0.939	2,15,50,59
8.	Enfield	0.997	2,7,15,50,59
9.	Haringey	0.992	4,16,48
11.	Havering	0.891	10,26,82,86,96
13.	Hounslow	0.961	2,7,22,50
14.	Kingston	0.965	2,19,48
17.	Redbridge	0.940	2,7,50,59
18.	Richmond	0.853	2,15,19,48,95
20.	Waltham Forest	0.853	7,16,22,48
21.	ILEA	0.788	4,16,48
24.	Dudley	0.979	19,23,50,64,86
27.	Walsall	0.895	28,48,46,50
31.	St Helens	0.929	46,60,54
32.	Sefton	0.953	19,50,64,86
33.	Wirral	0.934	19,50,64,86
34.	Bolton	0.910	48,50,78,95
35.	Bury	0.904	19,50,95
36.	Manchester	0.872	25,30,44,64
37.	Oldham	0.986	44,48
38.	Rochdale	0.834	46,48,78
39.	Salford	0.881	44,46,48
40.	Stockport	0.951	48,78,95
41.	Tameside	0.952	46,48,50
42.	Trafford	0.933	50,78,86,95
43.	Wigan	0.901	46,50,64,86
47.	Sheffield	0.909	26,28,46,50,59
51.	Leeds	0.987	48,50,78,95
53.	Gateshead	0.935	46,48,52
54.	Newcastle-Upon-Tyne	0.856	22,78,86
58.	Avon	0.922	59,78,86,95
63.	Cheshire	0.925	48,78,86,95
67.	Derbyshire	0.994	45,46,50,82,86
68.	Devon	0.958	48,86,92,96
69.	Dorset	0.985	50,59,86,95
70.	Durham	0.982	28,44,48,96
71.	E Sussex	0.958	48,78,86,95
72.	Essex	0.963	48,78,95
73.	Gloucestershire	0.969	61,81,86,95,96
74.	Hampshire	0.963	50,59,86,95
75.	Hereford and Worcester	0.973	48,78,86,90,95
76.	Herfordshire	0.903	2,19,48,95
79.	Kent	0.969	50,78,86,95
80.	Lancashire	0.992	65,82
83.	Norfolk	0.947	48,86
85.	Northamptonshire	0.973	48,86,90,96
87.	Nottinghamshire	0.937	44,46,48,86,96
88.	Oxfordshire	0.999	86,88,95,96
89.	Shropshire	0.929	81,86,90,96
91.	Staffordshire	0.926	44,48,78,86
	Mean inefficiency score	0.936	

Notes:(1)Only inefficient LEAs are included explicitly.
(2)Appendix 3.1 contains a full list of LEA names to assist in the identification of the peer authorities.
Source: Authors' calculations.

Of 96 LEAs in the cross section, 44 have a score of unity and thus are relatively efficient in their management of teaching expenditure. The remainder, 52 in all, are relatively input inefficient to varying degrees attaining an efficiency score less than unity. In the literature it is common practice to calculate the mean efficiency score as a representative level of performance (see e.g. Cubbin, Domberger and Meadowcroft (1987) in a study of local authority refuse collection). The approach taken in reporting results throughout this book is to quote the mean *inefficiency* score; that is, the mean of non-unit efficiencies. The inclusion of best-practice tends to overstate levels of performance since the mean including best-practice is greater than that excluding it. Thus the mean efficiency score including all 96 LEAs is 0.966; excluding best-practice it is 0.936, as in Table 3.3.2. This distinction is important from the point of view of adjusting funding at inefficient authorities. For if mean efficiency is calculated to *include* best-practice the representative target will suggest too small an adjustment in costs at the typical inefficient authority. Only the mean *inefficiency* gives an accurate definition of a representative target. Nevertheless, it is acknowledged that to get the broadest possible view of efficiency, i.e. of performance at *all* LEAs, the mean efficiency based on the *whole* sample may remain appropriate—particularly in the calculation of *total* available savings, rather than those at inefficient authorities alone.

The technical efficiency scores in Table 3.3.2 are defined relative to the standards set by the best-practice LEAs. These LEAs are not necessarily efficient in an absolute sense—rather no LEA belonging to this cross section performs better. In the stylised terms of Figure 3.3.1, these LEAs form the efficient isoquant (or reference technology) against which relatively inefficient production is compared. The DEA efficiency index is thus the ratio of best-practice performance to actual performance.

In Figure 3.3.1, 5 hypothetical LEAs are producing, for the sake of argument, one unit of output using different quantities of two inputs, X_1 and X_2. The efficiency ratio for each LEA is a radial measure. LEA *H*, for example, is inefficient relative to the best-practice LEAs *C* and *D* because the ratio of best-practice to actual input is less than unity. That is, its relative efficiency score *OG/OH* < 1.

Figure 3.3.1
The DEA efficiency score

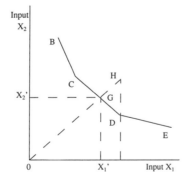

Given the comparison is of like-with-like and that linear combinations of best practice are feasible, an efficient target OG^* can be defined for the relatively inefficient LEA as:

(3.3.1) $OG^* = (OG/OH).OH$

where the contents of the brackets is the scalar efficiency score and OH is the vector reflecting the LEA's current usage of inputs.   The efficiency score implies an equi-proportionate contraction in each input of:

(3.3.2) $(1 - OG/OH)$

to $X_j^i, j = 1,2$, in Figure 3.3.1.

The adjustments to LEA funding implied by the efficiency score are summarised in Table 3.3.3.   LEA 43, for example, has an efficiency score of 0.901.   On the basis of the formula for efficient production in (3.3.1) this implies a lower target level of teaching expenditure, *viz.*:

$$OG^* = (0.901)\, 687 = 619.$$

619 pounds is the target spend per pupil which would put LEA 43 on the best-practice isoquant.   Essentially, DEA is predicting that LEA 43 can support existing levels of attainment with a reduction of $(1 - .901) = 9.9\%$ in its current teaching expenditure. The distribution of savings is not spread evenly through the cross-section.   LEA 21, for example, is overspending by one-fifth, given the levels of its outcome variables. Of course LEA 21 and some others may choose to argue that examination results do not adequately reflect the range of outputs they seek to provide.   These alternative outputs may be inconsistent with the centralised objectives outlined in the annual public expenditure White Paper (which have been used as a broad guide in the choice of variable set in this Chapter).

Unlike LEA 21, some (e.g. 8 or 9) would have to improve performance only marginally to be ranked along with the best-practice LEAs.   An average across all inefficient producers in the sample suggests a typical reduction in costs approaching 7%. It is worth noting in passing that the average target is consistent with the mean inefficiency score of 0.936 quoted earlier in Table 3.3.2.   This also implies a typical reduction in teaching costs of nearly 7%.   However the mean efficiency score including best-practice, 0.966, suggests that funding might be adjusted by under 3.5% which is clearly an understatement of the average potential for savings at inefficient authorities, but which is an accurate indicator of total available savings.

Note that on a simple administrative split between London boroughs (LEAs 1-21), Metropolitan boroughs (22–57) and English counties (58–96) the simple proportions of LEAs relatively inefficient in each of these categories are, respectively: 61.9%, 52.8% and 51.3%.   This could be taken as evidence of greater inefficiency in "urban" education producers or perhaps the greater difficulty of their task *vis-à-vis* rural education. (The relative efficiency of rural and urban education is discussed further in Chapter 7.)

Table 3.3.3
Targets and savings in teaching expenditure for inefficient LEAs

	LEA	Actual performance £ per pupil	Target performance £ per pupil	Savings £ per pupil	Savings %
1.	Barking	663	637	26	3.92
3.	Bexley	613	596	17	2.77
5.	Bromley	650	592	58	8.92
6.	Croydon	664	624	40	6.02
8.	Enfield	641	639	2	0.31
9.	Haringey	761	755	6	0.79
11.	Havering	681	607	74	10.87
12.	Hounslow	686	659	27	3.94
14.	Kingston	644	621	23	3.57
17.	Redbridge	668	628	40	5.99
18.	Richmond	707	603	104	14.71
20.	Waltham Forest	768	662	106	13.80
21.	ILEA	833	657	176	21.13
24.	Dudley	618	605	13	2.10
27.	Walsall	667	597	70	10.49
31.	St Helens	654	607	47	7.19
32.	Sefton	638	608	30	4.70
33.	Wirral	637	595	42	6.59
34.	Bolton	641	582	59	9.20
35.	Bury	652	589	63	9.66
36.	Manchester	749	653	96	12.82
37.	Oldham	589	581	8	1.36
38.	Rochdale	686	572	114	16.62
39.	Salford	684	603	81	11.84
40.	Stockport	617	587	30	4.86
41.	Tameside	620	589	31	5.00
42.	Trafford	632	590	42	6.65
43.	Wigan	687	619	68	9.90
47.	Sheffield	669	608	61	9.12
51.	Leeds	588	580	8	1.36
53.	Gateshead	638	593	45	7.05
54.	Newcastle-Upon-Tyne	739	634	105	14.21
58.	Avon	638	588	50	7.84
63.	Cheshire	632	584	48	7.59
67.	Derbyshire	605	601	4	0.66
68.	Devon	616	585	31	5.03
69.	Dorset	604	595	9	1.49
70.	Durham	625	608	17	2.72
71.	E Sussex	617	591	26	4.21
72.	Essex	602	579	23	3.82
73.	Gloucestershire	622	603	19	3.05
74.	Hampshire	618	595	23	3.72
75.	Hereford	602	586	16	2.66
76.	Herfordshire	664	599	65	9.79
79.	Kent	605	586	19	3.14
80.	Lancashire	641	609	32	4.99
83.	Norfolk	623	601	22	3.53
85.	Northamptonshire	609	592	17	2.79
87.	Nottinghamshire	637	597	40	6.28
88.	Oxfordshire	614	609	5	0.81
89.	Shropshire	639	594	45	7.04
91.	Staffordshire	635	588	47	7.40
	Average of inefficient LEAs	651	607	44	6.76

Notes: Target performance is given by the efficiency score and (where applicable) adjustments in input-slack variables.
Source: Authors' calculations.

The reductions in spending in Table 3.3.3 are recommended on Pareto welfare grounds.[1] That is, an LEA is efficient if it *cannot* be shown that some other LEA or combination of LEAs can produce the same amount of output with less of some input and no more any other (Charnes, Cooper and Rhodes (1981), Lewin and Morey (1981), Koopmans (1951)).

In Figure 3.3.1 (above) the best-practice LEAs B, C, D and E are clearly Pareto efficient on this definition. However, LEA H violates the Pareto efficiency conditions in comparison with LEA D, since for given output, D is using less of X_2 and no more of X_1 than H. The target defined in (3.3.1) is therefore advocated in the literature as defining a production plan which is Pareto efficient and which eliminates unnecessary consumption of resources at the inefficient LEA.

As has been noted in Chapter 2, the radial contraction path defined in (3.3.1) is not in all circumstances a rigorous enough definition for Pareto efficiency. Specifically, production on the isoquant but at the end of *horizontal or vertical facets* is not Pareto efficient. In Figure 3.3.2 for given output and X_2, LEA E would remain Pareto inefficient by the horizontal distance from D to C after the standard radial contraction in inputs. Thus, for given outputs, some other LEA, in this case LEA C, uses the same quantity of X_2, but *less* of X_1 and hence dominates production at D. The distance D to C is given by a non-zero slack variable (S_1^*) in the optimal solution of the DEA program. Accordingly, the formula for an efficient target in (3.3.1) can be rewritten (using Figure 3.3.2) as:

(3.3.3) $OC^* = (OD/OE).OE - S_k^*$

where S_k^* $(k = 1, \ldots, m)$ is the optimal value of the relevant input slack variable. Notice that the efficiency score is a scalar, being the ratio of the distances $d(O,D)$ to $d(O,E)$—where d is the usual Euclidean distance function. Similarly, the S_k^* $k = 1, \ldots, m$ are non-negative scalar quantities representing reductions in inputs. *OE*, however, is a *vector* of observed performance at LEA E.

Figure 3.3.2.
Slacks and Pareto efficiency

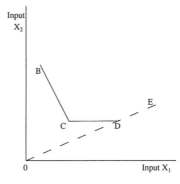

The *feasibility* of the target in (3.3.3) is given by an assumption that the production possibility set is convex. In particular any convex linear combination of observed inputs at best-practice LEAs is feasible.

Convexity ensures that the data is "enveloped" or packaged through the extreme (best-practice) LEAs in a piecewise manner. In practice, the result is a piecewise-linear approximation to the true production technology, as in Figure 3.3.1. Points along each facet of the isoquant are linear combinations of *observed* best-practice and on this basis are deemed feasible targets. Where the optimal values of the slack variables are equal to zero, the route to these targets is a radial contraction path (cf that for LEA *H* in Figure 3.3.1).

More specific qualitive information on precisely *how* targets can be obtained is derived by analogy from the peer groups identified in Table 3.3.2. For each LEA a comparable set of peers is selected by DEA. For relatively *efficient* LEAs this will contain none other than the LEA itself. But inefficient LEAs will have a distinct reference group of best-practice LEAs.

In Table 3.3.2, LEA 43, for instance, has LEAs 46, 50, 64 and 86 as "peers", which in linear combination define its target performance. In principle, LEA 43 can use these authorities as blueprints to improve performance since, other things being equal, they are likely to be implementing superior managerial procedures (Epstein and Henderson (1989)).

3.4. A preliminary evaluation of the peer group

This section examines the question of the use of best-practice results as peers for the improvement of inefficient production. It has been widely argued in the literature (in for example Charnes *et al* (1989), Thanassoulis *et al* (1987), Bowlin (1986)) that an inefficient organisation (or its auditors) should make comparisons with best-practice in order to extract and transfer relatively better managerial procedures to improve its productive performance. From the results in section 3.3 the inefficient LEA would inspect the best-practice peer group identified for it in Table 3.3.2.

Smith and Mayston (1987) suggest "an important supplementary measure in assessing the robustness of this result is the number of inefficient authorities for which the [best-practice] authority forms the efficient frontier". They continue that "*if this number is high the authority is genuinely efficient* with respect to a large number of authorities" (emphasis added). On this basis the most useful examples of best-practice are likely to be found in heavily cited instances of best practice. These can be extracted from Table 3.4.1. LEA 43, for example, would find that LEAs 50 and 86 in its peer group have been cited over 20 times. On the other hand LEA 64 could be argued to be a poorer peer in being cited only 7 times. Thus the informational contents of the peer group can be read in the light of what amounts to a citations index for best-practice in Table 3.4.1.

Table 3.4.1
Citations for best-practice LEAs

LEA		Citations in peer groups
2.	Barnet	8
4.	Brent	3
7.	Ealing	5
10.	Harrow	2
15.	Merton	4
16.	Newham	4
19.	Sutton	8
22.	Birmingham	4
23.	Coventry	2
25.	Sandwell	3
26.	Solihull	3
28.	Wolverhampton	4
30.	Liverpool	2
44.	Barnsley	8
45.	Doncaster	2
46.	Rotherham	11
48.	Bradford	27
50.	Kirklees	22
52.	Wakefield	2
59.	Bedfordshire	9
61.	Buckinghamshire	2
64.	Cleveland	7
65.	Cornwall	2
78.	Isle of Wight	15
81.	Leicestershire	3
82.	Lincolnshire	4
86.	Northumberland	26
90.	Somerset	4
92.	Suffolk	2
95.	West Sussex	20
96.	Wiltshire	8

Notes:Table 3.4.1 contains those efficient LEAs which appear in peer groups (not including their own) of inefficient LEAs. Several LEAs (numbers 12, 29, 49, 55, 56, 57, 60, 62, 66, 77, 84, 93 and 94) do not appear in either Table 3.3.2 or Table 3.4.1. These have input efficiencies equal to unity but appear in only one peer group, their own.

Source: Authors' calculations

The Smith-Mayston interpretation of best-practice can be discussed in the light of Figure 3.4.1. Figure 3.4.1 contains a hypothetical DEA isoquant for 2 inputs (with output given) where LEA performance has been deliberately bunched in the south west of the feasible set of production decisions. LEAs B, C, and D are best-practice with efficiency scores equal to unity. Targets for the resources X_2 and X_1 are defined for LEAs E, F, G, H and J which are inefficient relative to B, C and D. It is clear from Figure 3.4.1 that the reference or peer LEAs for most of the inefficient producers (other than LEA J) are LEAs C and D. For example, the target for LEA F is a weighted average of C and D.

But LEA J has unusual input proportions such that its target is an interpolation of LEA B and C. Clearly best-practice authorities such as LEA B which have relatively unusual input proportions will lie on the extreme parts of the isoquant. They will be cited infrequently (ignoring a trivial citation in their own peer group) since, with

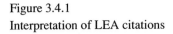

Figure 3.4.1

Interpretation of LEA citations

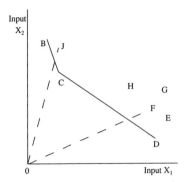

unusual input proportions, there is a lower probability of finding comparable inefficient LEAs.

It should be evident that each best-practice authority does not have an equal probability of citation *unless* inefficient LEAs are spread evenly through the feasible production space. This may not be the case. This possibility has been illustrated in Figure 3.4.1 where performance is bunched in such a way that some instances of best-practice will be cited less frequently than others. It follows that a *high* number of citations implies only *comparability* with a larger number of inefficient LEAs. Indeed in the application of DEA to financial statements Smith (1990) has made an analogous point arguing that the comparability of an observation conveys nothing *in and of itself* on the underlying efficiency in an organisation.

In general, it is true that the larger the number of citations for a DMU, the larger the "sample" of observations in the neighbourhood of that DMU. On the basis of traditional sampling theory, the larger is the sample in a particular neighbourhood, the closer is the sample frontier likely to approximate the true frontier. However, it is not at all clear *a priori* what would constitute an appropriately "high" number of citations and therefore at what point a dominant observation accurately conveys the attainments and practices which are possible on the true (unknown) frontier.

3.5. Appraisal

The existence of multiple non-homogenous inputs and outputs is a basic difficulty in the construction of total-factor productivity measures. In the trading sector market price weights can be used to yield summary profit and revenue measures. The additional problem of the non-trading sector (both public and not-for-profit) is the absence of market price weights: "the [input and output] indicators are given on different scales and we have no *a priori* set of weights with which to judge their relative importance, or functions with which to transform the indicators into common measures of utility" (Smith and Mayston (1987)). This supports the belief in, for example, Miller (1987) that there is a requirement for enhanced performance measurement to ensure greater accountability from public sector entities where performance cannot be fully tested by standard profitability criteria. In response, several authors, for example Boussofiane *et al* (1991), have suggested the application of the DEA approach in the public sector. In the absence of other weighting schemes, DEA identifies an objective set of "data-based" weights making minimal assumptions on the production technology *vis-à-vis* an econometric approach.

The broad applicability and acceptance of a non-parametric approach is attested by the diversity of empirical work emerging in the literature. Tulkens (1990) for example has investigated municipal efficiency, Ganley and Cubbin (1987) the prison service and Lewin *et al* (1982) courts. Grosskopf and Valdmanis (1987) and Banker, Conrad and Strauss (1986) have completed studies of hospital efficiency, while Bjurek *et al* (1986) have examined the performance of social security offices. Lewin and Morey (1981) contains a study of the cost effectiveness of military recruitment using DEA. More generally the approach is being applied to the analysis of private sector services, notably banking (Aly *et al* (1990), Vassilogou and Giokas (1990)).

Using data on 96 English local education authorities this Chapter has indicated the potential contribution of Data Envelopment Analysis to the existing set of educational performance statistics. After reviewing the relevant measurement problems in section 3.2, scalar measures of technical efficiency for each authority were presented in section 3.3 using DEA. These measures may be used to set targets for relatively inefficient LEA producers which, in principle, may utilise the peer group identified by DEA as a guide to achieving targeted improvements in resource consumption.[1] Independent findings by Barrow (1988) and Audit Commission (1986 b) appear to confirm the extent of inefficiency identified in these results.

In section 3.4 the first attempt in the published literature to develop a DEA-sensitivity "statistic" by Smith and Mayston (1987) was evaluated and re-interpreted as an indicator of the comparability (rather than the intrinsic quality) of the best-practice estimates.

Academic interest in DEA information has been paralleled during the 1980s in government initiatives on performance measurement and accountability for the public sector. Of most importance in the UK has been the Financial Management Initiative (FMI), heralded in 1982 in *Efficiency and Effectiveness in the Civil Service*.[2] The aim of the FMI has been "to promote in each department an organisation and system in which managers at all levels have a clear view of their objectives and means to assess and, wherever possible, measure outputs or performance in relation to those objectives" (para 13, Cmnd 8616). In a follow up report, the National Audit Office (1986) argues that departments should publish annual reports providing *intelligible* information (perhaps summary indicators) about their aims, objectives and performance.

---

(1)   Further aspects of the peer group and best-practice are discussed in Chapter 4.
(2)   Command paper, cmnd 8616. London: HMSO.

Accordingly, recent public expenditure White Papers have placed increasing emphasis on value for money and efficiency including a total of around 1800 output and performance measures for government spending programmes. Any selection of these reveals, however, that they are mainly traditional ratio measures such as unit costs and throughputs.[1]

More sophisticated summary measures of (total-factor) productivity do not appear to be widely used by government departments. This would seem to be restraining the potential for public sector accountability and evaluation. In the educational context there may be extra scope for the adoption of consistent total-factor measures of efficiency like DEA. In the first place, the 1980 Education Act has signalled a shift from professional to public accountability of education. This is being underwritten by the development of a national curriculum which should make inter-authority comparisons more robust. Equally important, the regular, standardised testing of pupils may eventually generate measures of value added for specific cohorts of school children.

With the collection of improved data in prospect, DEA is well placed to take advantage of this. In principle, DEA could form part of a set of key aggregate indicators summarising educational performance. Jesson, Mayston and Smith (1987) have argued that careful analysis of educational productivity using DEA might be used to settle funding disputes between the LEAs and central government. An additional role for summary performance measures like DEA may come as the authorities and the Education Department attempt to rationalise the surplus capacity which is currently being generated by falling school rolls.

---

(1) See, for example, those performance measures selected for *Economic Progress Report*, Number 188, January-February 1987, pages 6–7.

APPENDIX 3.1

Local Education Authority Data Set

	(a)	(b)	(c)	(d)	(e)	(f)	(g)	(h)
1 Barking	13.37	41.83	18.63	663	14.55	4.62	7.69	43.81
2 Barnet	35.85	65.46	8.81	707	44.11	3.85	30.86	32.78
3 Bexley	25.31	70.42	7.65	613	31.42	2.05	8.06	35.49
4 Brent	17.82	54.34	14.99	778	25.12	10.39	53.84	57.29
5 Bromley	28.83	64.35	9.03	650	48.37	2.03	9.06	19.54
6 Croydon	25.32	62.94	10.25	664	35.76	3.69	21.25	36.73
7 Ealing	19.28	56.09	13.89	721	25.65	9.88	45.10	50.45
8 Enfield	22.86	62.30	11.10	641	31.03	3.27	25.83	31.89
9 Haringey	14.75	51.32	19.99	761	24.61	7.93	50.21	67.16
10 Harrow	37.19	67.16	6.28	760	41.35	3.28	25.45	38.68
11 Havering	25.22	62.09	7.03	681	30.00	1.74	4.86	20.45
12 Hillingdon	21.39	64.65	10.92	653	32.26	2.84	13.20	20.83
13 Hounslow	22.24	60.41	12.87	686	25.65	6.27	29.69	34.32
14 Kingston	31.34	63.59	9.44	644	44.17	2.30	14.50	35.40
15 Merton	24.49	65.08	12.70	606	33.94	3.37	21.92	43.76
16 Newham	11.34	45.28	25.14	701	11.73	14.92	40.80	57.60
17 Redbridge	25.68	55.71	9.35	668	34.73	3.97	20.59	40.07
18 Richmond	27.64	66.76	11.83	707	48.36	3.19	15.36	28.90
19 Sutton	33.52	70.58	6.57	616	39.46	1.85	9.17	39.00
20 Waltham	16.20	51.39	15.27	768	20.96	8.50	30.86	54.45
21 ILEA	14.41	46.65	20.99	833	20.64	9.47	34.85	76.20
22 Birmingham	18.76	59.29	14.42	651	18.52	9.88	26.72	38.08
23 Coventry	21.68	65.99	11.63	639	19.91	5.91	17.25	32.51
24 Dudley	24.66	71.82	11.76	618	25.98	4.07	6.68	30.60
25 Sandwell	13.14	54.57	17.66	661	12.93	11.22	21.10	35.98
26 Solihull	26.34	77.06	4.53	613	37.39	1.68	4.34	11.07
27 Walsall	19.69	62.24	14.40	667	21.13	7.13	13.03	25.18
28 Wolverhampton	16.62	61.36	14.92	683	15.73	13.44	27.30	36.94
29 Knowsley	12.45	44.88	21.13	706	10.96	5.87	1.78	17.76
30 Liverpool	18.30	48.09	19.41	684	14.28	7.67	3.86	45.17
31 St Helens	22.62	62.79	13.48	654	22.36	5.04	1.68	14.22
32 Sefton	28.01	61.25	10.68	638	31.07	2.79	2.51	19.91
33 Wirral	25.81	66.77	8.42	637	28.97	2.40	2.89	21.53
34 Bolton	23.22	58.46	11.70	641	26.84	7.87	11.75	18.65
35 Bury	26.39	63.97	11.42	652	31.26	3.47	5.86	17.76
36 Manchester	15.78	42.18	21.14	749	14.72	8.24	14.68	38.61
37 Oldham	12.82	52.72	17.86	589	21.62	6.53	10.45	15.59
38 Rochdale	17.97	54.64	17.39	686	23.92	6.50	10.46	12.98
39 Salford	16.95	51.30	14.44	684	18.45	5.11	3.87	25.17
40 Stockport	26.88	64.87	9.27	617	40.06	2.28	4.36	23.04
41 Tameside	19.16	55.64	13.19	620	21.23	4.41	6.74	21.09

	(a)	(b)	(c)	(d)	(e)	(f)	(g)	(h)
42 Trafford	26.27	64.08	8.15	632	33.01	3.14	8.04	20.99
43 Wigan	22.95	64.46	10.98	687	21.76	2.87	1.69	15.54
44 Barnsley	15.83	58.75	15.99	617	15.92	3.53	1.88	6.85
45 Doncaster	17.56	63.84	11.02	640	18.72	4.36	3.96	4.98
46 Rotherham	18.18	69.42	10.27	608	18.07	4.22	3.74	8.90
47 Sheffield	20.43	68.94	9.66	669	22.75	4.77	7.56	14.63
48 Bradford	18.63	51.33	17.63	570	23.33	9.50	21.82	12.36
49 Calderdale	23.22	60.93	11.74	621	25.07	5.35	8.52	5.25
50 Kirklees	23.90	64.14	11.22	585	26.22	7.31	16.21	9.07
51 Leeds	22.60	62.98	11.40	588	27.27	3.29	8.48	12.54
52 Wakefield	16.85	62.08	14.65	590	20.61	3.02	3.14	9.36
53 Gateshead	17.46	64.31	14.65	638	19.72	4.15	2.14	14.76
54 Newcastle	20.43	66.38	13.17	739	23.51	4.43	6.21	24.83
55 N Tyneside	23.06	77.41	8.17	671	25.15	2.21	2.39	23.66
56 S Tyneside	18.58	74.12	10.44	694	16.87	4.26	2.11	25.23
57 Sunderland	18.81	71.51	9.95	645	17.16	3.61	1.92	21.42
58 Avon	22.94	67.08	7.99	638	32.59	1.95	6.09	6.80
59 Bedfordshire	21.23	63.76	6.81	613	31.82	3.70	15.64	4.11
60 Berkshire	25.44	72.05	5.96	627	39.68	3.65	13.17	5.41
61 Buckinghamshire	33.16	72.49	4.97	652	42.87	2.48	9.93	3.02
62 Cambridgeshire	25.85	66.10	7.86	626	32.60	2.93	8.53	1.70
63 Cheshire	25.12	66.29	10.02	632	33.50	2.73	3.02	3.99
64 Cleveland	22.73	69.44	12.09	629	19.90	4.48	4.16	9.74
65 Cornwall	25.32	65.78	10.26	624	28.00	3.66	3.39	1.21
66 Cumbria	23.95	68.93	10.02	641	25.68	2.68	2.03	0.72
67 Derbyshire	21.47	69.63	8.95	605	26.25	3.84	5.91	3.46
68 Devon	22.34	63.27	8.47	616	28.72	2.49	4.14	1.43
69 Dorset	26.77	72.53	6.96	604	33.42	2.07	5.21	2.24
70 Durham	19.15	65.33	13.08	625	20.91	3.64	2.27	2.49
71 E Sussex	27.61	65.53	9.24	617	36.85	2.88	6.58	3.66
72 Essex	23.69	60.88	9.76	602	35.21	1.74	4.92	4.02
73 Gloucestershire	27.35	67.07	8.02	622	33.58	2.49	5.72	1.90
74 Hampshire	24.89	70.54	7.29	618	32.57	1.95	6.79	3.88
75 Hereford	23.50	71.78	11.53	602	33.69	2.52	3.91	1.61
76 Hertfordshire	30.62	68.47	6.82	664	43.18	1.85	8.30	5.85
77 Humberside	20.61	62.26	13.83	628	23.89	4.57	3.11	2.43
78 Isle of Wight	20.13	71.06	9.82	571	30.53	2.41	3.10	3.12
79 Kent	25.58	69.25	8.49	605	32.95	2.94	6.30	3.93
80 Lancashire	21.93	58.23	12.38	641	27.04	5.80	8.31	4.49
81 Leicestershire	22.67	64.96	11.39	629	28.04	4.91	14.28	3.31
82 Lincolnshire	23.48	71.04	6.70	642	28.23	2.95	4.46	0.93
83 Norfolk	19.28	55.70	11.00	623	29.20	2.77	3.66	1.29

	(a)	(b)	(c)	(d)	(e)	(f)	(g)	(h)
84 N Yorkshire	28.54	71.30	7.95	637	33.93	2.03	4.29	0.80
85 Northamptonshire	18.79	70.44	9.09	609	28.47	2.65	7.05	2.23
86 Northumberland	25.56	78.15	7.44	591	29.19	2.34	2.37	0.60
87 Nottinghamshire	18.99	66.86	11.65	637	24.53	4.23	7.01	4.55
88 Oxfordshire	26.56	73.84	7.88	614	36.38	2.09	7.73	1.99
89 Shropshire	23.46	67.93	11.77	639	29.68	2.51	4.47	1.08
90 Somerset	20.51	64.99	10.63	580	31.09	2.19	3.58	1.24
91 Staffordshire	20.61	67.06	13.94	635	26.82	4.02	3.85	3.74
92 Suffolk	20.99	57.54	9.97	591	28.30	2.62	4.80	1.58
93 Surrey	33.01	74.42	5.80	653	50.04	2.12	9.02	5.98
94 Warwickshire	25.14	75.00	8.07	619	32.56	2.49	7.24	2.40
95 W Sussex	31.17	76.02	5.87	597	41.34	1.69	6.55	3.33
96 Wiltshire	24.14	68.40	7.48	599	28.77	2.08	8.04	1.49

Where variables (a) through (h) are defined as in Table 3.3.1.

Source: Department of Education and Science (1984).

CHAPTER 4

TOTAL FACTOR PRODUCTIVITY MEASUREMENT IN LOCAL PRISONS AND REMAND CENTRES: A FURTHER APPLICATION OF DATA ENVELOPMENT ANALYSIS

4.1. Introduction

Chapter 4 examines the relative efficiency of 33 UK local prisons and remand centres in the financial year 1984/85. Although the application of Data Envelopment Analysis to public sector production is increasing there has been no examination of prison relative efficiency other than in Ganley and Cubbin (1987). This Chapter extends the model used in that paper making an important distinction between remand and non-remand items. Because some local prisons carry large remand populations this alters the interpretation of performance at several establishments. For example Ganley and Cubbin (1987) originally reported that Wormwood Scrubs had an input efficiency of 0.66. The revised results presented in this Chapter indicate that this prison is best-practice. This underlines the importance of informed variable selection in efficiency modelling with DEA—an issue which is at last beginning to receive attention in the literature (Ahn and Seiford (1990), Seiford and Thrall (1990) and Epstein and Henderson (1989)).

In what follows section 4.2 briefly outlines the analytical background to the performance comparisons undertaken later in the Chapter. The nature of the prison, its environment and sources of data are discussed in section 4.3 together with an attempt to predict efficiency *"ex ante"* from a straightforward inspection of the data prior to the formal programming analysis.

The growing number of DEA applications shrouds the fact that a general framework for the implementation of DEA results in the public sector has not been suggested. In the context of the UK Financial Management Initiative a potential framework for the implementation of DEA is suggested. The results are based on a varying returns to scale technology. The nature of the efficiency coefficient is evidenced in the performance at Canterbury local prison. A normative development in the literature suggests that the peer group contains examples of better performance which the non-best practice establishment should emulate. The nature of the peer group is investigated in this connection.

Section 4.4 explores the writings of Leibenstein on X-efficiency and the concept of inert production. Traditionally much of Leibenstein's evidence for X-efficiency has been in the nature of casual empiricism and as Button (1985) commented: "the major problem of the X-inefficiency concept is that it focuses on relationships that are essentially unobservable". After formalising the concept of inert production, section 4.4 goes on to show that, *ceteris paribus*, the DEA relative efficiency coefficient can be interpreted as a *quantitative* guide to the scale of X-efficiency. This may represent a significant step forward for the credibility of X-efficiency theory. With the application of a quantitative measuring rod the concept becomes subject to formal testable hypotheses. The received Popperian view of knowledge acquisition as a process of error elimination indicates that the assertion of testable hypotheses is essential in scientific endeavour (Blaug (1980), Popper (1976)). Finally, section 4.5 summarises the results and conclusions reached in this Chapter and the Appendix contains the complete prisons' data set.

4.2. Analytical background to relative efficiency measurement

An analytical literature on the nature of technical efficiency measures has flourished in parallel with the development of empirical estimation procedures. Initially Fare and Lovell (1979) set out to define the axiomatic properties that a production technology must fulfil and how far the empirical estimates in Farrell (1957) and later work meet these requirements. A small and demanding literature has developed around the initial impetus of Fare and Lovell, the main contributions being Fare and Lovell (1981), Kopp (1981), Fare, Lovell and Zieschang (1982), Zieschang (1984), Fare, Grosskopf and Lovell (1985, 1983), Bol (1986) and more recently Russell (1989) and Fare and Grosskopf (1990). This section evidences in the briefest of detail the basic concept of a production correspondence as developed in this literature. Section 4.2 is not however an exhaustive guide to the theory of production and efficiency measurement since this can be found elsewhere—for example in the volume by Fare, Grosskopf and Lovell (1985).

The underlying objective of the work initiated by Fare and his associates has been to characterise efficiency measures as propositions on sets: Sets of input and output possibilities. This approach derives originally from the work of the American economist Shephard (1974, 1970, 1953) who developed the body of axioms which a production technology must ordinarily be required to satisfy.

Input and output correspondences

Productive activity, whether undertaken in the public or private sector, is constrained by the nature of the production process itself. Conceptually, a production unit transforms a vector of non-negative inputs into a vector of non-negative outputs, subject to the constraint imposed by a known, fixed technology. This transformation process is modelled analytically by an input correspondence which defines the subset of input vectors capable of producing a given output vector or, inversely, by an output correspondence specifying the subset of output vectors obtainable from a given input vector. Each of these correspondences must satisfy a basic set of axioms suggested originally by Shephard in order to provide a meaningful basis for a model of productive behaviour.

Consider a production process transforming inputs $x = (X_1, X_2, . . ., X_n) \, \varepsilon \, R_+^n$ into net outputs $y = (Y_1, Y_2, . . ., Y_m) \, \varepsilon \, R_+^m$. This process can be modelled by the input correspondence $L(y)$ which denotes the subset of all input vectors $x \, \varepsilon \, R_+^n$ which yield at least output levels y. Analogously $P(x)$ is the output correspondence denoting the subset of all output vectors $y \, \varepsilon \, R_+^m$ obtainable from input levels x. The inverse relationship between L and P is given by:

(4.2.1) $\qquad\qquad x \, \varepsilon \, L(y) < = = > y \, \varepsilon \, P(x)$

and may be computed or "enumerated" as (Fare, Grosskopf and Lovell (1985)):

(4.2.2) $P(\underline{x}) = [\ \underline{y} : \underline{x}\ \varepsilon\ L(\underline{y})\ ]$

and:

(4.2.3) $L(\underline{y}) = [\ \underline{x} : \underline{y}\ \varepsilon\ P(\underline{x})\ ]$.

It is easier to see the meaning of the input set $L(\underline{y})$ and output set $P(\underline{x})$ for the simple case of $n = m = 2$ in Figure 4.2.1. In part (a) the subset of all input vectors $\underline{x}\ \varepsilon\ R_+^2$ capable of producing at least output $\underline{y}$ is labelled $L(\underline{y})$, and consists of the subset of all input vectors on or above the curve AB. In part (b) the subset of all output vectors $\underline{y}\ \varepsilon\ R_+^2$ obtainable from input vector $\underline{x}$ is labelled $P(\underline{x})$, and consists of the subset of non-negative output vectors on or below the curve AB.

It is evident from Figure 4.2.1(a) that the boundary of the input correspondence AB is nothing more than a conventional isoquant (and analogously AB in part (b) is the production possibility frontier for given technology and input vector $\underline{x}$). In the results below in section 4.3 the estimated input correspondence is merely the four-dimensional counterpart of Figure 4.2.1(a) where $n = 4$ so that $L(\underline{y})\ \varepsilon\ R_+^4$. Again there is a corresponding output correspondence defined for four definitions of prison outputs, and so $P(\underline{x})\ \varepsilon\ R_+^4$.

Figure 4.2.1 a   Figure 4.2.1 b
The Input Correspondence, n=2   The Output Correspondence, m=2

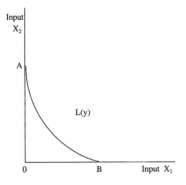
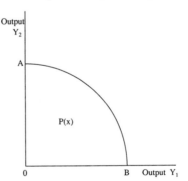

4.3. Empirical investigation of prison efficiency

Since the 1960s there has been a steady flow of contributions to a new literature on the economics of crime and justice. One of the best known and seminal contributions is Becker (1968), and later Carr-Hill and Stern (1979); for a survey see Lewis (1987) or Pyle (1983). More recently the literature has started to diversify. One of the newest strands of investigation is of the effectiveness of penal institutions, *viz.*, the police (Levitt and Joyce (1987)), courts (Lewin, Morey and Cook (1982)) and the prisons.

The background to the development of the modern prison is fascinating. One of the best introductions to the subject is Garland (1985) which could be very usefully supplemented with a read of Merquior (1985, Chapter 7) and Foucault (1977) who analyses the broader philosophical arguments for and against the existence of prisons.

The focus of this Chapter is the efficiency of prison production.   This has several analytical and policy-orientated dimensions.   For example much has been written about the possibilities for privatisation in UK prisons (Morgan and King (1987), Stern (1987)) and this debate continues as yet unresolved.   Privatisation, however, is only one aspect of a debate on prison costs and spending.

Several studies (e.g. Prison Department and PA Management Consultants (1986)) of the prison service have diagnosed excessive costs and overtime driven staffing in the service.   Shaw (1984) has identified the prison service as a public sector growth industry *vis-à-vis* other public programmes which have been subject to resource control.   In the context of the Financial Management Initiative (FMI) and the Prison Department's "Fresh Start" proposals attention has thereby focused on the allocation of resources in the service and their effectiveness in attaining penal objectives.

Some studies have deliberated on penal final outputs like deterrence (McAleer and Veall (1987)) and recidivism   (Schmidt and Witte (1988), Wilson and Hernstein (1985), Maltz (1984)).   Others have investigated efficiency and effectiveness at the level of intermediate output; [1]viz. Dessent (1987) who formalised a model for the cost effectiveness of the prison perimeter.   Ganley and Cubbin (1987) presented the first analysis of prison productivity using frontier techniques.

This Chapter extends the model in Ganley and Cubbin (1987) with greater disaggregation of costs and some redefinition of prison outcomes.   The remainder of this section discusses prison resources, objectives and data and how these have determined the specification of the prison production function underlying the analysis. It continues with a look at the possibility of predicting enterprise efficiency *ex ante;* that is, using simple descriptive statistics it attempts to identify best-practice production prior to the formal programming analysis which makes specific technology assumptions and has significantly greater computational requirements.   It also examines the potential role efficiency predictions have in the context of the Financial Management Initiative and the Prison Department's "Fresh Start" proposals.   This includes   discussions   of   the   appropriate   line-departmental   structure   and   the implications   for   branch   and   central   decision-makers   of   inefficient   production. Results   on   efficiency   in   33   representative   prison   establishments   using   Data Envelopment Analysis are tabulated based on an assumption of varying returns to scale in the reference technology.   Several important dimensions of the results are investigated including the nature of the peer group comparison and their congruence with Leibenstein's concept of the inert area in production.

The prison environment

Prisons constitute a labour intensive, continuous process industry providing a number of non-traded outputs.   The definition of prison outputs is especially difficult.   At the crudest level, a prison provides a level of incarceration to protect law-abiding citizens from potentially dangerous offenders.   The level of incarceration can be measured by the number of prisoner days (average inmates x 365).   The success of incarceration is

---

(1)   For a full discussion of the distinction between intermediate and final outputs see Gadrey (1988) and
       Bovaird (1981).

more subtle.   Again at the crudest level this can be approximated by the frequency at which prison security is breached—most notably in escape.   Escape, however, is just one form of behaviour which can be deemed unacceptable in a set of undesirable acts which will include a variety of punishable offences: For example assault of a prison officer or wilful damage to prison property.   These forms of behaviour are regulated and punished by prison officers.   The number of offences so recorded can be used as an indicator of the output of discipline and regulation within a prison.   However, the possibility of differences in local policy from one prison to another suggests that some incidents will be punished in one but not in another.   Consequently the "Offences" variable used below is defined as the number of serious offences.   This includes incidents of escape, assaults on staff and wilful damage to prison property.   These are fairly clearly defined and exclude less serious incidents.

A priori it is not clear whether larger numbers of offences represent stricter regulation and hence greater work effort or poorer standards of inmate behaviour which might be caused by a poorer regime.   For the purposes of this study the number of offences will be classified as an intermediate output or throughput measure of work done; in this sense, offences are a positive output or "benefit".   The more subtle final output connotations of offences for the rehabilitative work of the prison are acknowledged nevertheless.

In recent years UK prisons have become overcrowded.   The total prison population currently stands at over 50,000 with the estate designed to house about 42,000.   Each prison has a designated "Certified Normal Accommodation" (CNA).   The difference between CNA and the average inmate population over the year is usually negative, indicating overcrowding.   This is included in the model as an undesireable outcome of production.   From the prison governor's point of view, both CNA and the number of inmates he holds are given to him.   Hence overcrowding is usually unavoidable and is likely to have a profound effect on the attainment of the other objectives.   The education and rehabilitation of offenders can only be jeopardised in cramped conditions.   Some commentators subscribe to a "university of crime" interpretation of penal institutions.[1]   On this basis, dispersal of prisoners and their containment at lower densities is thought to be the most conducive environment for rehabilitation. Naturally on this argument overcrowding only serves to worsen the proclivity to re-offend.   Figures in *The Economist* (23/1/88) show that 60% of male offenders leaving overcrowded institutions are reconvicted within 2 years.

A joint Prison Department-PA Management Consultants' Report[2] found that manning in the service has been unwieldly and over-time driven.   The UK government's recent "Fresh Start" proposals are designed to "shake up" the service establishing a basic working week and satisfactory remuneration without excessive overtime.[3] Incarceration and supervision is labour intensive—the more so according to the

---

(1)   See Dennis Pawley *The Guardian*, 1/4/1988, page 21.
(2)   *Study of Prison Officers' Complementing and Shift Systems*, vol 1 (Report) and vol 2 (Appendices) April 1986.
(3)   See Home Office News Release, 31st July 1987,"New working arrangements in prisons in England".

category of inmates concerned.   Accordingly for the purpose of this investigation
costs have been broken down into manpower and non-manpower costs.

Non-manpower costs are a catch-all including all costs other than those attributable to
labour services.   These costs are current (running) costs and do not include capital
expenditures.   Manpower costs include direct labour expenses and will reflect the
effects of overtime, etc.   A first approximation to a case mix indicator is had in a
disaggregation of both cost variables into their remand and non-remand components.
Non-remand inmates are the "typical" sentenced prisoner.   Remand prisoners are
awaiting trial and/or sentencing.   During this period their incarceration is lightened
with privileges, e.g. extra visits, own clothes, etc. which add to their costs *vis-à-vis*
sentenced inmates.   In addition the courts control when the remand prisoner shall
appear for trial and sentencing.   The prison must provide escorts to and from the court
at the time determined by the court.   This may interfere with the rostering which
would otherwise be most efficient from the prison's point of view.   The court work
associated with remand prisoners is a further reason for the separation of remand
items.   This important distinction has also been incorporated into the prisoner days
outcome variable.

Sources of data

The inputs and outcomes suggested above yield a set of 8 variables.   They have been
chosen from first principles as the best indicators of the underlying production
process.   It is intended that they are broadly congruent with the objectives of
Government penal policy as framed in the Prison Department Report (Cm 264) and
Public Expenditure White Paper (Cm 288).   These objectives were interpreted by
Ganley and Cubbin (1987) as:

    1   Secure containment of offenders;

    2   The quality and rehabilitative effect of prison life; and

    3   Efficient use of resources.

Although severely criticised in the past (see e.g. Shaw (1984)) prison statistics are
improving.   Data by establishment on offences like escape and assault satisfies (1)
and has been taken from *Prison Statistics, England and Wales, 1984,* Tables 9.3 and
9.4.   Cost data has been derived from the annual *Report on the work of the Prison
Department, 1984/85,* Appendix 2, Table D and is intended to reflect achievement of
(3).   Currently there is no published data on (2), the state of the prison regime.   Yet
data of this sort is circulated internally to the Service and may ultimately be published
annually in the *Prison Department Report* or the *Public Expenditure White Paper* if
the recommendations of the Education, Science and Arts Committee in a recent
report[1] are accepted.   The quality of life and regime in the prison could be crudely
approximated by an indicator such as the number of non-statutory hours inmates are
allowed out of their cells for free association, games, learning etc.   As far as the

---

(1)   *Prison Education.   Second Report from the Education, Science and Arts Committee,* HC 138-9, session
        1986-87.

model's congruence with actual policy is concerned lack of data on regime quality is perhaps the less worrying of data deficiencies since in recent years a good, reforming regime appears to have been tacitly downgraded by policy-makers *vis-à-vis* the simple incarceration objective. (See *Prison Education*, HC 138-1, Session 1986–87.) The data used in the study below are based on a cross-section of 33 representative penal establishments. These are predominantly local prisons with large remand populations. However, seven remand centres (Ashford, Brockhill, Glen Parva, Latchmere House, Low Newton, Pucklechurch and Winchester) and one Category B closed training prison (Coldingley) have also been included to broaden the cross-section. Broadening the cross-section in this way assumes an acceptable level of homogeneity across establishments in order to make their relative efficiency assignments meaningful.

The cost and overcrowding data on these institutions are for the financial year 1984/85 and are derived from the *Prison Department Report, 1984/85*. The prisoner day and offences outcomes for 1984 do not overlap exactly with data from the *Report*: They are published annually for the calendar year only in *Prison Statistics, 1984*. For purposes of evaluation the incongruent overlap of relevant data is disappointing. An important and desireable future step forward in the development of prison statistics would be the accurate and timely reporting of all relevant performance data on a fully comparable basis.

Ex ante efficiency prediction

It is not uncommon in empirical work in the DEA literature to present descriptive statistics on the input-output data prior to formal modelling of the production process (see for example Rangan *et al* (1988), Fare, Grosskopf and Logan (1987), and Grosskopf and Valdmanis (1987)). This serves to provide some intuition on the plausibility of the derivative DEA-efficiency coefficients. These coefficients lack a simple test statistic such as would be output from conventional parametric procedures like Ordinary Least Squares. In a similar context Besley (1989) and Hammond (1981) have proposed the evaluation of efficiency *"ex ante"* and *"ex post"*. Thus the efficiency predictions in this section are termed *"ex ante"* in the sense that they are derived from descriptive statistics on the data prior to formal evaluation of performance with DEA. Analogously the DEA efficiency scores can be interpreted as *ex post* "predictions" of efficiency. Table 4.3.1 contains means, standard deviations, maxima and minima of the input-output data set based on the full cross section of 33 establishments. From the extreme values in the data it is possible to make crude *ex ante* efficiency predictions. Since Chapter 4 focuses on the input dimensions of prison production these predictions are based on the extreme values of the cost data alone. From Table 4.3.1 this would imply that Gloucester local prison and Thorpe Arch remand centre may be among the best-practice establishments with minimal observed costs. Analogously Brixton and Wandsworth locals might be anticipated to be poor efficiency candidates with respectively maximum remand and non-remand costs. However, it should be noted that Brixton did the bulk of London's remand work whilst Wandsworth had no remand prisoners in 1984/85: Their apparently excessive spending may be more a function of their inmate mix than of true cost inefficiency. Brixton moreover delivers the greatest prisoner throughput in the sample. The DEA results themselves will of course throw more light on this.

Table 4.3.1
Summary of Prison Costs (£M) and Outputs, 1984/85

	Manpower		Non-Manpower		Overcrowd	Days		Offence
	(a)	(b)	(a)	(b)		(a)	(b)	
Mean	2.24	3.47	0.64	1.05	-147	78	137	112
S.Devn	2.08	2.51	0.59	0.92	133	58	125	107
Max	11.85	10.55	3.24	3.80	-622	237	533	573
	6	*31*	*6*	*31*	*16*	*6*	*31*	*13*
Min	0.55	0.34	0.11	0.10	-3	0	13	16
	14	*30*	*14*	*30*	*9*	*20,31*	*30*	*9*

Notes:

1. Figures in italics denote the identity of the prison with the maximum or minimum value of the variable concerned—see Table 4.3.2 below for prison names.

2. Outcome variables: (i) Overcrowding is a negative outcome of production and hence is defined as the Certified Normal Accommodation (CNA) less the actual average prisoner population; (ii) "Days" is the number of prisoner days, a basic throughput variable, defined as 365 x average prisoner population, expressed in thousands. Like Manpower and Non-manpower costs it has been split to reflect the number of (a) Remand and (b) Non-remand prisoners; (iii) Offence is the number of serious *punished* offences and is a further indicator of staff activity (in the regulation of inmates' lives).

Source: *Prison Statistics, 1984* and *Report of the work of the Prison Department, 1984/85.*

A potential framework for the implementation of relative efficiency analysis in the public sector

DEA efficiency coefficients derived from formal programming procedures and based on the data summarised in Table 4.3.1 may be used to form part of a performance data-flow in managerial and productive evaluation in the public sector. The Financial Management Initiative (FMI), as manifested in the *Multi-departmental review of budgeting* (HM Treasury, March 1986), and the Home Office's "Fresh Start" proposals appear to place branch organisations (e.g. the prison) into an evaluation hierarchy linked to a central-managerial function, for example the Prison Department. Performance along the branches or lines of this hierarchy generates data. These can be extracted for the central evaluation function. In the highly stylised terms of Figure 4.3.1 the line manager is devolved financial responsibility for a budget. The line manager, for example a prison governor, discharges this budget in the knowledge that at year-end he is accountable to the centre (the Prison Department) for his performance.

Accordingly, data accrues to the centre at year-end and may be used in an efficiency evaluation and screening process. This could include an annual DEA evaluation of branch performance carried out by central management who will control next year's funding on the basis of these results. Best-practice organisations will be recognised in DEA terms by the recommendation that subsequent budgets can be fully justified. Poorer performers can be set cost targets derived from the efficiency coefficient.

Typically these will entail that existing levels of service be maintained at a reduced budget from which last period's inefficient expenditure has been deducted.

Figure 4.3.1
A stylised view of FMI & the Fresh Start scheme

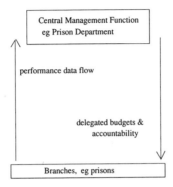

DEA results on prison relative efficiency with a VRS technolgy: Overview

Table 4.3.2 contains relative efficiency coefficients using Data Envelopment Analysis with a varying returns to scale (VRS) technology assumption embodied in the underlying linear program. The results have been estimated for the full cross section of 25 local prisons, 7 remand centres and 1 Category B closed training prison.

These prisons operate in an environment constrained by court decisions, crime rates and the statute book. Consequently many of the outcomes of prison production like prisoner days and overcrowding are wholly or partially beyond the control of the individual prison. In these circumstances the cost rather than the output dimensions of efficiency are more germane because it is only costs which are truly discretionary (after certain minima, of course) from the prison decision-maker's point of view. *A fortiori* targets for outputs in these circumstances would be unattainable. Accordingly the efficiency coefficients contained in Table 4.3.2 have been estimated using the input-minimisation version of the DEA program (in place of its output-maximising counterpart) assuming the prison decision-maker strives to minimise the cost of producing given levels of output. The analysis of efficiency on the input-side rather than the output-side is becoming common in DEA applications for a variety of reasons. In the context of constraints on output Dawson (1987) used an input-minisation program in the analysis of dairying where output is set exogenously through EC quotas.[1] Owing to the difficulties frequently encountered measuring public sector outputs several authors (Maindiratta (1990), Mersha (1989), Fare, Grosskopf and Lovell (1988), Kumbhakar (1988) and Mellander and Ysander (1987)) have recommended that efficiency studies focus as far as possible on the more reliably measureable aspects of production; that is, on the cost behaviour of organisations measured in money terms.

---

(1) The general problem of exogenously fixed inputs or outputs is discussed in Ray (1988) and Banker and Morey (1986a,b).

Table 4.3.2
DEA-efficiency coefficients under varying returns to scale in local prisons and remand centres in 1984/85

Prison	Cost efficiency	Peer group
1. Ashford	1.0000	1
2. Bedford	0.7095	15, 16
3. Brockhill	1.0000	3
4. Birmingham	0.8459	14, 16, 28, 31
5. Bristol	1.0000	5
6. Brixton	1.0000	6
7. Canterbury	0.8581	5, 16, 28, 29, 30
8. Cardiff	0.9782	5, 13, 16, 29
9. Coldingley	1.0000	9
10. Dorchester	1.0000	10
11.Durham	0.8817	5, 16, 30, 31
12.Exeter	0.8293	3, 5, 16, 21, 28, 30, 31
13.Glen Parva	1.0000	13
14.Gloucester	1.0000	14
15.Latchmere House	1.0000	15
16.Leeds	1.0000	16
17.Leicester	0.7806	14, 16, 29, 30
18.Lewes	0.9858	1, 3, 6, 16
19.Lincoln	0.8873	3, 16, 28, 31
20.Liverpool	1.0000	20
21.Low Newton	1.0000	21
22.Manchester	1.0000	22
23.Norwich	0.8896	13, 15, 16, 31
24.Oxford	0.9913	10, 14, 15, 16, 20
25.Pentonville	1.0000	25
26.Pucklechurch	1.0000	26
27.Reading	0.9514	16, 28, 30
28.Shrewsbury	1.0000	28
29.Swansea	1.0000	29
30.Thorpe Arch	1.0000	30
31.Wandsworth	1.0000	31
32.Winchester	0.8951	3, 5, 13, 16, 30, 31
33.W.Scrubs	1.0000	33

Mean inefficiency $(1/n \sum TE_i < 1)$: 0.8834
S. Dev'n.   : 0.0825

Note: The mean and standard deviation are calculated for technical efficiency scores less than unity.

Source: Authors' calculations.

Thus Table 4.3.2 summarises the cost behaviour of prisons relative to a best-practice cost frontier defined by prisons with unity technical efficiency *(TE)* scores.   There are 20 best-practice prisons in Table 4.3.2 which form peer groups for inefficient prisons along a piecewise linear average cost function.   Thirteen prisons of the full cross section of 33 have been identified as technically inefficient relative to the peer prisons on the cost frontier.   At some establishments inefficiency is quite marked: Bedford has *TE* = 0.71 and Leicester *TE* = 0.78. By contrast there are near trivial divergences from best-practice in others, *viz.*, at Oxford with *TE* = 0.99.   The mean technical inefficiency is 0.88.   As a representative value for inefficiency this suggests there are substantial excess costs through the cross section as a whole. That is, there are average cost reductions of around 12% for a representative prison with a non-unity efficiency score. Ignoring additional slack adjustments, this implies next period's budget (for 1985/86) might have been adjusted downwards by 12% at the representative establishment.

Costs at Canterbury

Canterbury has a representative level of technical inefficiency, 0.86, which is close to the mean level of 0.88. It is therefore a useful example of the typical correction to resource consumption required in this cross section for boundary production. In Table 4.3.3 targets have been estimated for each cost item at Canterbury. The largest wastage at Canterbury is associated with the manpower aspects of the containment of remand prisoners. This is intuitively reasonable given the extra work generated by untried and unsentenced prisoners.

Table 4.3.3
Costs at Canterbury local prison

	Actual £M	Target £M	Saving %
Manpower costs			
(1)Remand	1.845	1.463	21
(2)Non-remand	2.060	1.767	14
Non-manpower costs			
(1)Remand	0.418	0.358	14
(2)Non-remand	0.466	0.376	19
Total costs	4.789	3.964	17

Source: *Prison Department Report, 1984/85* and authors' calculations.

Summing the cost targets suggests a scaling down of total costs at Canterbury of approximately 17%. This reduction in total costs includes a radial contraction (reflecting the efficiency score) and a slack component. The efficiency score at Canterbury is 0.86 which implies an equal 14% scaling down in each of the cost variables. It is the presence of non-zero input slacks in particular cost items which raises the overall reduction in total costs to 17%.

The peer group comparison

The nature of the efficient subset of production possibilities has been developed rigorously and on an axiomatic basis by Fare and Hunsacker (1986). To date, however, the definition and meaning of a peer establishment in empirical applications has often been left unclear in the literature. This section clarifies the definition of a peer and provides a further assessment of its usefulness to inefficient establishments in the light of claims in the literature and the results tabulated above. The definition and meaning of the peer group have also been discussed in Chapters 2 and 3.

It is argued throughout the literature (see e.g. Bowlin and White (1988), Bowlin (1987), Charnes, Cooper and Rhodes (1981, 1979, 1978)) that attainment of boundary performance is facilitated by appeal to the peer group attainments identified by DEA.

The peer establishments have best-practice costs and are likely to be producing at broadly similar scale. The target is a weighted average of their performance. Given that it is genuinely comparable with the peers selected by DEA, the inefficient prison like Canterbury should be able to modify its performance to levels defined by them—borrowing the better productive and managerial procedures which they are presumably implementing.

L.P. definition of the peer group
These peer units can be defined in terms of the linear program (L.P.) underlying the results in this Chapter.

The prisons' cross section contained $j = 1,. . .,p,. . .,33$ establishments. If X_{ip} is the *i*th input for a branch p and Y_{kp} its *k*th output the varying returns dual program for input efficiency for a unit p becomes:

(1)
$$MIN\ h_p - \varepsilon \left[\sum_{i=1}^{4} s_i + \sum_{k=1}^{4} s_k \right]$$
$$\lambda_j$$

subject to

(2)
$$h_p X_{kp} - s_k = \sum_{j=1}^{33} \lambda_j X_{kj} \qquad k = 1,2,3,4$$

(3)
$$Y_{ip} + s_i = \sum_{j=1}^{33} \lambda_j Y_{ij} \qquad i = 1,2,3,4$$

(4)
$$1 = \sum_{j=1}^{33} \lambda_j$$

and

$$\lambda_j \ge 0, \quad j = 1,...,p,...,33 (\text{branches})$$

$$s_i \ge 0, \quad i = 1,...,4\ (\text{output slacks})$$

$$s_k \ge 0, \quad k = 1,...,4\ (\text{input slacks})$$

The λ_j are the weights on branches (or intensity variables—see Fare, Grosskopf and Logan (1987, 1985)), the s_i are output slacks and the s_k input slacks; and where the RHS of the constraints (2) and (3) define the peer group. This is apparent on consideration of the implications of $h_p^* = 1$ and $h_p^* < 1$, where (*) denotes the optimal value of a variable in the basic solution of the DEA program. If the unit p has $h_p^* = 1$ and $s_i^* = s_k^* = 0$, for all i and k then it is relatively efficient. In this case the definition of the peer group becomes trivial since $\lambda_p^* = 1$ and $\lambda_j^* = 0$, for $j \ne p$. Essentially the efficient unit p has no peers (other than itself). However, where $h_p^* < 1$, $\lambda_p^* = 0$ and some subset of the remaining λ_j^* ($j \ne p$) are non-zero. These non-zero λ_j^* are weights on units with $h_p{}^* = 1$ and constitute the peer group for p. For example Canterbury (unit 7) has five peer units. These are Bristol, Leeds, Shrewsbury, Swansea and Thorpe Arch. In terms of the program this means $\lambda_5^*, \lambda_{16}^*, \lambda_{28}^*, \lambda_{29}^*$, and λ_{30}^* are all non-zero in the optimal solution to the program for Canterbury. The constraints in the program for Canterbury are thus:

(2) $$0.86X_{k7} - s_k = \lambda_5^* X_{k5} + \lambda_{16}^* X_{k16} + \lambda_{28}^* X_{k28} + \lambda_{29}^* X_{k29} + \lambda_{30}^* X_{k30,} \quad k = 1,2,3,4$$

(3) $$Y_{i7} + s_i = \lambda_5^* Y_{i5} + \lambda_{16}^* Y_{i16} + \lambda_{28}^* Y_{i28} + \lambda_{29}^* Y_{i29} + \lambda_{30}^* Y_{i30,} \quad i = 1,2,3,4$$

(4) $$1 = \lambda_5^* + \lambda_{16}^* + \lambda_{28}^* + \lambda_{29}^* + \lambda_{30}^*$$

The constraints (2) and (3) define both the peer group for Canterbury and in addition the feasible production space; that is (2) and (3) are hyperplanes in the production space which together constitute an efficient, eight-dimensional surface against which interior production at the prison can be compared to estimate an efficiency score (see Banker, Charnes and Cooper (1984)). Constraint (4) is the "technological constraint"; its absence would imply that the intensity variables (λ_j, $j = 1,. . .,n$) are calculated unconstrained in the program which amounts to an assumption of constant returns to scale (see Grosskopf (1986), Fare, Grosskopf and Lovell (1985) and Chapter 2). The restriction that they should instead sum to unity originates in Banker (1984) and allows local variations in scale over the production surface.

The peer group and its interpretation in the literature

One of the major normative propositions in the literature (see Bowlin (1986), Bessent, Bessent, Elan and Long (1984), Bessent, Bessent, Charnes Cooper and Thorogood (1983), Lewin, Morey and Cook (1982), Lewin and Morey (1981), Charnes, Cooper and Rhodes (1979, 1978) for example) entails that the inefficient decision-maker such as Canterbury should be able to compare itself with the units identified in the constraints (2, 3 and 4) in order to extract examples of better managerial and productive behaviour. This could take the form of on-site inspection of peer prison procedures or greater disaggregation of costs at the modelling stage. It is likely however that expansion of the input-output variable set would lead to a significant reduction in the ability of DEA to identify non-unit efficiency scores. Bowlin (1987, page 133), Parkan (1987) and Nunamaker (1985) have shown that for a given number of establishments the *a priori* expectation after this kind of modification would be for an increase in the number of best-practice establishments, for: "the more variables considered, the greater the chance some inefficient [unit] will dominate on the added dimension and thus become efficient" (Nunamaker (1985, page 54)). In addition Nunamaker demonstrates that the addition of variables will produce an upward "trend" in the efficiency scores. The discriminating power of DEA is correspondingly reduced since an establishment can raise its efficiency rating without increasing effort but rather by expanding the variable set used in the programming analysis. In this connection Nunamaker argues that, *ceteris paribus,* the *a priori* model of the production process should be kept as compact as possible in order to maximise the discriminating power of DEA.

It is not at all clear then that simply disaggregating the input-output variables or adding to them would enhance the information provided by the peer group for the inefficient establishment.   An interesting study by Parkan (1987) undertook the comparison of bank branches in Alberta, Canada.   The results were laid before managers who offered their own criticisms. They declared that: "the comparison of a branch which was declared relatively inefficient to a hypothetical composite branch, [that is, to a weighted average of the peer group as in constraints (2) and (3)] did not allow for convincing arguments as to where the inefficiencies lay" (Parkin (1987, page 242).

Table 4.3.4
Costs at Canterbury and of its relatively efficient peers

Costs (£M)	Cantbry	Bristol	Leeds	Shrswby	Swansea	T. Arch
Manpower						
(1)remand	1.845	1.061	4.453	0.832	1.019	1.936
(2)non-remand	2.060	4.989	4.230	1.456	2.225	0.344
Non-manpower						
(1)remand	0.418	0.231	1.196	0.204	0.192	0.543
(2)non-remand	0.466	1.087	1.136	0.357	0.419	0.096
Total	4.788	7.368	11.015	2.849	3.854	2.919

Note: Columns may not sum to totals exactly because of rounding.

Source: *Prison Department Report, 1984/85.*

In this connection Table 4.3.4 summarises the target variables for Canterbury and its peer institutions.   At this level of cost aggregation precise indications as to potential sources of improvement are not conspicuous, despite contrary claims in the literature. Comparing the cost profiles of all six prisons it is not the case that Canterbury spends the largests sums and hence the claim of Thanassoulis *et al* (1987, page 403) that "comparing an inefficient unit with the efficient units in its reference set *shows up clearly how the former's performance is weak*" (emphasis added) is too enthusiastic an interpretation of the peer group without a much more detailed investigation of procedures at the individual prisons themselves.

Greater detail of procedures may be obtained through finer disaggregation of costs at the modelling stage but as indicated earlier this may alter the efficiency scores and so make the scale of the associated targets ambiguous.   In some cases, then, inspection of the peer group can only provide limited suggestions as to how performance can be improved.   More precise lessons may only come through *on-site inspection* of operations at the inefficient prison itself.

Comparison of *ex ante* and *ex post* efficiency predictions
Prior to the formal programming analysis with DEA, *ex ante* predictions of prison efficiency were made in Table 4.3.1.   These predictions were based on the levels of

costs in the prisons and were summarised in Table 4.3.1. Thorpe Arch and Gloucester were singled out on this *"ex ante"* basis as establishments that were likely to prove efficient under DEA. The results in Table 4.3.2 suggest that these prisons are indeed efficient or "best-practice". Brixton and Wandsworth on the other hand also attain best-practice status in DEA which contradicts the crude *ex ante* prediction that these prisons were likely to be inefficient.

This apparent contradiction can probably be explained by the contribution of all input and output variables in the estimation of the DEA cost-efficiency coefficient: Heavy costs notwithstanding, Brixton and Wandsworth produce substantial prisoner throughputs (prisoner days). That all dimensions of production contribute to the efficiency score marks it out as equitable *vis-à-vis* traditional productivity measures. As Todd (1985) and Ruchlin (1977) have argued, production and output are the result of all inputs applied in combination and not the application of inputs in isolation as is suggested by the partial-productivity measure like output-per-head.

The correlation between DEA-efficiency and the data

The link between DEA-efficiency and the levels of costs at prisons can be examined further on the basis of the following hypothesis. For given outcomes, the DEA technical-efficiency score *(TE)* is some function of the vector of target variables. Using the input-minimisation version of the DEA program outputs are taken as given and costs are targeted. Thus if:

(4.3.1) $$TE_{inp} = f(\underline{C} \; ; \underline{Y})$$

where $\underline{C}$ is a vector of prison costs (the target variables) and $\underline{Y}$ is a vector of (fixed) outcomes; then a reasonable efficiency hypothesis might be:

(4.3.2) $$\frac{\delta TE_{inp}}{\delta C_j} < 0, \quad j = 1,...,4.$$

That is, *ceteris paribus*, increases in the 4 cost items will be negatively associated with movements in the input efficiency score, TE_{inp}. Analogously, other things being equal, technical efficiency might be related to higher outputs:

(4.3.3) $$\frac{\delta TE_{inp}}{\delta Y_i} > 0, \quad i = 1,...,4.$$

(4.3.2) and (4.3.3) can be translated into the simple linear correlation hypothesis:

$$Ho : a = 0$$

$$H_A : a \gtrless 0$$

where a is the linear correlation coefficient between the efficiency score and the relevant input/output variable. Naturally the negative version of the alternative hypothesis is consistent with (4.3.2) and the positive version with (4.3.3).

Table 4.3.5 summarises calculated values of a for two different types of efficiency score.   Column 1 contains the correlation of input and output variables with the efficiency scores based on a varying returns to scale (VRS) assumption in the production technology.   In column 2, comparable results are presented assuming a constant returns (CRS) technology.

Table 4.3.5
Linear correlation matrix for efficiency scores and the input-output variables in the prison model

	VRS	CRS
Target variables:		
Manpower Costs		
(1) Remand	0.0497	-0.4583*
(2) Non-remand	0.0114	0.2107
Non-manpower costs		
(1) Remand	0.0751	-0.4255*
(2) Non-remand	0.0640	0.2290
Outputs:		
Prisoner Days		
(1) Remand	0.0609	-0.2248
(2) Non-remand	0.0717	0.2902**
Offences	0.2169	0.2982**
Overcrowding	0.1092	0.1155

Notes:

(1) The critical value of the linear correlation coefficient with $n-2 = 31$ degrees of freedom is ± 0.2961 at the 5% level.

(2) * denotes a significant variable at the 5% level.

(3) ** denotes a variable which is almost significant at the 5% level.

Source: Authors' calculations.

The critical value of the correlation coefficient at the 5% level is   0.296.   On this basis, the null hypothesis that there is no linear association between VRS efficiency and costs cannot be rejected.   However, this is not the case for the constant returns to scale efficiency measure.   Both the remand cost items are significantly negatively associated with CRS-efficiency at the 5% level.   On the output side, non-remand prisoner days and the offences variable are almost significant *vis-à-vis* CRS efficiency. Prison efficiency on a constant returns basis is discussed fully in Chapter 5. Note that CRS versions of the DEA program usually identify fewer best-practice establishments when compared with a VRS version of the program on the same data set. Consequently there is more variation in the CRS-efficiencies since there are more non-unity efficiency scores.   This may go some way to explain the greater significance of the CRS-efficiency scores in a linear correlation analysis.   In addition, of course, there may be non-linear relationships between efficiency and the target variables which cannot be identified here.

Nevertheless the bulk of the correlation coefficients—for both CRS and VRS efficiency are statistically insignificant (at the 5% level). This suggests that the *"ex post"* efficiency prediction by DEA does not follow trivially from the level of the (target) variables. In particular, *it would appear that high costs per se are as likely to be found at best-practice establishments (e.g. Brixton and Wandsworth) as they are elsewhere.*

4.4. Inert production: A new interpretation with DEA

Chapter 2 outlined the importance of a frontier measure of efficiency and noted its congruence with economic theory as far as maximising behaviour is concerned. DEA provides a means for estimating frontier performance and in this sense it is an appropriate tool for efficiency measurement. It is important to clarify the overlap between DEA and economic concepts like optimising behaviour. Much of the development of DEA has been undertaken in the case-oriented Operations Research literature, outside the economics mainstream. Consequently it has developed without full justification in economic theory. In particular, no analytical rationale has been advanced as to why one organisation gets a higher efficiency score than another. However, the concept of an "inert area" originally proposed by Leibenstein (1987, 1980, 1975, 1969) in his work on X-efficiency can be re-interpreted to provide, in economic terms, a firmer picture of the nature and variations in efficiency. It is the objective of this section to develop such an interpretation of inert production which could be offered as a tentative explanation of the causes of the differences in efficiency identified by DEA in Table 4.3.2.

Definition of the inert area

Specifically, economic agents may behave so as to yield non-maximising outcomes because different groups within the enterprise have conflicting priorities and may have equilibrium effort levels below those which are optimal from the whole organisation's point of view (cf Bös and Peters (1991)). Leibenstein's concept of the inert area addresses these possibilities and brings a utility dimension to efficiency measurement in much the same way that Debreu (1951) first tried to define inefficiency in utility terms. Thus in Leibenstein (1969, page 607) an inert area is defined as: "a set of effort positions whose associated levels of utility are not equal but in which the action required to go from a lower to a higher [effort] level involves a utility cost that is not compensated". Unlike non-human inputs, labour suppliers have preferences and may voluntarily alter their performance. Subject to certain constraints, these preferences will determine the amount of effort attached to units of labour time purchased by the employer which maximises their utility. Given that work is not completely meaningless this level of effort will be non-zero but may be below that which would otherwise maximise the surplus from production.

This perspective on the organisation has been embraced in models of the principal-agent relationship and in Williamson's transactions cost framework. The key point in this literature is that contracts are neither complete nor self-enforcing because the principal has incomplete information on agents' effort, preferences and abilities. Thus while the labour contract may stipulate a fixed amount of labour time purchased per period effort remains a variable, so output is unpredictable *ex ante*. From the employer's point of view, a straightforward relationship between labour purchases, output and remuneration is lost—the essential ingredient being that labour effort and purchases of labour time are not the same thing.

Sources of inert production

Saraydar (1991), Frantz (1988) and Button (1985) have indicated the sources of inert production. Supervisors or "principals" may have a desire to extract higher levels of effort from supervisees than the latter are willing to offer (Rees (1985)). Equally, to obtain increased levels of effort implies that supervisors themselves must work harder in policing and regulation. This engenders a utility penalty for the supervisor such that he may feel it too costly in terms of his own utility to move to a higher effort point. Consequently subordinates have an opportunity to labour at an intensity that may be lower than that which is optimal for the performance of the organisation as a whole.

Several other factors may influence the extent of the inert area. Its scale can be expected to be determined by the "shelter" available to agents to buffer demands on their labour. Absence of competitive pressures in both public and private sectors is a major determinant of shelter (cf Stevenson (1983)). But for a given competitive background to the enterprise, the key influences are the internal organisation, regime and policing arrangements which prevail upon agents: "Full motivation, as implied in the maximisation concept, may work as long as we are thinking about one-man firms or very small firms with an over-dictator-manager [*sic*] in charge. But *differential motivation* becomes especially important once we consider large firms" (Leibenstein (1979), emphasis added). Once effort strategies vary in this way, the possibility of maximal frontier attainments—whether of costs or outputs—diminishes. Maximal attainments are the outcome of a well-behaved *Rational Economic Man* (Leibenstein (1980)).

Assuming the sources of inert production can be found in most organisations, it is not unreasonable to suggest that it is reflected in prison efficiencies reported in Table 4.3.2. This in turn would lend support to the Leibenstein (1975) reinterpretation of internal enterprise behaviour. That is:

(1) The individual agent, and not the enterprise itself, is the basic decision unit from an efficiency point of view; and

(2) There exist differing, unallied priorities among agents within the enterprise.

(1) and (2) are the result of the fact that labour is able to choose its preferred effort-levels, subject to certain constraints. Because these effort-levels may not be consistent with the levels of the enterprise as a whole Leibenstein coined his term "inert area" as an indicator of wasted labour potential. That is, as an indicator of the difference between that level of effort preferred by the individual and that preferred by the enterprise. Insofar as variations in performance reflect wasted labour potential, the DEA-efficiency score can be thought of as a measure of the inert area in production.

An elementary stylisation of the inert area

It is useful to formalise a model of the inert area at this point to illustrate the idea of wasted labour potential and its connection with the DEA-efficiency score. Leibenstein's basic thesis is that *the organisation typically requires greater effort than will maximise individual utilities.* Thus whilst increased labour effort might lower costs onto the cost function, the marginal utility gain of doing so to the individual may be trivial or even negative.

This motivates Figure 4.4.1 which depicts a stylised relationship between an individual's total utility and labour effort; it is based on Leibenstein (1980). *Ceteris paribus*, a typical agent has a utility function defined on labour effort *(L)*, *viz.*, $U = U(L)$. He derives satisfaction from additional effort up to the point (L^*, U^*) in Figure 4.4.1. Beyond L^* his total utility decreases monotonically because extra effort is tiresome for him and produces a negative marginal utility.

Figure 4.4.1

Utility and effort

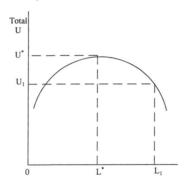

Leibenstein (1969) suggests that the enterprise can reduce its costs by extracting greater effort per unit of labour time purchased. If the organisation succeeds in obtaining greater effort levels it can reduce the total units of labour time purchased. Thus, *ceteris paribus*, it may prefer an effort level, say L_1, from individuals. The difference between this level of effort, which is optimal from the employer's point of view, and that preferred by the employee (L^*), is the inert area. From Figure 4.4.1 this translates into $(L_1 - L^*) > 0$. In general, any effort level beyond L^* will not be desired by individuals because it has a negative marginal utility and a non-zero inert area, reflecting wasted labour potential.

In principle, the difference between L^* and L_1 can be thought to reflect the difference between best-practice and inefficient production defined by a (non-unity) DEA-efficiency score. Attainment of the DEA target for an inefficient organisation then requires the elimination of the inert area by increasing agents' effort levels from L^* to L_1. By increasing effort levels the organisation can reduce the number of employee-hours it requires to produce a given output. This immediately lowers the wage bill and total costs. Given the traditional arguments about the flexibility of factors of production in the short run—that is, that labour is variable while other factors are not—suggests short-run adjustments onto the cost frontier can only take

place through reductions in the wage bill. These could be achieved either by making
some of the workforce redundant and asking large increase in effort levels from the
remainder. Or, the organisation can keep all its existing employees and ask each one
for a relatively smaller increase in work intensity.

To fix ideas, these arguments may be recast in Figure 4.4.2 which illustrates a stylised
frontier for average costs. Consider for example a hypothetical prison producing at
point *i* with average costs *OB*. Its DEA-efficiency score is *OA/OB* and the associated
target *OA*. Costs *OB* are relatively inefficient and presumably reflect agents preferred
effort levels, as at L^* in Figure 4.4.1. In principle, the only way the employer may be
able to reduce costs in the short run is to employ less labour. If the employer can
persuade agents to raise effort levels then the number of hours of labour purchased to
deliver output *OY* can fall. For a given wage rate, this will reduce the wage bill
because wasted labour potential is eliminated; that is, the reduction in average costs
(OB-OA) for best-practice could be achieved if labour effort per hour rose to remove
the inert area $L_1 - L^*$.

Figure 4.4.2

DEA & inert production

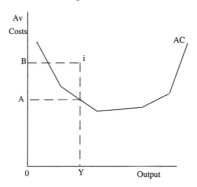

The main qualification falling on this argument would be that it suggests the whole of
the improvement in average costs suggested by DEA, *(OB - OA)*, is attainable through
increases in labour effort. As suggested earlier this relies on the likelihood of other
factors being fixed in the short run. If this is indeed the case then the only facet of
operations which may be able to absorb inefficiency will be the work intensity of
employees. However, if other adjustments are possible (e.g. in procedures,
equipment, etc.), then some or all of the DEA adjustment to costs may be attainable
without increases in work intensity.

The attainability of DEA targets

It has become clear that to attain a point of best-practice may require individuals to
work with an intensity greater than they would prefer. This is evident if the inert area
is expressed explicitly in utility terms. For effort points such as L_1 and L^* in Figure
4.4.1 the inert area would then be given by $[U(L_1) - U(L^*)] < 0$; that is, as the
difference between total utilities at non-preferred and preferred effort levels. The
expression is negative and indicates that there would be a net utility cost to the
individual of increased effort. In these circumstances the attainment of boundary
performance implies that individuals within an organisation would have to accept a

lower total utility from their work. Presumably such a situation could only be achieved after increased monitoring and regulation of work. Of course if individuals desired effort levels are coincident with those preferred by the organisation, best-practice production would not mean lower utility. Leibenstein's key (1979) point, however, is that such a situation (i.e. $L^* = L_1$) is unlikely unless in small owner-managed firms because of reasons of shelter and looseness in labour contracts in larger organisations. The possibility that achieving higher work intensities could mean lowering individual utilities underlines the difficulties that may be encountered in the implementation of targets. Individuals may resist voluntary calls to increase their effort such that costly increases in monitoring arrangements might become necessary. If the budgets are not available to develop stricter monitoring then inefficiency is likely to persist because individuals are unlikely to *voluntarily* increase their effort to a point of lower utility (Reifschneider and Stevenson (1991)).

Management may however be able to achieve some fraction of targeted savings by *bribing* employees into accepting lower utilities. In principle, management could "buy out" their lost utility by offering a higher wage rate which could be offset by greater effort on the part of workers.

DEA, X-efficiency and the inert area

Leibenstein's concept of an inert area has proven useful in permitting a tentative exploration of the inefficiencies identified by DEA in a traditional economic framework based on utility concepts. Furthermore, this utility-based interpretation of DEA suggests an economic rationale to explain why the targets by DEA might not be achieved. In particular, efficiency may persist because best-practice costs may require levels of effort from individuals which would lower their utility. A "rational" agent would not ordinarily be expected to volunteer lower utility and so if efficiency is not to persist this implies some form of coercion of agents might be necessary.

The framing of DEA in X-efficiency terms as an inert area suggests the first sense in which the extent of X-efficiency might be quantified. Button (1985, page 85) has written that "the problem of the X-efficiency concept is that it focuses on relationships that are essentially unobservable. Traditional economic methodology, involving the establishment of testable hypothesis, is particularly difficult to apply in such circumstances. Leibenstein himself tends to rely upon casual empiricism and sites a series of *ad hoc* case studies, examples and impressionistic findings to support his stance". However, if the inert area is a transactions failure caused by imperfect information, DEA can then be regarded as a method of measuring (and reducing) the extent of this organisational failure by providing indirect information on agents' effort levels.

4.5. Conclusion

This Chapter has implemented the revised DEA program of Banker (1984) on a representative cross-section of 33 local prisons and remand centres for the financial year 1984/85. The Banker approach represents a step forward on the original Farrell/Charnes and Cooper methodology which imposed constant returns to scale over the whole production surface. Banker added an additional constraint to the original DEA program (that the sum of the intensity variables is exactly unity) which permits the returns to scale to vary locally. It has thus been possible to estimate the efficient production correspondence for prisons without requiring restrictive assumptions on the underlying production technology. This is in contrast to classical econometric methods that estimate production correspondences using a prespecified parametric functional form which involves implicit assumptions about the nature of the underlying production technology. An interesting comparative study of efficiency in North Carolina hospitals by Banker, Conrad and Strauss (1986) has confronted non-parametric DEA estimates with a translog version of the production function. The translog results suggested that constant returns prevailed in the hospital sample, whereas the DEA procedure indicated that both increasing and decreasing returns to scale may be observed in different segments of the production correspondence, in turn suggesting that the translog model may have been "averaging" diametrically opposed behaviour. This comparative study provides evidence in favour of the non-parametric approach as used in this Chapter since the DEA estimates appear to be able to identify production behaviour more accurately.

On this basis thirteen establishments in the sample were diagnosed as operating with technical inefficiency. The mean level of the efficiency coefficient for inefficient prisons was 0.88 suggesting that these institutions could, on average, reduce their operating costs by around 12%. In some cases however, substantially greater orders of inefficiency were identified: For example at Bedford $TE = 0.71$ and at Leicester $TE = 0.78$.

The definition of the peer group which "drops out" of the solution to the DEA program was clarified in section 4.3. It is argued that there is no straightforward link between the peer group and improvements in performance at inefficient establishments, contrary to suggestions in the literature. Standards at peer establishments may only be dominant in one dimension (Nunamaker (1985)) and so certain cost items at an inefficient establishment may actually be lower than costs in the peer group—recall the comparison of Canterbury with its peers in Table 4.3.4.

The nature of inefficiency and its relationship with the level of costs was examined. A linear correlation analysis suggested that costs attributable to remand prisoners are significantly associated with the CRS efficiency coefficient. Simple inspection of the extreme values of the costs data does not provide enough information *ex ante* to predict an establishment's efficiency status in the DEA program. Gloucester and Thorpe Arch dominated on (respectively) the remand and non-remand cost variables in Table 4.3.1 and achieved best-practice status in the DEA results. This is consistent with Nunamaker (1985) who demonstrated that dominance on a single variable is enough to confer full technical efficiency in DEA.

However, *ex ante*, it is not possible to predict the consequences of sub-dominance on efficiency. Brixton and Wandsworth had the highest remand and non-remand expenditures (see Table 4.3.1). Nonetheless they were identified as technically efficient in the DEA program. It follows that *sub-dominance in a particular variable (that is, excess costs or deficient outputs) implies of itself neither efficiency or inefficiency.* This can be attributed to the total-factor view embodied in the underlying DEA-efficiency ratio.   The inefficiency coefficient is effectively a weighted average of performance on all variables and so sub-dominance on a single variable cannot in its own right determine   an establishment's efficiency status. Herein lies the advantage of a total-factor approach over the more traditional partial view which defines productivity as a ratio of a single output to a single input.   The use of methods embodying a total-factor view in performance measurement is now widely recommended in the literature—see for example the volume edited by Cowling and Stevenson (eds.) (1984), Pickering (1983), Richardson and Gordon (1980) and Craig and Harris (1973).

Harvey Leibenstein's ideas on X-efficiency have for two decades remained on the periphery of the analysis of productivity.   Experience in any organisation suggests the existence of slack and that inputs—in particular labour—may not be fully employed. This apparently innocuous proposition has eluded empirical estimation leaving X-efficiency theory as little more than an addendum to the literature.

Section 4.4 formalises X-efficiency in terms of the concept of an inert area (an idea also proposed originally by Leibenstein); it argues that, *ceteris paribus*, the efficiency coefficient can be regarded as a quantitative guide to inert production.   This is a significant step forward in that the concept is now brought within the domain of empirically quantifiable hypotheses and may lead to its incorporation into empirical research more generally.   A development of this nature is all the more remarkable given that Leibenstein himself has tended to draw support from casual empiricism and *ad hoc* case studies (see for example Leibenstein (1970, 1966)).

Finally, section 4.4 suggested a utility-based interpretation of technical inefficiency. Consistent with recent research (e.g. Singh and Frantz (1991)), it was argued that inefficiency may be the result of agents lowering their effort levels to maximise individual utilities.   If these effort levels are not consistent with minimum costs, the organisation will face a motivational problem because individuals have no incentive to work harder if this lowers their personal utilities.   Consequently inefficiency may be a persistent phenomenon making DEA targets unobtainable without coercion or bribes.

APPENDIX 4.1

Local Prisons and Remand Centres Data Set

PRISON	(1)	(2)	(3)	(4)	(5)	(6)	(7)	(8)
1 Ashford	3.24324	1.8564	0.911196	0.52156	-88	108405	62050	185
2 Bedford	1.7108	2.11406	0.5096	0.62972	-139	51100	63145	65
3 Brockhill	1.73316	0.35178	0.609232	0.123656	-68	73730	14965	110
4 Birmingham	2.961244	5.627232	0.904332	1.718496	-419	124465	236520	139
5 Bristol	1.060904	4.9894	0.231088	1.0868	-5	36865	173375	41
6 Brixton	11.84555	2.902068	3.239808	0.793728	-299	236885	58035	96
7 Canterbury	1.844856	2.059668	0.41756	0.46618	-65	53290	59495	44
8 Cardiff	1.34992	3.27184	0.27612	0.66924	-65	43070	104390	73
9 Coldingley	0.89908	2.8899	0.2548	0.819	-3	25550	82125	16
10 Dorchester	0.6435	1.4274	0.1716	0.38064	-51	20075	44530	30
11 Durham	2.1931	6.3882	0.639132	1.861704	-235	87965	256230	80
12 Exeter	1.5288	3.40704	0.4004	0.89232	-100	51100	113880	77
13 Glen Parva	1.239576	4.451616	0.42744	1.53504	-28	50005	179580	573
14 Gloucester	0.554944	2.485184	0.10764	0.48204	-59	16790	75190	18
15 Latchmere Hse	0.840008	0.962936	0.264368	0.303056	-48	29930	34310	109
16 Leeds	4.452552	4.229576	1.196208	1.136304	-622	233235	221555	123
17 Leicester	1.989104	3.092648	0.409968	0.637416	-174	53290	82855	36
18 Lewes	3.101956	1.730872	0.978692	0.546104	-159	116435	64970	150
19 Lincoln	2.116296	3.085524	0.594048	0.866112	-227	86870	126655	75
20 Liverpool	0	9.52224	0	3.536832	-307	0	477420	90
21 Low Newton	1.585012	0.915408	0.515372	0.297648	-107	68255	39420	230
22 Manchester	3.966768	7.26024	1.296828	2.37354	-360	178485	326675	125
23 Norwich	1.50696	4.10904	0.510692	1.392508	-121	58765	160235	80
24 Oxford	0.938184	1.286376	0.282464	0.387296	-107	35405	48545	18
25 Pentonville	1.794208	6.04656	0.755456	2.54592	-163	82855	279225	128
26 Pucklechurch	1.55064	0.915616	0.41496	0.245024	-8	38325	22630	113
27 Reading	1.646268	1.33224	0.440804	0.35672	-136	63145	51100	23
28 Shrewsbury	0.832	1.456	0.20384	0.35672	-50	29200	51100	32
29 Swansea	1.019096	2.224612	0.19188	0.41886	-23	29930	65335	62
30 Thorpe Arch	1.936116	0.34398	0.542932	0.09646	-67	71905	12775	89
31 Wandsworth	0	10.55288	0	3.796	-202	0	532900	361
32 Winchester	1.828008	4.01388	0.511056	1.12216	-116	68985	151475	116
33 W. Scrubs	5.494944	7.075536	1.64309	2.115724	-239	189070	243455	179

(1) Manpower Costs (remand element), £m.
(2) Manpower Costs (non-remand element), £m.
(3) Non-manpower Costs (remand element), £m.
(4) Non-manpower Costs (non-remand element), £m.
(5) Overcrowding (designated population less actual).
(6) Prisoner Days (remand element).
(7) Prisoner Days (non-remand element).
(8) Serious Offences by Inmates.

Source: *Prison Statistics, 1984* and *Report of the Work of the Prison Department, 1984/85.*

CHAPTER 5

PROGRAMME-EFFICIENCY IMPLICATIONS OF DATA ENVELOPMENT ANALYSIS

5.1. Introduction

Since its inception, Data Envelopment Analysis has often been used as a measure of technical efficiency within larger organisations with a branch structure. However in many contexts it is the performance of the larger organisation of which the branch is only a part which is of most relevance. A good example occurs in the determination of public expenditure. Government departments in the UK make a bid each year to the Treasury for resources. The reaction of the Treasury to this bid will depend on many considerations, not the least of which is the perceived value for money of the programmes[1] operated by the department. In evaluating the efficiency of a spending programme, central decision-makers will not usually have the resources to consider the detailed performance outcomes of the smaller operating units within the programme. Quite simply, as Nelson (1981, page 1,039) has remarked: "top management is limited in the number of things it can control or attend to in any detail". It follows that the control of production for efficient outcomes requires information to summarise branch-level operations to a point which gives a more concise, summary picture of the operation of the programme as a whole.

In 1980 a system known as MINIS (Management Information System for Ministers) was set up at the UK Environment Department to provide top management with key data on "low-level" operations within the Department. For similar purposes, this Chapter seeks to summarise the branch-level (or "line") information provided by DEA into indicators of the performance of the whole programme. It is argued that this summary information on programme performance could play an important dual role in public sector decision-making. First, in top management systems like MINIS; and second in the operation of the annual Public Expenditure Survey (PES) where the Treasury requires summary performance data to evaluate proposed departmental spending bids.

Section 5.2 of this Chapter develops a methodology for the aggregation of branch-efficiency scores and examines the aggregate efficiency of the prison spending programme by way of its illustration. This is extended in section 5.3 which examines the implications for costs and efficiency of an alternative constant returns to scale assumption in the underlying linear program. The causes of differences in costs under varying and constant returns are explained in section 5.4.

Building on the work of Rangan *et al* (1988), section 5.5 shows that excess costs in a spending programme can be decomposed into a scale and technical efficiency component. Together with the Banker (1984) scale indicator, this enables the joint

---

(1) "Programme" denotes a government budget on prisons or health care for example. "Program" refers to a linear program (L.P.).

identification of the *magnitude and direction* of change required to bring operations to the optimal scale. To date many studies in the empirical DEA literature have attributed the total variation in excess costs to technical efficiency alone. The results presented in section 5.5 suggest this may be a misleading diagnosis of inefficient production since scale inefficiencies are an important determinant of excess costs in prison operations. Section 5.6 develops the analysis of scale efficiency, taking into consideration the argument of Banker and Thrall (1989) that there may be *multiple* points of maximum average productivity in an empirical VRS boundary. Banker and Thrall (1989) have proposed the identification of these points through estimates of the bounds on the slopes of line segments (facets) in the production frontier. This suggestion is evaluated alongside our own solution to this problem which involves identification of maximum and minimum values of the scale indicator. Section 5.7 draws the Chapter to a close, noting the main conclusions for prison management and efficiency policy and measurement more generally.

5.2.   The cost efficiency of a multi-branch public spending programme: The case of local prisons and remand centres

The problem of programme evaluation

Farrell's original (1957) empirical contribution investigated the relative performance of agriculture across whole states in the USA. In a similar way, section 5.2 sets DEA into a more aggregative context to provide information on the performance of whole spending programmes. This is a departure for DEA which hitherto has been largely a tool for the measurement of branch efficiency alone.

Many spending programmes are made up of a complex web of branches which deliver final services to the client. The performance of individual branches within the programme can be measured using DEA in the manner outlined in Chapters 3 and 4. Analysis of spending and delivery at the programme-level however, is potentially more difficult owing to the diversity of institutions and activities which may be involved. Zeleny (1974) concluded that "human ability to arrive at an overall evaluation by weighting and combining diverse attributes is not very impressive". Other studies like Balachandran and Steuer (1982) indicate that the optimal set of weights required to summarise productivity measures is typically dependent upon variable measurement scales and the decision-maker's preference function. In the presence of non-marketed outputs with a merit significance decision-making for the prisons' spending programme is no less problematic than these studies suggest.

Consequently at the programme-level, performance evaluation requires a form of "informational reductionism" to condense large volumes of information into quantities tractable enough for decision-makers. One means of summarising information in this context may be Data Envelopment Analysis and, more generally, total-factor productivity measures. These are effectively condensed performance statements in which productivity is defined in a summary fashion, thereby avoiding the complexity and potential ambiguity of multiple single-factor measures. A good example of the difficulties posed by traditional measures is a UK database on local authority performance containing 400 indicators of activity and resource use (see Department of Health and Social Security (1985, 1983)). The existence of such a large volume of indicators may conceivably hinder as much as it assists senior-management decision-making. Thus Mersha (1989, page 164) argued that "the derivation of *a single overall performance index* will provide a more operational and practical basis for evaluating the relative performance of competing agencies" (emphasis added). Like Mersha, Fare, Grosskopf and Lovell (1988, page 79) have argued that efficiency measures may play a broader role "in circumstances in which a public agency oversees the operation of a number of service providers. Examples are state departments of education overseeing many school districts, state departments of justice supervising local courts and the like".

In principle, DEA provides an overall performance index—such as Mersha (1989) and others have sought—which eschews several common public sector measurement difficulties. For example, it does not require the decision-maker to express his own weighting scheme for inputs and outputs. Equally however, research by Beasley (1988), Beasley and Wong (1989) and Golany (1988) has shown that, where appropriate, the constraints in the DEA program may be re-formulated in order to permit *a priori* restrictions on input and output weights: For example where inputs or outputs have a meritocratic or legal significance their *unconstrained* weighting as in the conventional DEA program may be inappropriate. Moreover, it may be useful in some contexts to simulate the effects on performance ratings of different value systems, i.e., of different weights.

Furthermore, in normal circumstances, the DEA relative-efficiency coefficient is derived unaffected by units of measurement in the underlying data (see Charnes and Cooper (1984) for formal proof of the latter proposition). Most significantly however, it summarises performance into a single measure and thereby avoids the ambiguity of multiple productivity ratios.

Modernisation of public sector accounting methodologies

The importance of DEA to productivity measurement has been quite widely recognised for the evaluation of branch-level efficiencies. However, it is clear that similar benefits are likely to accrue from the application of DEA at higher levels of aggregation. Charnes and Cooper (1980a,b) recommend DEA in their concept of a broader "comprehensive audit" for public programmes in the modernisation of public sector accounting and evaluation. Indeed Charnes and Cooper argue that in this context DEA fulfils a need and a tradition for servicing third-party requirements for information, together with additional professional requirements for objectivity, care and validation. This view, that DEA can be seen as a development of the public-sector auditing function, is now widely supported by economists in this literature. Thus Smith (1988), Greenberg and Nunamaker (1987), Smith and Mayston (1986) and Sherman (1984) have developed arguments which support the use of DEA in the analysis of *broader* public sector budgets.

The UK government's White Paper on efficiency policy[1] is significant here because it advocates change in the structure of public institutions which is consistent with the application of DEA at a more aggregate level. Specifically, the White Paper proposes

---

(1)   *Civil Service Management Reform: The Next Steps.* Cm 524, London: HMSO. November, 1988.

that the bulk of departments' non-policy-making functions be re-organised as "executive agencies". Agencies are designed to have a large degree of financial autonomy, surviving on budgets devolved to them from the parent department. This initiative broadens the scope for public sector monitoring and evaluation because some degree of central control over budgeting will be lost to the agencies. As the White Paper puts it: "Agencies will be expected to install robust management systems, including proper measures of efficiency, as a basis on which ministers can confidently delegate as much responsibility as possible to them. Stretching performance targets will be set and monitored regularly. The Government's aim is that controls should be few but effective, and it agrees that, provided demanding performance targets are set and monitored, and firm overall controls are maintained, it should be possible to reduce the degree of detailed control of agencies" (CM 524, page 9).

It is in this context of the modernisation and development of public sector auditing that section 5.2 proposes a new methodology for the aggregation of branch performance in a manner which summarises the implications of agency (i.e. branch) performance for programme-level costs. It will be argued that DEA-derived measures of programme performance may be used as accounting rules in the annual public-expenditure round where programmes compete for resources out of the planning total.

The structure of multi-branch public spending programmes and a further role for DEA

DEA enables the estimation of technical efficiency for each organisation within public-spending programmes with a branch structure. This information is important to the line manager of each branch who must be aware of its potential implications for funding next period. In the spending of public monies, the line (branch) manager is accountable to his sponsoring department which may play a judicial role analogous to the functioning of the market in the private sector. Thus if a DEA evaluation of performance by the sponsoring department is unfavourable this could be the basis for budget reductions at branches next period. Incidentally, many public sector organisations have a "sponsoring department". Prisons are managed by the Prison Department at the Home Office; hospitals by the Department of Health; job centres by the Department of Employment; local authorities by the Department of the Environment and so on.

Ultimately, the sponsoring department is itself responsible to the Treasury in the use of public funds. Performance measurement of departmental activity by the Treasury should acquire greater importance now that budgets are being increasingly devolved to "lower" levels of public sector management. The maintenance of central (Treasury) control over spending in this context requires a more aggregative view of performance than is provided by branch efficiency scores. Information on individual branch performance is generally too voluminous to be considered in detail at the Treasury in the allocation of broad spending totals to sponsoring departments. However, the branch structure of many public spending programmes may permit a second, broader role for the use of DEA evaluation. In particular, Mersha (1989, page 163) has observed that "most public service programmes are designed to achieve their objectives through lower level operating units and a programme's performance is eventually determined by the efficiency and effectiveness of such operating units".

Hence, where the performance of a spending programme is ultimately constituted by the performance of its sub-branches, it is possible to derive *aggregate* technical efficiency measures for the programme itself—simply by summing over branch performance.   Such measures overcome the excessive detail of branch-level performance indicators.   Hence they could be used by central funding institutions, such as the Treasury, in the allocation of broad spending totals to the sponsoring departments managing multi-branch spending programmes.

The methodology of multi-branch programme performance measurement

Consider then a multi-branch public expenditure programme.   Resources are disbursed through its n branches.   The programme is simply defined as the sum of spending at each branch i:

$$\sum_{i=1}^{n} C_i$$

The Aggregate Technical Efficiency *(ATE)* of the whole programme can be defined by the identity:

$$(5.2.1) \qquad ATE = \sum_{i=1}^{n} C_i^* / \sum_{i=1}^{n} C_i$$

where C_i^* is the DEA target (or best-practice) cost level for each branch; and C_i is its actual spend.   Disaggregated cost items within total costs may also be identified and so programme efficiency in each of these separate *(m)* classes may be defined:

$$(5.2.2) \qquad ATE_j = \sum_{i=1}^{n} C_{i,j}^* / \sum_{i=1}^{n} C_{i,j}, \quad j = 1, \ldots, m$$

where $C_{i,j}^*$ is the target cost level for item j at establishment i and $C_{i,j}$ is similarly defined for actual spending on j at i.

The main difference between the conventional branch efficiency and aggregate technical efficiency *(ATE_j)* scores is that the former vary over establishments while the latter are indexed on the input or output variables (having summed over establishments).   Their interpretation however is the same, *mutatis mutandis*.   As the efficiency of a branch approaches unity so technical efficiency is eliminated from its operations.   Equally, as ATE_j approaches unity (for $j = 1, \ldots, m$), technical inefficiency is eliminated in the m separate cost items within the programme.   When $ATE_j = 1$ for all j, the programme is operating at full cost efficiency with best-practice performance prevailing in all its constituent branches.

Programme performance and allocative efficiency

It should be noted that programme efficiency has been defined as the sum of branch-level technical efficiencies.   There is however an additional allocative element to overall economic efficiency *(OE)*.   Hence Farrell (1957) suggested the efficiency identity:

$$OE \equiv TE.AE$$

That is, overall efficiency is the product of technical efficiency *(TE)* and allocative efficiency *(AE)* measures.   In Figure 5.2.1 technical efficiency is the ratio *OB/OC* and measures the extent of "interior production".   Allocative efficiency reflects the discrepancy between the cost-minimising factor price-ratios at *D* and those observed at *A*.   Hence *AE = OA/OB* and *OE = OA/OC*.   Thus overall economic efficiency may be lower than technical efficiency.   This is because costs at *B*, C_1, are greater than those at *D*, C_0.   It follows that if technical efficiency is adjusted to take account of allocative efficiency, the implied cost adjustments for overall economic efficiency are greater than those necessary for technical efficiency alone.   Only in the unique case of production at *D*, will the adjustment to achieve technical efficiency be identical to that required for full economic efficiency.

Figure 5.2.1

Technical & allocative efficiency

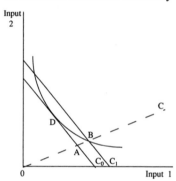

The methodology adopted in this Chapter for programme evaluation focuses on technical efficiency to the exclusion of allocative efficiency because of problems in the measurement of public sector prices.   These problems include: (1) There may be distortions in (non-competitive) factor markets due to monopoly or monopsony power —see Fare, Grosskopf and Lovell (1988).   This may mean that the prices ruling in markets are not genuine representations of the opportunity costs of inputs and hence allocative efficiency cannot be meaningfully defined against prevailing factor prices; (2) Particularly in a public sector context, prices may not exist or be intractable to definition (Sengupta (1982) and Margolis (1971)).   In this case the optimal factor price ratios for inputs *i* and *j*, (P_i^* / P_j^*), and hence the slope of the associated isocost hyperplane will be undefined; (3) Finally, some authors of efficiency studies have suggested that losses due to allocative inefficiency are small relative to technical efficiencies.   See McGuire (1987), Alessi (1983) and Leibenstein (1980), for example.

In these circumstances, programme performance has been defined in this section in terms of technical efficiency alone.   It is acknowledged that an adjustment for allocative efficiency, where possible, could increase the size of excess costs which might be identified in public spending programmes.   Subsequently, the analysis will be extended in section 5.5 to include the implications of scale inefficiencies for programme performance.

Estimates of Aggregate Technical Efficiency in the local prison spending programme under varying returns to scale

The prisons' model estimated in Chapter 4 identified four cost variables ($m = 4$) at 33 local prisons and remand centres. The Aggregate Technical Efficiency of the programme in each of these four items is defined:

$$ATE_j = \sum_{i=1}^{33} C_{i,j}^* / \sum_{i=1}^{33} C_{i,j} \quad j = 1, \ldots, 4$$

In this way Table 5.2.1 summarises the actual and target spending for manpower and non-manpower costs in local prisons in the financial year 1984/85. The cost targets derived in Chapter 4 assumed that the costs technology exhibits varying returns to scale. Table 5.2.1 also includes the implied total cost efficiency by summing costs and targets over j (cf the initial version of the aggregate efficiency identity (5.2.1)).

These results suggest about 5% of the aggregate prisons' budget addressed by these results is not spent efficiently. Moreover, in terms of the potential percentage gains the extent of cost inefficiency appears to be fairly evenly distributed across manpower and non-manpower costs. This implies that over the programme as a whole there are no substantial slack variable adjustments to be made in the cost variables. That is, the existence of vertical or horizontal facets in the VRS production surface is uncommon. It should be stated that the savings identified in Table 5.2.1 may be very much potential long-run gains. Lewis (ed.) (1986) argued that improving efficiency might require *increases* in budgets initially to assist in re-organisation, re-equipment, etc. For example, redundancy payments will swell costs in the present before a reduction in employment brings costs down in the future.

Table 5.2.1
The programme implications of prison cost inefficiency in 1984/85 under varying returns to scale

Costs	Actual £m	Target £m	ATE %	Saving %
Manpower				
(1) remand	69.41	66.30	95.5	4.5
(2) non-remand	114.38	109.06	95.3	4.7
Non-manpower				
(3) remand	19.85	18.78	94.6	5.4
(4) non-remand	34.51	32.96	95.5	4.5
Total costs	**238.15**	**227.15**	**95.4**	**4.6**

Notes:
Column 1 is the sum of actual spending on item j for all $i = 1, \ldots, 33$ prisons, ΣC_{ij}; column 2 is the sum of best-practice costs at these prisons for item j and is defined as $\Sigma C_{i,j}^*$, where * denotes best-practice costs; column 3 is the Aggregate Technical Efficiency of programme items in percentage terms, *viz.*, $ATE_j = (\Sigma C_{i,j}^* / \Sigma C_{i,j})100$; column 4 is the potential percentage saving which could result from best-practice production, that is, $(1-ATE_j)100$.

Source: Authors' calculations and *Prison Department Report, 1984/85.*

There is also the question of the quality of service and efficiency. Higher costs may be the result of a better service which will suffer from future budget restrictions. In the evaluation of the target itself, it will be useful for decision-makers to have well-defined norms and references against which to assess quality. If conventional standards of service delivery cannot be attained from existing resources, then a budget cut-back in funding is inappropriate. Higher quality of outcomes in prisons might be identified in the amount of time devoted to the educational rehabilitation of inmates and the number of hours per day allowed for association—both of which have implications for manning, costs and quality of service. Consequently a straightforward implementation of cost targets amounts to the existence of a maintained hypothesis that considerations of quality and adequate levels of service are satisfied.

It follows that *cost targets may be meaningful in the short run where standards of attainment in outcomes are acceptable and constant with respect to the reductions in funding implied by the target.* In these circumstances, DEA information on programme performance may be fed into a policy environment like the annual public expenditure planning cycle. This could assist in the bidding process between Treasury and line departments, with poorer performing programmes being curtailed in favour of more efficient spending. Accordingly reductions in spending at the programme level such as suggested in Table 5.2.1 can be thought of as potential adjustments to the public sector planning totals for departments in the Public Expenditure Survey (PES).[1]

A number of further caveats must be added at this point. A target for programme funding in period $t + 1$ based on performance in time t must be adjusted to take account of anticipated future price movements. Given that prices have a tendency to rise, a target which has not been adjusted for anticipated inflation will unfairly penalise a programme next period. Second, the structure of some spending departments may not permit evaluation by DEA. For example, unitary departments like the Foreign and Commonwealth Office lack a comparable branch structure and are not therefore tractable within DEA at the programme level. In such cases, programme performance evaluation will have to follow an alternative route.

Finally, the results in Table 5.2.1 are based on spending at only 33 local prisons and remand centres while the *Prison Department Report* for 1984/85 identifies 118 penal establishments of one sort or another. From these, only those (33) institutions with a significant remand population have been included. The presence of remand prisoners was taken as an indicator of reasonable homogeneity among institutions. The inclusion of other types of establishment (e.g. open prisons) in a broader analysis of the total programme might give a different picture of performance.

It was felt however that that the sample should be restricted to homogeneous establishments with similar functions and objectives. Clearly the comparison of performance with a production frontier would be meaningless if the relevant facet is a weighted average of a dissimilar production process. Some form of criterion (such as a significant remand content) which carefully differentiates between different forms

---

(1)   A synopsis of existing procedures in the annual UK Public Expenditure Survey can be found in HM
         Treasury *Economic Progress Report*, no. 200, February, 1989.

of production has—of necessity—been used in most empirical DEA studies.   For example Tomkins and Green (1988) sought to compare production in 36 UK university departments but limited their final sample to 20 because the remaining 16 were part of economics or management departments.   Likewise several other studies have restricted the size of the relevant cross section.   Sengupta (1987a) in a study of high-school education in California selected only 25 out of a feasible sample of 50 schools in order to preserve homogeneity.

Whether in actual practice enough comparable units can be identified to make "programme" evaluation a reality will depend on the nature of the activity in question. It can be said, however, that the input efficiency defined in cost terms has a profound advantage over the output efficiency score where programmes are widely diffentiated internally.   Specifically, the efficiency of subgroups of organisations—however small —can be aggregated in relation to the whole programme provided efficiency is additive: That is, costs (both actual and targeted) measured in monetary units can be summed over any number of subgroups in the programme; outputs, by contrast, usually may not, because in the public sector they are mostly non-traded and therefore cannot be valued financially.   In this context, targets for outputs remain in the original units of measurement which makes aggregation of output efficiency to the programme level intractable.   Of course in a programme which is made up of branches with identical outputs, programme-level aggregation is unproblematic because output can be measured in the same units throughout the programme.

Despite these qualifications, the dissent sometimes aroused during the public expenditure round suggests some rationalisation of PES proceedures for multi-branch programmes may be in order.   Careful use of DEA throughout applicable programmes in the PES could facilitate Treasury allocations to sponsoring departments on the principle that future resources are based on current performance.   Departmental bids for funds could be judged on a consistent total-factor basis with DEA efficiency measurement.   By contrast, under existing arrangements, programme performance is evaluated through a range of *ad hoc* criteria which can lead to divergent conclusions on future funding—see the extensive range of measures used in recent public expenditure White Papers in the United Kingdom.

An alternative measure of aggregate efficiency

The foregoing discussion has focused on the measurement of aggregate technical efficiency in multi-branch public expenditure programmes through the summation of performance in the underlying target variables.   An interesting paper by Beasley (1988) prompts the suggestion of an alternative definition of efficiency for programme evaluation.

Beasley examines two methods of calculating efficiency scores for all establishments using the *same* set of weights.   This is in contrast to the standard approach *à la* Charnes, Cooper and Rhodes (1978) who advocate the solution of the linear program *n* times generating a separate set of optimal weights for each establishment.   Beasley describes what he calls a Global and an Incremental approach to the simultaneous solution of the DEA program for all units.   The most interesting of these is the Global approach.   This involves the solution of the standard DEA program choosing weights under a new criterion.   That is, *the optimal solution to the program is that set of weights which maximises the sum of the efficiencies of the individual units.*   This is a very useful idea which can be generalised to other contexts.   In particular, the sum of individual technical efficiency scores can be interpreted as an alternative (ordinal) measure of aggregate efficiency.   Thus for n establishments, the Aggregate Technical Efficiency *(ATE)* becomes:

$$(5.2.3) \qquad\qquad ATE = \sum_{i=1}^{n} TE_i$$

where TE_i is the branch-level technical efficiency score.   For n establishments, the maximum value of *ATE* is n.   The minimum value of *ATE* is not so evident.   But assume the simplest branch structure conceivable, $n = 2$.   (A unitary spending programme *without* a line structure would imply $n = 1$.)   If both branches are best-practice then full efficiency exists throughout the spending programme and $ATE = 2$.   Where there is technical inefficiency in the sample, i.e. $\Sigma TE_i < 2$ ($i= 1, 2$) one establishment must dominate the other.   In the limit as the dominance of one establishment increases indefinitely over the other, $\Sigma TE_i \to 1$.   For $n > 2$, the same result follows, for there must be at least one dominant (i.e. best-practice) establishment.   As the performance of the non-best-practice units worsens indefinitely, their efficiency scores both individually and collectively fall towards zero.   Hence $ATE \to 1$ as performance in the programme deteriorates.   However it is always possible to find at least one dominant unit, so *ATE* can never fall below unity. Then:

$$(5.2.4) \qquad\qquad 1 < ATE \leq n$$

In most applications of DEA, it is very unlikely that only one unit would be dominant. Rather, several are likely to be dominant in one or more input (or output) dimensions (see Nunamaker (1985)).   Additionally, *ATE* is never likely to be *exactly* equal to unity except in the irrelevant and trivial case of $n = 1$ (i.e., where there is no branch structure).   If there are n establishments where unit 1 is dominant with best practice costs C_1 and $n - 1$ units are relatively inefficient then:

$$(5.2.5) \qquad\qquad ATE = 1 + \frac{C_1}{C_2} + \frac{C_1}{C_3} + \ldots\ldots + \frac{C_1}{C_n}$$

As inefficient costs $C_2, \ldots, C_n$ rise indefinitely, the implied efficiency ratios $TE_2, \ldots, TE_n$ fall towards zero.   Only where there exists an extraordinary and improbable range in performance (i.e. in spending) would this be observed in actual practice.

On this new basis, derived from Beasley (1988), the aggregate technical efficiency of the prison spending programme is summarised in Table 5.2.2.   Two variants of the *ATE* are presented.   The first, *ATE (CRS)*, is the sum of efficiency scores under a new constant returns to scale assumption (the underlying CRS efficiency scores will be reported in full in the next section).   Second, *ATE (VRS)*, has been calculated from the prison efficiencies reported in Chapter 4, based on varying returns to scale.   Each of these results is an ordinal measure of the proximity of the programme as a whole to a situation of best-practice production at all prisons.

Table 5.2.2
Aggregate Technical Efficiency in the local prison spending programme:
The sum of efficiency scores under constant and varying returns to scale

	ATE(CRS)	ATE(VRS)
Sum of efficiency scores	29.4	31.5
Best-practice share in ATE		
—actual	11.0	20.0
—per cent	37.4	63.5
Non-best practice share in ATE		
—actual	18.4	11.5
—per cent	62.6	36.5

Note: For a sample size of 33 establishments, $1 < ATE \leq 33$.

Source: Authors' calculations.

Under CRS, *ATE* is 29.4 and under VRS *ATE* is 31.5 out of a possible maximum score in each case of 33. As would be expected, the VRS-based measure is higher because of the greater preponderence of unity efficiency scores (that is, of best-practice) under VRS. A noteworthy feature of the results is the asymmetric role played by the best-practice establishments. Under VRS 20 such units are identified, making a contribution of 63.5% to the efficiency rating of the whole programme. Only 11 prisons were earmarked best-practice with CRS which contribute 37.4% to programme efficiency. This contribution or share in aggregate efficiency is very close to that made by non-best practice units $(TE_i < 1)$ under VRS.

The alternative measure of *ATE*, inspired by Beasley, indicates a marked change in the significance of best-practice performance. A VRS assumption typically identifies a greater number of best-practice establishments which then make up the bulk of the contribution to aggregate efficiency. Under CRS the best-practice share in efficiency is substantially lower.

The decision-maker's objective in this context will be to improve the performance of inefficient units towards unity in order to raise the aggregate efficiency of the programme towards its maximum (where $ATE = n$). In this regard a study by Parkan (1987) suggests that a drawback of the VRS results is their relative lack of discriminating power among units. Clearly no distinction can be made among best-practice on the basis of DEA alone. CRS results by contrast find fewer best-practice operations and therefore give a distinct (non-unity) performance rating to a greater proportion of the sample. Thus, although the CRS results give a rather poorer overall picture of performance they offer a finer ranking and identification of efficiency levels which may be of use in decision-making. It also follows that inasfar as the peer group comparison is of any significance this will be clarified under CRS because, quite simply, there are fewer examples of "best-practice" to assimilate.

The importance of the *ATE* measure prompted by Beasley is its simplicity and ease of interpretation for decision-makers.   Little (1971, page 483) argues: "the biggest bottleneck in the managerial use of models is not their development but getting them used.   I claim that the model builder should try to design his models to be given away. In other words, as much as possible, the models should become the property of the manager, not the technical people [;] . . . . . .   to be used by a manager, a model should be simple, robust, easy to control, adaptive, as complete as possible and easy to communicate with".   These broader dimensions of measurement are of great importance for the ultimate success of efficiency modelling and policy of any kind. The simple summation of efficiency scores as a measure of programme performance is offered with these broader dimensions in mind.   The resulting measure is reasonably intuitive and in a policy-making context it could probably be implemented without being overwhelmed by traditional performance measures to which decision-makers are more accustomed.

5.3.   Evaluation of the impact of a new reference technology on branch and programme efficiency

Chapter 4 and the discussion above in section 5.2 assumed that the underlying costs' technology in prisons exhibits varying returns to scale (VRS).   Many of the earlier empirical applications of DEA, by contrast, assumed constant returns to scale (CRS) until Banker (1984) developed the first varying returns program.   Each of these variants of the DEA program has its own distinctive implications for branch and programme-level costs.   These have been ignored in the empirical literature on DEA. Accordingly section 5.3 explores the effects of a constant returns to scale assumption on costs and attempts to reconcile differences in the CRS and VRS results based on an interpretation of DEA-efficiency first proposed in Grosskopf and Valdmanis (1987).

Background

Grosskopf (1986) and Fare, Lovell and Zieschang (1983) were the first to show that there is no unique measure of efficiency in a frontier context.   That is, the efficiency measure is not invariant to the scale and disposability assumptions which have been made with regard to the nature of the production processs.   Essentially this means there exists a number of different reference sets against which to measure the efficiency of a given input-output vector, and each reference set implies its own efficiency measure.

Grosskopf (1986) for example, has shown that the efficiency measure is nested in the sense that a strongly disposable technology contains its weakly disposable counterpart. That is, a weakly disposable technology defines a higher technical efficiency than strong disposability (this has been illustrated fully in Chapter 2).

An additional source of efficiency variation that will be discussed in this section are changes in the returns to scale assumption.   Farrell's original (1957) contribution to the literature set a trend in much of the later work on frontier estimation in making the assumption that the underlying reference technology exhibits constant returns to scale (CRS). In particular new American work on frontier estimation via DEA initially made this assumption—see Bessent, Bessent, Kennington and Reagan (1982), Lewin, Morey and Cook (1982), Charnes, Cooper and Rhodes (1981, 1979, 1978), Bessent and Bessent (1980), etc. Only later contributions exposed the possibility of non-constant returns technologies. Of these Fare, Grosskopf and Lovell (1985) and Banker (1984) are among the most important. However, subsequent empirical applications of DEA have tended to adopt either the CRS program (cf Thomas, Greffe and Grant (1988), Bowlin (1987, 1986), Todd (1985) and Sherman (1984a,b)) or the non-CRS variant (e.g. Fare, Grosskopf and Logan (1987) and Grosskopf and Valdmanis (1987)) without investigation of which is appropriate and their differing effects on branch- and programme-level efficiency.

The DEA results presented in Chapters 3 and 4 on local education authorities and prisons are predicated on an underlying assumption of varying returns to scale (VRS) and strong disposability in the production process. That is, for VRS the "intensity variables" (or weights on branches) are constrained to sum to unity in the Banker (1984) DEA program, i.e., $\Sigma \lambda_c = 1$ as in (2.5.1) in Chapter 2. Alternative assumptions, in particular constant returns to scale (CRS), are feasible and in the DEA program the optimal weights will be unconstrained for a CRS technology.

New results on prison efficiency based on a constant returns to scale technology

Technical efficiency coefficients were estimated in Chapter 4 assuming the reference technology exhibited varying returns to scale and strong disposability of inputs and outputs. These coefficients have been re-estimated for the whole sample based on an alternative technology assumption of constant returns to scale with strong disposability.

The new results are contained in Table 5.3.1. It is immediately noticeable in comparison with the coefficients in Table 4.3.2 that there are significantly fewer best-practice establishments (11 as against 20 previously) and that the non-unit efficiency scores on the whole are lower. The mean inefficiency in the new results is 0.83 which is around 5 percentage points lower than the mean varying returns score in Table 4.3.2. This suggests that under constant returns a typical inefficient establishment could be expected to save 17% of its current expenditure *vis-à-vis* the minimal possibilities observed along the CRS frontier. By contrast, a representative VRS prison with non-unit efficiency could be asked to save only 12% of its current budget.

In some cases under CRS, costs have advanced significantly beyond this. Brixton, for example, has $TE = 0.53$, losing its VRS best-practice status, and for Bedford $TE = 0.59$ (against 0.71 under VRS). It is noteworthy that these potential gains in cost efficiency at Bedford and Brixton are greater than the largest savings suggested by VRS: The lowest efficiency score reported in Chapter 4 is at Bedford with $TE = 0.71$. Apparently the CRS results give a poorer picture of prison performance with a lower mean inefficiency and fewer best-practice establishments being identified.

Table 5.3.1
DEA efficiency coefficients under constant returns to scale

Prison	Cost efficiency	Peer group
1. Ashford	0.9393	3,5,13,26,30
2. Bedford	0.5858	16,21,31
3. Brockhill	1.0000	3
4. Birmingham	0.8358	5,16,31
5. Bristol	1.0000	5
6. Brixton	0.5303	16,30
7. Canterbury	0.8493	16,29,30
8. Cardiff	0.9766	5,13,16,21
9. Coldingley	1.0000	9
10. Dorchester	0.7215	5,16,21,31
11. Durham	0.8817	3,5,16,31
12. Exeter	0.8037	3,5,16,21,31
13. Glen Parva	1.0000	13
14. Gloucester	0.9750	5
15. Latchmere House	0.8317	5,13,16,21,30,31
16. Leeds	1.0000	16
17. Leicester	0.7333	5,16
18. Lewes	0.8638	3,5,13,16,30
19. Lincoln	0.8517	3,5,16,21,31
20. Liverpool	0.9929	31
21. Low Newton	1.0000	21
22. Manchester	0.9667	3,5,13,16,31
23. Norwich	0.8505	3,13,16,31
24. Oxford	0.7285	16,31
25. Pentonville	1.0000	25
26. Pucklechurch	1.0000	26
27. Reading	0.8284	5,16,29,30
28. Shrewsbury	0.8777	3,5,16,21,30,31
29. Swansea	1.0000	29
30. Thorpe Arch	1.0000	30
31. Wandsworth	1.0000	31
32. Winchester	0.8950	3,5,13,16,30,31
33. W. Scrubs	0.8335	3,5,13,16,30,31

Notes:
Mean inefficiency ($1/n\Sigma TE_i$, for $TE_i < 1$: 0.8342; Standard Deviation: 0.1180.   The mean and standard deviation are calculated from only those efficiency scores less than unity.
Source: Authors' calculations.

Cost implications of CRS for programme efficiency

It would seem to follow that a poorer picture of performance at the micro-level will impair the behaviour of the prison spending programme as a whole.   Accordingly, using the aggregate efficiency identity (5.2.2) further results on programme efficiency have been collected together in Table 5.3.2.   Under the VRS assumption, the potential aggregate savings in costs were around 5% and evenly distributed between manpower and non-manpower items (cf Table 5.2.1).   The picture is now quite different, for each item the potential gain from boundary production across all prisons is larger. Non-remand savings have doubled to around 10% whilst savings in remand items have more than tripled to around 18%.   (This implies an overall reduction in total costs of around 13.1%: Savings which could in principle have been attained were costs best-practice throughout the sample.)   Clearly the distribution of inefficiency across the various cost measures is no longer even, and has swung against the remand items.

This particular picture is consistent with the more cost intensive nature of untried and unsentenced remand prisoners who are entitled to greater care and priviledges *vis-à-vis* ordinary inmates. It also suggests that there may be substantial slack adjustments on the remand variables at the micro-level.

Table 5.3.2
The programme implications of prison cost inefficiency in 1984/85 under constant returns to scale

Costs	Actual £m	Target £m	ATE %	Saving %
Manpower				
(1) remand	69.41	56.75	81.8	18.2
(2) non-remand	114.38	102.72	89.8	10.2
Non-manpower				
(1) remand	19.85	16.29	82.1	17.9
(2) non-remand	34.51	31.29	90.7	9.3
Total costs	238.15	207.05	86.9	13.1

Notes: See Table 5.2.1
Source: Authors' calculations and *Prison Department Report, 1984/85.*

Interpretation of the CRS results: Long-run and short-run measures of efficiency

Given that the differences between the CRS and VRS results are apparently marked, it is important to examine how this might affect the usefulness and interpretation of DEA in the allocation of funds within and across public programmes. In particular, some reconciliation of the large differences in efficiency status between the two sets of results is required. One of the most useful arguments in this regard is the interpretation of DEA efficiency found in Grosskopf and Valdmanis (1987). Essentially they argue that the CRS technology should be interpreted as reflecting long-run performance possibilities. Analogously, the VRS assumption indicates feasible attainments in the short run. On this basis the long-run CRS adjustments to costs will be greater than those suggested by the VRS technology. The CRS targets are effectively adjustments towards long-run equilibria, i.e., the minimum point of a U-shaped average cost curve. In the short-run even best-practice costs will be greater than those attainable in the long-run and so VRS cost adjustments will be smaller than their CRS counterparts.

The problem of the decision-maker is not then in deciphering two seemingly contradictory sets of results on efficiency status, but in the initial choice of technology assumption. Once this is motivated, the nature of the "bias" imparted to the efficiency measure is explicable *a priori*. In particular the CRS results can be taken as indicators of the proximity of the prisons to a long-run notion of best-practice. It follows that the finding of fewer examples of best-practice (11 out of 33 prisons) is to be expected from the CRS results because long-run cost attainments are likely to be lower than those set by best-practice in the short run. Analogously, a larger share of the cross section (20 out of 33 prisons) are efficient under VRS. This suggests prison establishments, and hence the spending programme as a whole, are closer to the less demanding attainments along a short-run VRS best-practice boundary.

This interpretation is of course a neoclassical argument based on the supposed effects of market competition on costs in the short and long run. It is not without relevance in a public sector context: Grosskopf and Valdmanis (1987) argued for this interpretation when comparing performance in public and private hospital care in California. Inefficiency is less likely to be tolerated and, acceptable performance standards will, if anything, be raised by public sector policy-makers in the long run. The stream of efficiency-related White Papers in Britain over the past ten to twelve years suggests the level of performance-consciousness has been raised both within and outside government. *A fortiori* the latest developments in efficiency policy suggested in *Civil Service Management: The Next Steps* (Cm 524) include the widespread creation of quasi-autonomous governmental agencies with considerable financial independence. The devolution of financial resposibility is to be counterbalanced by greater emphasis on efficient performance through increased evaluation of line-behaviour. The scope for a neoclassical interpretation of public sector cost behaviour as in Grosskopf and Valdmanis (1987) is correspondingly increased because greater managerial accountability and scrutiny can be interpreted as a proxy for a market discipline on line costs.

Market ideas and public sector efficiency —a short digression

It is worth recognising at this point that the use of market-based concepts of analysis in the public sector performance literature is becoming increasingly common. The appropriation of private sector ideas comes out of the quest for a single-value calculus in public sector performance. Without traded outputs there is no revenue-based measure like profit or surplus. Yet Sengupta (1987a), for example, has cleverly restyled the DEA ratio. If the optimal values of the input and output weights in the DEA program, W_k^* and V_i^* respectively, are positive for each k and i then these can be interpreted as prices of inputs and outputs defining a pseudo-profit function for public sector production. For a cross section of n organisations write:

$$(5.3.1) \qquad \Pi_j = \sum_{i=1}^{t} V_i^* Y_{i,j} - \sum_{k=1}^{m} W_k^* X_{k,j}, \quad j = 1, \ldots, n$$

The function is the absolute rather than the ratio difference between the t weighted outputs and the m weighted inputs in organisation j. Again with a neoclassical flavour to the analysis Sengupta proposes a pricing rule based on the surplus function:

$$(5.3.2) \qquad \frac{\delta \Pi_j}{\delta X_{k,j}} = \sum_{i=1}^{t} V_i^* \frac{\delta Y_{i,j}}{\delta X_{k,j}} - W_k^* = 0$$

for $k = 1, \ldots, m$ and $j = 1, \ldots, n$.

In principle, the decision problem now involves maximisation of (5.3.1) by setting the derivatives in (5.3.2) equal to zero and ensuring the second derivatives of the maximand are negative. This constitutes maximisation of the surplus accruing to public sector production and Sengupta (1987a) argues that the size of the (non-monetary) surplus generated in (5.3.1) may be used as an indicator of the efficacy of public production in organisations whose performance could be ordered according to the scale of these pseudo-profits.

5.4. Excess costs and the nesting of empirical DEA technologies

Section 5.3 introduced results on prison efficiency based on a constant returns to scale assumption in the underlying linear program. It was observed that this led to differences in both branch and programme-level efficiencies. This section seeks to clarify the causes of these differences by investigating how empirical DEA technologies differ under alternative scale assumptions. It develops the work of Fare, Grosskopf and Njinkeu (1988) and Grosskopf (1986) who have demonstrated that the various definitions of the production boundary (the reference technology) can be "nested". This implies that the efficiency score associated with each technology can also be nested. A consequence of technological nesting is that the excess cost implications of alternative technologies can be predicted in qualitative terms *prior* to empirical implementation of DEA.

This information is important for decision-makers in a policy-making context since it clarifies the effect on proposed cost adjustments of alternative scale assumptions in the underlying linear program.

Technological nesting and excess costs: An exposition

It is easiest to grasp Grosskopf's (1986) argument from Figure 5.4.1 which contains stylised examples of three possible empirical variants of boundary which can be constructed from DEA. Consider then a branch of a spending programme, i, producing one output from one input on the interior of the production set. The simple one input/one output case represented in Figure 5.4.1 can be thought of as a two-dimensional section through an n-dimensional production possibility set (Banker (1984)). Output is given at $0Y$ from consumption of input $0X_2$. The efficiency of operations at this point can be evaluated relative to any of three alternative reference technologies. In terms of Figure 5.4.1 these are:

(1) $0D$ with constant returns to scale (CRS);

(2) $0BC$ with non-increasing returns to scale (NIRS); and

(3) $XABC$ with increasing, constant and decreasing (i.e., "varying") returns to scale (VRS).

Each of the technologies described above in (1), (2) and (3) can be constructed empirically from DEA which implies that there are at least three definitions of (input) technical efficiency *(TE)* for performance at i. That is:

(1) $TE_{crs} = 0X_0/0X_2$;

(2) $TE_{vrs} = 0X_1/0X_2$;

(3) $TE_{nirs} = 0X_0/0X_2 = TE_{crs}$ for $Y < Y^*$ but

$TE_{nirs} = TE_{vrs}$ for $Y > Y^*$.

Figure 5.4.1

Nesting of reference technologies

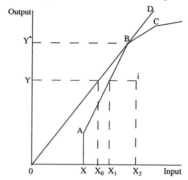

Naturally where $Y = Y^*$, $TE_{crs} = TE_{nirs} = TE_{vrs}$ since all 3 technologies overlap at this point. It follows immediately that the technical efficiency of branch i can be ordered. *Viz.:*

(5.4.1) For $Y < Y^*$, $TE_{crs} = TE_{nirs} < TE_{vrs}$;

and

(5.4.2) For $Y > Y^*$, $TE_{vrs} = TE_{nirs} > TE_{crs}$.

Clearly technical efficiency is greatest when evaluated relative to the closest technology. At i in Figure 5.4.1 this is the varying returns boundary $XABC$ where both the NIRS and CRS efficiency scores are equal but lower than TE_{vrs}. This arises because the VRS boundary is literally contained or "nested" within the CRS and NIRS alternatives. At output levels above Y^* the relationship between the efficiency scores changes in as much as NIRS is conincident with VRS (rather than with CRS) along the nested facet BC. Clearly, NIRS and VRS efficiency must be equal to each other but greater than CRS efficiency for output levels greater than Y^*. A general relationship governing the efficiency score and the scale characteristics of the estimated boundary is apparent here. *Viz.*, for given performance, a nested technology implies a higher relative technical efficiency score than a non-nested alternative. Equally, a non-nested technology implies a lower relative efficiency score than a nested counterpart. The qualitative ranking of technical efficiency which this implies is summarised above in (5.4.1) and (5.4.2) and is of important practical relevance, because the excess cost implications of alternative technologies can be ranked in an analogous way.

This can be established by defining excess costs in the sense suggested by Dawson (1987). That is, as the difference between actual costs and interpolated best-practice costs. Total (variable) costs are simply the unit price of an input *(p)* multiplied by the number of units purchased *(X)*. Assuming that the price does not vary with quantity purchased, then, from Figure 5.4.1, excess costs for branch i under the CRS and VRS technologies have the relationship:

$$(p.X_2 - p.X_0)_{crs} > (p.X_2 - p.X_1)_{vrs}$$

That is, excess costs are smaller under the nested VRS boundary. At all points along the VRS boundary (other than where it coincides with CRS at *B*), VRS best-practice costs *(BP_vrs)* are higher than those predicted along its CRS counterpart. In general, the relationship $BP_{vrs} \geq BP_{crs}$ will be true in all DEA applications because a CRS boundary will always (weakly) dominate its VRS counterpart, as in Figure 5.4.1.

The programme-efficiency ordering

The ordering of efficiency of branch operations is equally applicable to the measurement of programme-level efficiency. Section 5.2 showed that programme efficiency can be defined in terms of branch-level technical efficiency scores. Hence the Aggregate Technical Efficiency *(ATE)* of a multi-branch public expenditure programme was given by:

$$ATE = \Sigma C_i^* / \Sigma C_i$$

where C_i^* is the target (i.e. best-practice) cost at branch *i*, and C_i is the actual costs incurred at that branch. Because of the nesting of branch-level technologies, best-practice costs have the relationship $C_{i,vrs}^* \geq C_{i,crs}^*$. Accordingly the programme efficiency score *(ATE)* can be ordered under alternative technology assumptions. For example:

(5.4.3) $ATE_{vrs} \geq ATE_{crs}$

The implied excess cost adjustments for the programme have the same relationship. Programme-level excess costs *(EC)* are defined as the difference between the outturn for the programme, ΣC_i, and the best-practice expenditures implied by the *ATE* score (compare Tables 5.2.1 and 5.3.2):

$$EC = \Sigma C_i - ATE.(\Sigma C_i) \equiv \Sigma C_i - \Sigma C_i^*$$

Noting the properties of *ATE* under alternative assumptions in (5.4.3) implies that excess costs in the programme are greater when measured relative to a non-nested CRS technology:

(5.4.4) $\Sigma C_i - ATE_{crs} . (\Sigma C_i) \geq \Sigma C_i - ATE_{vrs} . (\Sigma C_i)$

The relationship between CRS and VRS excess costs in (5.4.4) is consistent with the results on programme-level efficiency which were reported in sections 5.2 and 5.3. Under constant returns to scale, excess costs in prison spending amounted to £31.1million. The comparable VRS figure is, at £11.1million, barely over one third of the recommended CRS adjustment in programme costs. The size of the difference between excess costs under the two definitions is enough to reinforce the Grosskopf and Valdmanis (1987) argument that CRS adjustments to performance are of a longer-run nature.

Moreover, the ability to nest both branch and programme-level efficiency estimates from alternative technologies is significant because it demonstrates to the decision-maker the "bias" or direction of change imparted to the results by the choice of one reference technology over another. Indeed nested efficiency concepts constitute a form of efficiency spectrum: At the one end the least savings that can be expected are established under VRS; at the other end, CRS results indicate to the decision-maker the upper limit on financial and efficiency gains.   In this way the differences in the VRS and CRS prison efficiency results presented in Chapters 4 and 5 can be reconciled given that each set of results is based on a distinct technology assumption with its own separate implications for costs.

5.5.   Additional sources of variation in excess costs: The identification of scale inefficiencies

The analysis of efficiency and costs in Chapters 3 and 4 and through Chapter 5 has assumed that the total variation in costs over best-practice levels is attributable to technical inefficiency alone.   This is common in applied work in the literature, as for example in Sherman and Gold (1985).   Recent work has shown, however, that the sources of excess costs can be more accurately identified.   In particular, Rangan, Grabowski, Aly and Pasurka (1988) have developed a methodology which distinguishes between excess costs due to technical inefficiency and those due to scale inefficiency.   Surprisingly, very little attention has been devoted to this distinction in the literature—although see Sengupta and Sfeir (1986) for a provisional attempt to incorporate the analysis of scale efficiency for a sample of Californian high schools. Section 5.5 seeks to apply the methodology developed by Rangan *et al* (1988) to the determination of excess costs in the prisons.   This enables a further analysis of costs at both the branch and programme levels and further clarifies the relative significance and interpretation of the VRS and CRS assumptions.

Scale efficiency measurement

The Rangan *et al* (1988) scale efficiency indicator is derived very simply from the VRS and CRS efficiency scores.   In Figure 5.5.1 CRS efficiency for the branch i is $0X/0X_1$ and its VRS efficiency is $0X_0/0X_1$.   As was shown in section 5.4 the VRS boundary is nested within its CRS counterpart and so—other than where the two frontiers coincide—CRS efficiency is always the lower.   The "discrepancy" between the two measures is defined according to the extent of the gap between the two frontiers.   This can be expressed as the ratio:

$$\frac{0X/0X_1}{0X_0/0X_1} = \frac{0X}{0X_0}$$

This is simply the ratio of the CRS and VRS efficiency scores and is proposed by Rangan *et al* as an indicator of scale efficiency *(S)*; whence for a branch i:

(5.5.1) $S_i = CRS_i \, / \, VRS_i$

In Figure 5.5.1 S_i is less than one, indicating that production at this point is not scale efficient.   Moreover, were production displaced onto the VRS boundary at *C, S_i* would remain less than unity.   Accordingly Rangan *et al* have made the distinction between "Pure Technical Efficiency" *(PTE)* and Scale Efficiency.   *PTE* is actually no more than the VRS efficiency score and hence is defined in terms of the nearer VRS boundary.   At a point such as i, $PTE_i = 0X_0/0X_1 < 1$.   However, $PTE_i = 1$, as at C in Figure 5.5.1, is not sufficient to generate scale efficient production.   At this point the VRS boundary is nested, and *PTE* efficiency will always be greater than CRS efficiency such that the scale ratio in (5.5.1) must be less than unity.

Figure 5.5.1
Decomposition of CRS efficiency

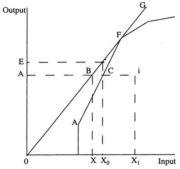

The "weakness" of production at C (where $PTE_i = 1$) can be examined in terms of its average productivity or scale properties (cf Banker (1984)). Specifically, this point is scale inefficient because average productivity—the ratio of output to input—has not been maximised. That is, for output $0A$, $0A/0X_0$ is less than its theoretical maximum $0E/0X_0$ which is defined along the CRS frontier. Thus in order to attain maximum average productivity *for output 0A* an additional contraction in input, $0X_0-0X$, would be necessary to bring production to point B on the CRS boundary. This contraction in inputs (further to that, $0X_1-0X_0$, to eliminate Pure Technical Efficiency) eliminates that wastage attributable to scale inefficiency.

The distinction of purely technical and scale efficiency suggests further insight into the policy-maker's choice between CRS and VRS targets. In the first place it explains that CRS targets suggest larger reductions in resource consumption because they include an additional scale element in efficiency. By the same token VRS targets suggest smaller reductions because VRS best-practice production is defined *without* the elimination of scale inefficiencies.

The decomposition of excess costs into technical and scale components
The identification of a distinct measure of scale is useful in the analysis of efficiency because it permits the division of excess costs into their separate technical and scale components. This is a significant step forward in the analysis of costs. Hitherto many papers in the literature have used a CRS assumption and attributed variations in performance *entirely* to differences in technical efficiency (among many references see Thomas, Greffe and Grant (1988) and Sherman and Gold (1985)). It is clear now that this is misleading in as much as some of the variation in performance may be the result of scale inefficiencies.

In order to decompose total excess costs into their various components it is convenient to recall briefly the definition of excess costs *(EC)*. These are the difference between actual spending and best-practice expenditure. For branch i in Figure 5.5.1 this definition gives total excess costs as:

$$EC_i = p.X_1 - p.X$$

where p is the unit price of X. This is the total excess costs of production for branch i. These can be decomposed into those attributable to scale inefficiency and to pure technical inefficiency. Excess costs due to pure technical efficiency alone are:

$$EC_i = p.X_1 - p.X_0$$

and these can be eliminated with a reduction in spending given by the VRS (or *PTE*) efficiency score. Thus production on the VRS boundary defined by:

$$0X_0 = 0X_1.(0X_0/0X_1)$$

would remove this element in excess costs. However a further element $(p.X_0-p.X)$ in excess costs remains. This is due to scale inefficient production and implies a further reduction in excess costs which is defined by the Rangan *et al* (1988) scale efficiency score. Thus the complete elimination of excess costs would require a further proportional reduction in total excess costs of $(1-0X/0X_0)$; or in absolute monetary terms of $(p.X_0-p.X)$.

In summary then total excess costs at a branch i (EC_i) can be broken down into two elements:

$$EC_i = EC_{i,vrs} + EC_{i,scale};$$

That is, those attributable to pure technical efficiency, $EC_{i,vrs}$ and those due to scale inefficiencies, $EC_{i,scale}$. In terms of Figure 5.5.1 this gives:

$$(p.X_1 - p.X) = (p.X_1 - p.X_0) + (p.X_0 - p.X)$$

Table 5.5.1 provides an exhaustive decomposition of excess costs on this basis for the whole prison spending programme. The excess costs due to technical and scale inefficiencies have been summed over all institutions to yield a summary picture of performance. As a share of total excess costs those attributable to scale inefficiency are almost two thirds of the total. However in both of the remand items scale inefficiency is noticeably greater; in manpower costs attributable to the incarceration of remand prisoners the share of scale inefficiency is three quarters of the total excess costs in this item. By contrast the excess costs in the non-remand items are more evenly split between scale and technical inefficiencies.

Table 5.5.1
Excess costs in the prison spending programme: An exhaustive breakdown

	Total (CRS) £m	PTE (VRS) £m	Scale (Rangan) £m	Scale (%)
Manpower				
(1) remand	12.66	3.11	9.55	75
(2) non-remand	11.66	5.32	6.34	54
Non-manpower				
(1) remand	3.56	1.07	2.49	70
(2) non-remand	3.22	1.55	1.67	52
Total excess costs	31.10	11.05	20.05	64

Notes:
Column 1 is total excess costs defined from the CRS boundary and is derived from Table 5.3.2.   Column 2 is excess costs due to pure technical efficiency defined from the VRS boundary and is derived from Table 5.2.1. Column 3 is the scale component in excess costs and is simply the remainder after *PTE* excess costs have been accounted for.   Hence column 3 = column 1 less column 2.   Column 4 gives the scale component in excess costs as a share in total excess costs.

Source: Authors' calculations.

It is clear from the results in Table 5.5.1 that scale inefficiency is a significant cause of wastage in the prison spending programme.   In this context it could be nothing other than an outright misdiagnosis to attribute total excess costs *in the context of a constant returns to scale assumption* to "technical efficiency" alone—as has been so common in the applied DEA literature.

Returns to scale in the prison spending programme

One of the most important papers in the DEA literature, Banker (1984), is useful at this point.   Banker demonstrated that the sum of the weights on branches in the optimal basis of the CRS version of the DEA program can be used as an indicator of the local returns to scale at the current level of operations.   This result, together with the Rangan *et al* (1988) scale efficiency indicator form the basis of Table 5.5.2.[1] The Rangan *et al* indicator shows by what proportion total costs could be reduced after the attainment of Pure Technical Efficiency on the VRS boundary and indicates that 21 out of 33 prisons are scale inefficient.   The mean reduction in total costs from a point of Pure Technical Efficiency at scale inefficient prisons would be (1–0.89) or 11%.   However in some cases, most notably Brixton, Dorchester and Oxford, the relevant figure is much higher.   Brixton deserves special comment since the scale indicator suggests that elimination of pure technical inefficiency would still allow a further cut of almost a half in the resources that remained.

The Rangan *et al* scale indicator is useful in suggesting the percentage reduction in total costs at a position of pure technical efficiency to achieve scale efficient production.   It is also useful for policy-making purposes to ascertain whether the local returns to scale at the prevailing level of operations are increasing or decreasing.

---

(1)   Bowlin (1988) has used the Banker measure of scale variations for the evaluation of the efficiency of fighter wings in the US Air Force.

Table 5.5.2
Scale efficiency and returns to scale in the local prison spending programme

Prison	Scale efficiency Rangan *et al*	Returns to scale Banker (1984)
1. Ashford	0.9393	1.7235 (DRS)
2. Bedford	0.8257	0.3440 (IRS)
3. Brockhill	1.0000	1.0000 (CRS)
4. Birmingham	0.9881	0.8046 (IRS)
5. Bristol	1.0000	1.0000 (CRS)
6. Brixton	0.5303	3.0135 (DRS)
7. Canterbury	0.9897	0.9327 (IRS)
8. Cardiff	0.9984	0.6655 (IRS)
9. Coldingley	1.0000	1.0000 (CRS)
10. Dorchester	0.7215	0.2257 (IRS)
11. Durham	1.0000	0.9952 (IRS)
12. Exeter	0.9691	0.6613 (IRS)
13. Glen Parva	1.0000	1.0000 (CRS)
14. Gloucester	0.9750	0.4322 (IRS)
15. Latchmere House	0.8317	0.4413 (IRS)
16. Leeds	1.0000	1.0000 (CRS)
17. Leicester	0.9394	0.4074 (IRS)
18. Lewes	0.8762	1.3476 (DRS)
19. Lincoln	0.9599	0.5621 (IRS)
20. Liverpool	0.9929	0.8959 (IRS)
21. Low Newton	1.0000	1.0000 (CRS)
22. Manchester	0.9667	1.9954 (DRS)
23. Norwich	0.9560	0.8505 (IRS)
24. Oxford	0.7349	0.1808 (IRS)
25. Pentonville	1.0000	1.0000 (CRS)
26. Pucklechurch	1.0000	1.0000 (CRS)
27. Reading	0.8707	0.4921 (IRS)
28. Shrewsbury	0.8777	0.3633 (IRS)
29. Swansea	1.0000	1.0000 (CRS)
30. Thorpe Arch	1.0000	1.0000 (CRS)
31. Wandsworth	1.0000	1.0000 (CRS)
32. Winchester	0.9999	0.9983 (IRS)
33. W. Scrubs	0.8335	2.5951 (DRS)
Mean	0.8941	0.9675 (IRS)

Summary: The Banker indicator suggests that:
17 prisons have IRS
11 prisons have CRS
 5 prisons have DRS

Notes:
1. The Rangan *et al* (1988) scale efficiency is the ratio of CRS to VRS efficiency scores derived from, respectively, Tables 5.3.1 and 4.3.2.
2. The mean of the Rangan *et al* scale indicator is calculated for only those (21) prisons for which $S_i < 1$.
3. Banker's (1984) measure of returns to scale is the sum of the weights on branches in the unconstrained CRS program, (2.4.3*).
4. The mean of the Banker measure is calculated on the sum of the weights at all 33 prisons.

Source: Authors' calculations.

With this information planners are able to reallocate the "total task" around the programme, running down establishments with decreasing returns in favour of those where returns are increasing (cf Maindiratta (1990)). Guidance of this nature is furnished in Banker's (1984) measure of returns to scale. Quite simply, if the sum of the weights on branches in the (unconstrained) CRS program is greater (less) than unity, then the returns to scale at this point are diminishing (increasing). (Recall the dual program (2.4.3*) and the discussion of returns to scale in Chapter 2.)

It is interesting to compare the Banker measure for Brixton with that of Dorchester and Oxford. Brixton's very low scale efficiency is reflected in a very marked diminishing returns to scale. By way of contrast both Dorchester and Oxford with low scale efficiencies are experiencing marked increasing returns to scale. Overall this measure suggests 17 prisons are experiencing IRS and a further 11 appear to have CRS. The mean returns to scale, calculated as an average of all 33 prisons, suggests the typical institution in this sample does indeed have a slight tendency to increasing returns.

From the policy-making point of view, one third of the sample appears to have CRS which suggests that their current level of operations can be maintained. Equally, however, the fact that around one half of the sample has IRS suggests that the scale of operations at these prisons could be increased. In actual practice, adjustments of this kind would probably entail some reallocation of responsibilties within the prison programme. Thus operations might be curtailed at overcrowded institutions such as Brixton and Wormwood Scrubs, but expanded elsewhere—at Dorchester, Oxford and Reading for example where there are marked increasing returns to scale.

5.6. Sensitivity of the returns to scale measure

The presentation of CRS results in section 5.3 subsequently enabled identification of scale efficiency as the ratio of CRS to VRS efficiency scores. As a supplement to the Rangan *et al* ratio, the Banker (1984) measure of returns to scale takes the sum of the weights in the CRS program as a guide to the *direction* of change needed to bring operations to the optimal scale. Using the Banker measure it was concluded in section 5.5 that over half the prisons in the data set have IRS, a further third have CRS and five have DRS.

These conclusions on returns to scale are based on the existence of a unique point of maximum average productivity. Banker and Thrall (1989) have argued that the existence of a supporting hyperplane passing through a *unique* point (such as *F* on the ray *OG* in Figure 5.5.1) may be a special or unusual case. In actual empirical applications, they argue, there may be more than one optimal solution to the linear program used to calculate DEA efficiency scores: That is, a given optimal score (a minimum score in the CCR primal problem, a maximum in the dual) can arise from distinct sets of reference groups. One effect of this could be that, on the CRS formulation, the Banker measure of returns to scale would take on any value within a range.

Naturally, this possibility has implications for the conclusions on returns to scale presented in section 5.5. These are explored in section 5.6 which examines the Banker and Thrall approach and which in addition suggests our own solution to the problem based on the maximum and minimum values of the scale indicator.

Nature of the problem

The analysis in section 5.5 is based on the premiss of a unique point of maximum average productivity. This point, termed the most productive scale size (MPSS) by Banker (1984), is defined at the tangency of a ray drawn from the origin to a point on the production possibility set—such as F on the ray OG in Figure 5.5.1. In a development of the original argument, Banker and Thrall (BT) (1989) have suggested that there is no reason *a priori* why the tangency should be unique—and indeed that there may be an infinite number of MPSS's along a facet in the production frontier. (The feasibility of multiple MPSS's has also been recognised in Maindiratta (1990).)

This possibility is examined in Figure 5.6.1 where the ray drawn from the origin intersects the production possibility set at an infinity of points forming a line segment BD in the production frontier.

Figure 5.6.1

Multiple MPSS

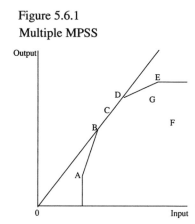

Between DMUs B and D there exists a region of constant returns (or multiple most productive scale sizes). Along this line segment, combinations of B, C and D can equally give rise to the same target input mix for inefficient DMUs such as F. This creates an arbitrariness in the selection of the reference group which, in principle, curtails the managerial information content of DEA.

Maximum and minimum values of the returns to scale

BT's (1989) solution to this problem involves identification of bounds on the slopes of the line segments *AB, BD,* and *DE* in Figure 5.6.1 to reveal the returns to scale. However, a more direct approach of our own is to find the maximum and minimum values of the returns to scale measure for each DMU. For a DMU p in the input-minimisation problem, this suggests a linear program of the following form:

(5.6.1)   MAX (MIN) S_p

subject to

(1) $\displaystyle\sum_{c=1}^{z} \lambda_c X_c \leq \mu X_p$

(2) $$\sum_{c=1}^{Z} \lambda_c Y_c \geq Y_p, \qquad c = 1, \ldots, p, \ldots, Z$$

(3) $$S_p = 0$$

and S_p, $\mu \geq 0$ and $\lambda_c \geq 0$ for all c where μ is obtained from a conventional first-stage DEA program.

By way of illustration, the L.P. in (5.6.1) has been implemented on a data set reproduced in Table 5.6.1. The Rangan *et al* scale ratio is tabulated with the associated CRS and VRS efficiency scores. Alongside these are the maximum and minimum values of the returns to scale measure derived from (5.6.1), together with the associated reference groups. For each DMU there are large differences between the maximum and minimum values of S_p. These are most significant in the case of DMUs C and F where the maximum and minimum values of S_C and S_F straddle unity. This strongly suggests the existence of a CRS line segment such as BD in Figure 5.6.1. The original Banker measure of returns, tabulated in the last column of Table 5.6.1, shows the sum of the weights identically equal to unity—with no hint of ambiguity in the reference groups or the shape of the frontier.

Table 5.6.1
Maximum and minimum values of the returns to scale indicator— sample results

DMU	Input	Output	Efficiency scores			Returns to scale				Banker measure
			CRS	VRS	Scale efficiency	Min S	Peer group	Max S	Peer group	
A	8	60	0.75	1.00	0.75	0.30	D	0.60	B	0.40
B	10	100	1.00	1.00	1.00	0.50	D	1.00	B	0.67
C	15	150	1.00	1.00	1.00	0.75	D	1.50	B	1.00
D	20	200	1.00	1.00	1.00	1.00	D	2.00	B	1.33
E	30	240	0.60	1.00	0.60	1.20	D	2.40	B	1.60
F	25	150	0.60	0.60	1.00	0.75	D	1.50	B	1.00
G	24	210	0.88	0.94	0.93	1.05	D	2.10	B	1.40

When the program in (5.6.1) was implemented using the prisons' data set the variations in the scale indicator were, on the whole, small. The largest variation in the scale indicator was 0.026. This was for Reading which had minimum and maximum values of 0.466 and 0.492 respectively. The only difference in its peer group was the exclusion of Swansea which had a weight of 0.677 in the standard program, while there were slight amendments to the weights of Bristol, Leeds and Swansea. These results, based on real data, would appear to provide little firm evidence of a CRS line segment in the production frontier.

The main limitation of the formulation in (5.6.1) is that it requires any alternative reference group to give *exactly the same* efficiency score as the original solution. With real world data, as opposed to artificial examples, it is unlikely that more than one linear combination of DMUs would give exactly the same score. Accordingly a modified version of (5.6.1) can be implemented, replacing constraint (1) with:

$$(1^*) \qquad \sum_{c=1}^{z} \lambda_c \, X_c \leq \mu \, X_p^*/(1+\gamma)$$

The inclusion of γ reflects the error propensity of empirical frontiers based on extreme observations. (Sengupta (1990a), among others, has highlighted the significance of errors in the extreme observations.)   With $\gamma = 0.02$ the alternative reference groups (with their associated S_p) would raise the reported score by 2%. Clearly different values of γ can be tried, but a value of 0.02 represents a sensible lower limit on the margin of error that might be expected in DEA frontiers. The results of calculations using the modified version of (5.6.1) are set out in Table 5.6.2.

Table 5.6.2
Maximum and minimum values of S_p for $\gamma = 0.02$

Prison	Maximum S_p	Peer group	Minimum S_p	Peer group
1. Ashford	1.824	3,5,13,26,28,30	1.501	1,3,5,13,26,30
2. Bedford	0.417	13,15,16,21,31	0.280	13,16,31
3. Brockhill	1.008	3,26,30	0.997	1,3,6,21
4. Birmingham	1.107	14,16,28,31	0.753	16,22,31
5. Bristol	1.000	5	1.000	5
6. Brixton	3.277	16,28,30	2.968	6,16,30
7. Canterbury	1.082	5,16,28,29,30	0.709	1,5,16,30
8. Cardiff	1.355	5,14,16,21,28,29,31	0.583	1,5,13,16,33
9. Colingley	1.000	9	1.000	9
10. Dorchester	0.299	5,14,16,21,28,31	0.178	5,13,16,22,31
11. Durham	1.437	5,16,28,30,31	0.881	5,16,22,31
12. Exeter	0.883	3,5,16,21,28,30,31	0.547	5,13,16,22,31
13. Glen Parva	1.000	13	1.000	13
14. Gloucester	0.875	14,16	0.342	5,16,31
15. Latchmere	0.516	3,5,13,14,16,21,28,31	0.372	5,13,16,21,30,31
16. Leeds	1.204	15,16,28,30	1.000	16
17. Leicester	0.755	14,16,29	0.308	5,16,31
18. Lewes	1.595	3,5,13,16,28,30,31	1.227	1,3,5,13,16,22
19. Lincoln	0.783	5,16,28,30,31	0.510	5,13,16,22,31
20. Liverpool	0.948	20,31	0.896	31
21. Low Newton	1.033	3,15,21,26,30	0.994	6,13,21
22. Manchester	2.291	3,13,14,15,16,31	1.420	3,5,13,16,22,31
23. Norwich	0.876	3,13,15,16,31	0.568	13,16,22,25,31
24. Oxford	0.241	3,15,16,31	0.179	16,22,31
25. Pentonville	1.181	3,13,16,25,31	0.989	13,25,31,33
26. Pucklechurch	1.000	26	1.000	26
27. Reading	0.598	16,28,30	0.415	1,5,16,30
28. Shrewsbury	0.456	5,16,28,29,30,31	0.299	1,5,13,16,22,31
29. Swansea	1.012	9,26,29	0.887	5,13,16,29,30
30. Thorpe Arch	1.007	26,30	0.996	1,3,6,30
31. Wandsworth	1.000	31	1.000	31
32. Winchester	1.203	3,5,13,16,28,30,31	0.819	1,3,5,13,16,28,30,31
33. W. Scrubs	3.087	3,5,16,28,30,31	2.249	1,3,5,13,16,22,30

This revised program, with $\gamma = 0.02$, reveals a very different picture. Large differences between the maximum and minimum values of the scale indicators are evident at the majority of prisons. In particular, at 10 institutions the scale indicators straddle unity, consistent with the Banker-Thrall conjecture of multiple most productive scale sizes. These institutions should be classified as having neither increasing or decreasing returns. One such institution is Cardiff. The original DEA solution (in Table 5.5.2) suggested increasing returns, the Banker measure equalling only 0.6655. The maximum value of the scale indicator for Cardiff in the modified program is 1.335. This new result appears to be based on the introduction into the peer group of Swansea (with a weight of 0.859) and Gloucester (weight = 0.250). These are both smaller prisons than Cardiff, measured in terms of prisoner-days.

More generally, the earlier conclusion that 5 prisons have DRS still appears to hold. However the new results suggest 12 prisons, as against 17 formerly, have IRS. Of the remaining 16, 5 appear unambiguously to have CRS with both maximum and minimum values of the scale indicator equal to unity. A further 11 establishments have scale indicator values straddling unity allowing no firm conclusion regarding their returns to scale.

The Banker and Thrall approach

The BT approach relies on the identification of bounds on the slopes of the multiple supporting hyperplanes to the production possibility set. It proceeds via the VRS formulation. Using vector rather than sigma notation for compatibility with BT suggests the folowing program for the pth DMU:

(5.6.2) $MAX \ b_p = \underline{V}.\underline{Y}_p + u_p$

subject to

(1) $\underline{V}.\underline{Y}_c - \underline{W}.\underline{X}_c + u_p \leq 0, \quad c = 1, \ldots, p, \ldots, Z$

(2) $\underline{W}.\underline{X}_p = 1$

where $\underline{V}, \underline{W} \geq 0$ and u_p is unconstrained in sign.

The graphical interpretation of (5.6.2) is convenient and straightforward for the single input/single output case. Specifically, $-(u_p{}^*/\underline{U}^*)$ can be thought of as an intercept term emanating from non-CRS facets of the production frontier, as in Figure 5.6.2 (cf Proposition 3 in Banker and Thrall (1989) and note that asterisks denote optimal values of variables.) A positive value of $u_p{}^*$ therefore implies a negative intercept and an IRS ray forming a line segment AB in the frontier. Equally, a negative value of $u_p{}^*$ defines a positive intercept and a ray with DRS joining the production frontier at C through D. It follows that the CRS facet is defined from the origin where the intercept term disappears, i.e. where $u_p{}^* = 0$.

The slopes of the line segments, and hence the returns to scale, of AB, BC, CD, etc. are given by the scale elasticity of output with respect to inputs. That is, in terms of (5.6.2), by $(1/1-u_p{}^*)$ or ρ for short. However, where there are multiple supporting hyperplanes, along facets such as BC, the scale elasticity is not uniquely defined and estimation requires determination of bounds on u_p. Consequently, the linear program in (5.6.2) is modified through the addition of a further constraint and a new objective function which alternately estimates the maximum and minimum values of u_p:

(5.6.2*) $MAX \ (MIN) \ u_p$

Figure 5.6.2
Banker & Thrall program

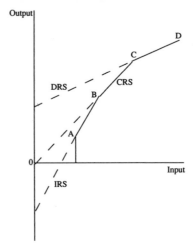

subject to

(1*) $\underline{V}.\underline{Y}_c - \underline{W}.\underline{X}_c + u_p \leq 0, \quad c = 1, \ldots,p, \ldots ,Z$

(2*) $\underline{W}.\underline{X}_p = 1$

(3*) $\underline{V}.\underline{Y}_p + u_p = 1$

where $\underline{V},\underline{W} \geq 0$ and u_p is unconstrained in sign.

The second and third constraints together imply that the efficiency score of the DMU is unity. Attempts to run this program on the complete prisons' data set (including both efficient and inefficient institutions) typically results in a large number of failed LPs. Indeed, the fact that u_p is unconstrained in sign makes standard algorithms for linear programming fail. Nevertheless results using the BT procedure were obtained for technically efficient DMUs using the sample data set in Table 5.6.3.

Table 5.6.3
Scale elasticity in the Banker and Thrall program

DMU	Input	Output	Maximum u_p		Minimum u_p	
			u_p	ρ	u_p	ρ
A	8	60	1.00	infinity	6.25	2.67
B	10	100	0.50	2.00	0.00	1.00
C	15	150	0.00	1.00	0.00	1.00
D	20	200	-1.50	0.40	0.00	1.00
E	30	240	-infinity	0.00	-1.00	0.50
F	25	150	no solution		no solution	
G	24	210	no solution		no solution	

The results suggest IRS for DMU *A*. The value of infinity for ρ_A is the counterpart of the vertical line segment in the envelope in Figure 5.6.1. Analogously the value of zero for branch *E* represents the flat segment of the envelope. More generally, if a production plan *(Xₚ,Yₚ)* at the *p*th DMU is technically efficient:

(1) IRS prevail at *(Xₚ,Yₚ)* iff $\rho_{max} \geq \rho_{min} > 1$;

(2) CRS prevail at *(Xₚ,Yₚ)* iff $\rho_{max} \geq 1 \geq \rho_{min}$;

and

(3) DRS prevail at *(Xₚ,Yₚ)* iff $1 > \rho_{max} \geq \rho_{min}$.

BT: A valedictory
Although some sample results have been presented, the computational intractability of the BT procedure is both frustrating and disappointing. The limitations of the procedure, despite its *prima facie* appeal, have prohibited corroboration of the RTS results in section 5.5. Our own measure—being based on an intuitive extension of Banker's original definition of returns to scale and embodying a computationally tractable linear program—would appear to be of greater practical relevance to the policy-maker.

5.7. Conclusion
Chapter 5 has sought to examine the efficiency of whole spending programmes on a consistent total-factor basis. Section 5.2 has shown that aggregate efficiency identities may be derived as summary indicators of *programme* performance. These indicators are significant in being consistent with the "micro-efficiency" scores implied by operations at the level of individual establishments. Several authors, for example Charnes and Cooper (1980a,b), have argued for the modernisation of public sector evaluation in the face of more complex production environments and constrained processing and decision-making abilities. The formulation of summary aggregate-efficiency concepts can help to reduce decision-making complexity. Moreover they may fulfil a role in a policy setting like the Public Expenditure Survey wherein resources may be diverted away from less effective programmes in favour of more efficient alternatives. This broadens the scope for measures such as DEA.

Using the cost identities proposed in section 5.2 it was estimated that about 5% of total costs in local prisons could be deducted while maintaining existing levels of service (assuming varying returns to scale). Section 5.3 looked at costs on an alternative CRS assumption. Potential non-remand savings doubled to around 10% and in remand items more than tripled to approximately 18%. Savings in all items rose to a potential figure of 13.1% of total costs under CRS. In absolute terms this implied excess costs of £31.1million under CRS against only £11.1million under VRS. It was noted that the distribution of these savings across the various cost measures is no longer fairly even as under VRS: In particular, savings in remand items appeared greater than before. This suggests that there may be greater scale inefficiency in the remand variables.

The existence of alternative scale assumptions suggested a potential ambiguity as to whether VRS or CRS results are a more accurate reflection of levels of inefficiency.

In the DEA literature to date there is little guidance on the implementation of scale assumptions. Section 5.4 examined the nature of the "bias" imparted to DEA results by the choice of one scale assumption over another. It was demonstrated that best-practice notions of cost can be nested according to the scale assumption and that best-practice CRS costs must be less than their VRS counterparts because the VRS production set is nested within the CRS set. This implied that the scale of savings (excess costs) under VRS must be less than under an alternative like CRS. This was borne out in the performance comparison in section 5.3 where potential savings in the programme as a whole under VRS reached a little over a third of those predicted from the CRS boundary.

The implications of the CRS and VRS boundaries were explored further in section 5.5. In particular the attainment of best-practice on a VRS boundary denotes only pure technical efficiency. Best-practice targets on a CRS boundary include in addition a contraction in resources to account for scale inefficiencies. The distinction between purely technical and scale inefficiencies enabled the breakdown of total excess costs in prison spending. This revealed that nearly two thirds (64%) of total excess costs are accounted for by scale inefficiencies. The Banker measure suggested that of those prisons which are scale inefficient, the bulk of these have increasing as against decreasing returns to scale. That is, 17 prisons were identified operating in regions of increasing returns to scale, 5 with decreasing returns and the remaining 11 had constant returns. The prevalence of non-constant returns suggests that a general policy of adjusting the scale of operations might yield substantial cost benefits to the prison service as a whole.

Section 5.6 examined the Banker and Thrall conjecture that there may be multiple (indeed infinite) points of maximum average productivity in the frontier. From a computational point of view the BT procedure proved disappointing and appears to offer little advantage over the original Banker measure. Our own proposal to deal with multiple MPSS is couched in terms of the maximum and minimum values of the original Banker measure. In practice, this looks more promising than the BT procedure, producing results on returns to scale broadly consistent with those already reported in section 5.5.

Before closing this Chapter it is worth reflecting on the future potential of DEA in the public sector. Sections 5.2 and 5.3 noted the developments in the UK government's efficiency White Paper *Civil Service Management Reform* which will allow greater financial autonomy to spending "agencies". In principle any branch of a spending programme such as a prison, a school or a hospital can be thought of as an agency. Regular application of DEA could be used to monitor the success of agencies in the control of their own budgets. The results of regular performance analyses of this nature could in turn be used as a "test" of the famous Averch-Johnson result that efficiency rises as the degree of government regulation of production falls (Hollas and Stansell (1988)). Although Averch and Johnson were concerned particularly with the regulation of public utilities it would nevertheless be of interest to discover whether less central involvement in the spending of funds by agencies does indeed lead to increased efficiency in the longer term.

CHAPTER 6

THE INTERPRETATION OF EFFICIENCY IN DATA ENVELOPMENT ANALYSIS

6.1. Introduction

"The standard economic doctrine is that, provided certain conditions are satisfied, efficiency (in the sense of Pareto efficiency) will be attained under a system in which individual economic agents egoistically maximise their own utility. This is the central insight of microeconomic theory. A large part of the literature of economics is concerned with the question exactly how stringent the conditions are in order for it to hold" —Matthews (1981).

The objective of Chapter 6 is to examine the meaning of efficiency in Data Envelopment Analysis (DEA). Typically the DEA literature identifies best-practice production with Pareto Efficiency. Chapter 6 discusses objections to this interpretation of best-practice. These are derived from two main sources: One is empirical and includes studies which suggest that best-practice operations are themselves capable of improving performance (Ganley and Cubbin (1987), McGuire (1987), Danilin *et al* (1985)). The other is based on *a priori* and analytical problems which have been raised by, among others, Sobel (1992), Talley (1988), Fare, Grosskopf and Lovell (1985), Thrall (1985), Tinbergen (1985), Peston (1980), Leibenstein (1978, 1975, 1966) and Margolis (1971) concerning the nature of efficiency and public sector measurement difficulties.

Chapter 6 sets these problems in the context of the formal conditions for technical, allocative and Pareto efficiency. It is demonstrated that in general the best-practice reference technology defined in the DEA estimates cannot be reliably identified with Pareto efficiency. In response, a new Utility-Dominance concept is proposed as a more appropriate justification of normative DEA prescriptions to replace the standard usage of the Pareto Criterion in the literature. This has not been suggested previously in the literature and represents a major re-interpretation of the validity and justification of DEA targets and efficiency scores. Later, Chapter 7 provides empirical evidence to support a more cautious interpretation of DEA efficiency in the replication of the education results in Chapter 3 on a "clustered" basis. The number of best-practice local education authorities (LEAs), targets and peer groups is seen to vary unpredictably, strengthening the impression of ambiguity in DEA efficiency and providing an additional rationale for abandoning the Pareto interpretation of the estimates.

Chapter 6 develops the conditions for the Pareto Criterion to hold in the context of a stylised 2-good economy. It is apparent that these conditions, particularly the broader requirements of allocative efficiency, are exacting to the extent that it is extremely misleading to label real world decision-making as Pareto efficient. Best-practice decision-makers in the education authority, for example, are clearly not implementing neoclassical decisions. To suggest otherwise may insulate relatively poor best-practice performers from remedial intervention and other scrutiny. This would be a serious restraint on the new ethos of evaluation and accountability for public sector decision-making enshrined in the Financial Management Initiative.

In his inaugural lecture at Cambridge, Frank Hahn (1973) adopted a comparable approach to a different problem.   He argued that the sophisticated and abstruse techniques (such as the famous fixed-point theorems of Brouwer[1]) required to demonstrate the existence of a competitive equilibrium were the focus of research precisely to demonstrate just how intractable (and therefore unlikely) are the assumptions underpinning the existence of a competitive equilibrium.

In outline, Chapter 6 proceeds as follows.   Section 6.2 is taken up with a discussion of the definition of best-practice and why this is no guarantee in itself of productive excellence.   The possibility of poor performance being identified with best-practice is justified with a discussion of the many sources from which inefficiency may spring. This covers arguments due to, among others, Fare, Grosskopf and Lovell (1985), Tinbergen (1985), and Leibenstein (1966).   Section 6.3 examines the definition of Pareto efficiency and shows that there is nothing in principle which can guarantee best-practice and Pareto efficiency will coincide—despite arguments in the literature to the contrary.   The discussion focuses on the importance of allocative efficiency.   It notes that technical efficiency is defined independent of factor prices and hence excludes the allocative requirements of Pareto efficiency.

The distinction between Pareto and DEA efficiency is formalised in terms of dominance concepts in section 6.4.   These are used to draw out the utility implications of production decisions.   From this it is argued in section 6.5 that although a DEA target may not be Pareto efficient it can nevertheless be justified as a Pareto Improvement.   This is an important re-interpretation of the normative basis for DEA targeting.

Some additional difficulties in DEA are discussed in section 6.6 regarding the coherence of targets, the problem of noise and the difficulties encountered in trying to compare like-with-like.

6.2.   The definition of best-practice

Many authors in the DEA literature (e.g. Charnes and Cooper (1985), Charnes, Cooper, Golany, Seiford and Stutz (1985), Nunamaker (1985), Johnson and Lewin (1984), Charnes, Cooper and Rhodes (1981), Lewin and Morey (1981)) have argued that best-practice decision-making units (e.g. LEAs with a unity efficiency score) can be regarded as Pareto efficient.   Lewin and Morey (1981), for example, identify Pareto efficiency with best-practice production in a manner characteristic of the literature on DEA: "DEA is based upon the economic notion of Pareto Optimality.   A given Decision Making Unit (DMU) is not efficient if some other DMU, or some combination of other DMUs [i.e. the peer group] can produce the same amounts of outputs with less of some resource and not more of any other resource; conversely, a DMU is said to be Pareto efficient if the above is not possible."   Notice that for consistency with the LEA and prison-efficiency results the input-based definition of

---

(1)   On which see Debreu (1959).

Pareto efficiency is cited here. There is, of course, an analogous output-based definition used in the DEA literature by, among others, Charnes, Cooper and Rhodes (1981). That is to say, a decision-making unit is Pareto efficient if it is impossible to increase an output without simultaneously increasing an input or decreasing another output. More generally, Lewin and Morey have argued that "the relative technical efficiency of any particular DMU is calculated by forming the ratio of a weighted sum of outputs to a weighted sum of inputs, *where the weights for both outputs and inputs are to be selected in a manner that calculates the Pareto efficiency of the unit*" (emphasis added).

Limits to the interpretation of best-practice

Best-practice in a given cross section of decision-making units (whether LEAs, local prisons, job centres or whatever) is the best performance found within that data set. Since the resulting DEA frontier is an observed or "revealed" frontier it is clearly possible to make an analogy with consumer theory; that is, observed consumption bundles reveal preferences and thereby in principle the utility function. However, in a production context the level of performance revealed as best-practice may itself be quite unexceptional. Thrall (1985) has coined the term "DEA-efficient" in order to distinguish best-practice production from true Pareto efficiency. Accordingly, he maintains that "in using DEA, one must take account of the fact that a DMU can be DEA-efficient without being meritorious." Analogously Greenberg and Nunamaker (1987, page 340) recognise that best current practice is not necessarily fully optimal and argue that "one must be careful not to conclude that because an institution is operating on the efficient frontier, its achievement level on all measures is necessarily desirable".

There is evidence in the public sector that there may be a pervasive lack of incentives and managerial excellence. In a translog comparison of Scottish hospital performance in 1983/84 McGuire (1987, page 793) argues that transactions costs and other characteristics of hospital production make full cost-minimising behaviour improbable: "The fact that the hospital sector is non-profit-making [in the UK] immediately attenuates the system of incentives held to underlie the neoclassical system. As such it is probable that cost-minimising production processes in this sector will involve the acquisition of information and the monitoring of contracts. That is to say that the sector will exhibit positive transactions costs"; thus "*a priori* consideration of the constraints [on optimising behaviour] in this sector would suggest that the estimated function is *not* the production frontier" (emphasis added).

Peston (1980) argues that in British education many of the conditions necessary for Pareto-efficient choices are unsatisfied because "it is a producer dominated system with great monopoly power . . . it is a satisficing, not an optimising system." In these circumstances best-practice production should not in general be expected to satisfy the "very extreme assumptions needed in order for a utility maximising outcome to be reached" (Matthews (1981))—even granted that that outcome remains technologically feasible. The Pareto Criterion compares (production) states of the world such that a Pareto-efficient state occurs where it is impossible to make one economic agent better off (as judged by himself) without simultaneously worsening the utility of another (as judged by himself). But clearly with non-optimising educational producers such as identified in Peston (1980), best-practice production will contain Pareto-inferior states when simultaneously other technically feasible optimal states exist at which unambiguous welfare gains could be derived: For example at given levels of educational attainment one agent (e.g. the taxpayer) could be made better off whilst no one else (e.g. pupils, teachers or parents) is made worse off from an improvement in the cost performance of a *best-practice* (that is, supposedly Pareto efficient) LEA.

Research in other areas leads to similar conclusions. In Ganley and Cubbin (1987) and in an independent field report[1] on staffing in the Prison Service, it is argued that even the best prison establishments might be targeted substantial reductions in manpower costs. Analogously so-called "best-practice" LEAs may themselves be expected to be capable of improvements relative to a maximal production boundary. Moreover it is this maximal standard which is the true Pareto standard, because for given vintages of the technology it cannot be dominated (see Figure 6.3.1 below).

The possibility of inefficient production decisions

Complementary arguments to these are to be found in several areas. Sobel (1992), for example, has argued that even ostensibly trivial tasks such as counting may be imperfectly performed, reflecting the error-propensities of agents. Much earlier, Leibenstein (1966) observed that conventional production theory presumes inputs have a fixed specification and yield a *fixed* performance when in actual practice inputs, especially labour services, may yield a variable performance. Traditional analysis excludes this possibility because it presumes that production units will only take optimal input decisions. From an *a priori* standpoint it cannot be denied that optimal decisions are possible, but equally it is conceivable that circumstances arise in which managers perform poorly. This may be because managers determine their own productivity in addition to that of the other inputs of labour and capital services. As a consequence, "firms [or more generally DMUs] and economies do not operate on an outer-bound production possibility surface consistent with their resources. Rather they actually work on a production surface that is well within that outer bound. This means that for a variety of reasons people and organisations normally work neither as hard nor as effectively as they could . . .[and] many people will trade the disutility of greater effort, of search, and the control of other people's activities for the utility of feeling less pressure and of better interpersonal relations" (Leibenstein (1966, page 413)). The evidence which Leibenstein presented was the first stride towards acknowledging that technical inefficiency is both possible and widespread. It follows that deviations from optimal Pareto production plans may be common enough to make the blanket Pareto interpretation of best-practice production in the DEA literature especially difficult to sustain.

Leibenstein's recognition of an inner production boundary for observed producer behaviour is consistent with this Chapter's thesis as to the sub-optimal nature of best-practice. A modern and important study, Danilin, Materov, Rosefielde and Lovell (1985), has drawn the same distinction between notional Pareto and best-practice frontiers: "Enterprise efficiency is a concept that expresses the degree to

---

(1)   *Study of Prison Officers' Complementing and Shift Systems*, vols 1 (Report) and 2 (Appendices), Home
       Office Prison Department and PA Management Consultants, April, 1986.

which the observed enterprise performance approaches its potential. This potential may be defined operationally in terms of prevailing technology and prices, or hypothetically with reference to arrangements under a generally competitive regime. Both interpretations are of interest . . ." (pages 225–226). Danilin *et al* were keen to stress this distinction because their study of Soviet cotton refining found a remarkably small dispersion of efficiency scores below best-practice. This, in itself, they argued, could not be taken as evidence of managerial and productive excellence as "*enterprises may still be inefficient to some unknown degree because the best-practice standard used to measure the production frontier may understate true engineering production*" (emphasis added). That is to say, had the efficiency comparisons been made including data from *several* countries, then domestic best-practice would in all probability have appeared poorer because a larger cross section may have revealed examples of better performance in enterprises operating in competitive Western environments.

Counterproduction

Leibenstein (1966, page 392) remarked that "a major element of X-efficiency is motivation". In a recent volume of his collected papers, Tinbergen (1985, Chapter 4) has stressed similar considerations in his theory of "counterproduction". This arose in his work on the problems of estimating production functions which suggested to him the possibility of *negative* marginal production of inputs; that is, in effect, a production decision on a positively sloped segment of the isoquant. Tinbergen's own empirical work suggests that blue collar workers in the United States have had negative marginal products and thus that deviations from first-best efficient production are, as Leibenstein has also maintained, common in real-world production environments. Tinbergen suggests that these deviations arise because of deficiencies in organisational structures and design. These deficiencies have a negative impact on job satisfaction and productivity in a manner which makes the first best Pareto outcome unattainable (Hammond (1987)).

Tinbergen (1985) has argued for an enrichment of economic science through a form of "territorial expansion" which will increase the realism of economic analysis by accounting for modes of behaviour and circumstances which traditional theory has ignored. It is in this context that he has proposed the theory of counterproduction for sub-optimal production decisions: A phenomenon "which economic theory has hardly analysed so far" (*ibid.*, page 38). A new theory of *inefficiency* such as Tinbergen suggested has been advocated most persuasively by Fare, Grosskopf and Lovell (1985). Fare *et al* have dichotomised Farrell's original notion of efficiency in a manner which enlarges the potential sources of inefficiency to account for a broader set of sub-optimal production decisions.

Fare, Grosskopf and Lovell (1985) efficiency decomposition

Farrell (1957) split efficiency into two components, technical and allocative. Fare, Grosskopf and Lovell (FGL) (1985) have shown that this is not exhaustive and that efficiency can be usefully disaggregated into purely technical, structural, allocative and scale components.

This decomposition is illustrated in Figure 6.2.1.   Given input prices *RR* and the long-run Pareto reference technology *PP*, the point of overall efficient production is the input choice at *G*.   But suppose that production is possible in the interior of the input set, for example at *F*.   Overall (i.e.   Pareto) efficiency (*OE*) is then:

$$OE = 0A/0F < 1$$

The purely technical component (*PTE*) in overall efficiency due to production on the interior of the input set is:

$$PTE = 0D/0F$$

The structural component, otherwise known as congestion (*C*), is due to production on a positively sloped stretch of the isoquant.   That is to say, in the non-economic region, identified by Tinbergen (1985) as counterproduction, where the marginal products of factor services are negative:

$$C = 0C/0D$$

Figure 6.2.1

FGL efficiency decomposition

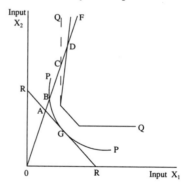

Deviations from scale efficiency (*S*) occur because a DMU is not operating at the scale of operations consistent with long-run equilibrium, i.e. at a point consistent with constant returns to scale.   Scale efficiency is thus the discrepancy between the true constant returns technology *PP* and the estimate of the intermediate or short-run technology *QQ*:

$$S = 0B/0C$$

Allocative efficiency (*A*) is price-dependent and defined relative to the input price line *RR*:

$$A = 0A/0B$$

All four of these potential sources of inefficiency can be combined into a multiplicative identity to define overall efficiency (OE):

$$OE = PTE.C.S.A$$

That is:

$$OE = \frac{0A}{0F} = \frac{0D}{0F} \cdot \frac{0C}{0D} \cdot \frac{0B}{0C} \cdot \frac{0A}{0B}$$

FGL observe that in the absence of price information, as in the case of non-traded outputs in the public sector, a more concise price independent measure of overall technical efficiency (OTE) can be defined as:

$$OTE = \frac{0B}{0F} = \frac{0D}{0F} \cdot \frac{0C}{0D} \cdot \frac{0B}{0C}$$

The FGL efficiency identity OE differs from the simpler Farrell version in the addition of the scale measure and the decomposition of his technical efficiency into the *PTE* and *C* components. The product of *PTE* and *C* gives the original Farrell definition of technical efficiency.

The FGL (1985) decomposition of efficiency is significant in that it represents an exhaustive taxonomy of the sources of inefficiency in production. They argue that it broadens the scope of testable hypotheses in production theory and injects a realism regarding the existence of new forms of sub-optimal managerial decision which have been ruled out in traditional neoclassical analysis.

The broadening arguments proposed by Fare *et al* (1985), Tinbergen (1985), Leibenstein (1966, etc.), and others, are further indication of the mounting evidence for the possibility of inefficient production and an estimate of a sub-optimal reference technology—an estimate which cannot therefore be considered to fulfil the first best, full information conditions of Pareto efficiency.

6.3. The definition of Pareto efficiency and the DEA efficiency score

The definitions and origins of Pareto efficiency go to the heart of neoclassical economics (Matthews (1981), Debreu (1959)). Conventional neoclassical analysis has used the differential calculus to develop stylised optimisation problems as the basis for decision-making in production (see for example Varian (1978), Chapter 1). If the local education authority successfully processed the neoclassical optimisation problem it would have chosen an optimal input and output mix which is technically and allocatively efficient.

On the basis of the arguments suggested in Ganley and Cubbin (1987), Prison Department (1986), Danilin *et al* (1985), Thrall (1985), Peston (1980), the minimal costs (C_{min}) of the neoclassical solution are likely to be less than best-practice costs (C_{bp}); that is, the LEA could not ordinarily be expected to solve the neoclassical decision-problem. Only costs C_{min} are Pareto efficient, with no unrealised welfare benefits attainable through the transfer of resources either to different LEAs or to different (non-education) sectors elsewhere in the economy.

Section 6.3 shows that best-practice costs may be greater than Pareto-efficient costs for two reasons. In the first place the best-practice boundary may be made up of poorly performing DMUs. This is explored below through Figure 6.3.1. If this is the case, best-practice does not define a true frontier (which by definition must be undominated). As a consequence best-practice targets will not suggest the full feasible reduction in costs defined from the underlying Pareto technology.

Second, where the best-practice frontier is an accurate estimate of the Pareto technology (as in Figure 6.3.2) costs may still exceed their minimum because of allocative inefficiencies. As Sexton, Silkman and Hogan (1986) have pointed out, DEA efficiency is narrowly defined in terms of the technology, ignoring the allocative dimension defined by the factor prices. These broader, price-based considerations have recently begun to receive more attention in the literature. Thompson, Langemeier, Lee, Lee, and Thrall (1990), for example, have developed their Assurance Region concept as a means of eliminating technically efficient organisations from a subset of DMUs satisfying more demanding allocative criteria. In this "post-DEA" analysis, Thompson *et al* found that the number of inefficient units rises appreciably. Hence the existence of deficiencies in best practice and/or allocative inefficiencies will ordinarily divorce Pareto and DEA efficiency. This does not, however, deny that best practice can be Pareto efficient. Rather it is to suggest that in most applications this is unlikely.

A best-practice "boundary"

Figure 6.3.1 demonstrates the possibility that in general best-practice efficiency scores of unity with costs C_1 do not necessarily imply full cost minimisation and Pareto efficiency. This is because best practice is defined relative to the best performance in the cross section at that time. There is nothing which can guarantee *ex ante* that this is "meritorious"—to use Thrall's (1985) term.

The best-practice technology BB' is nested in (and thereby dominated by) the Pareto technology PP'. The best-practice efficiency score at C is unity, when clearly costs

Figure 6.3.1

Best-practice & Pareto technologies

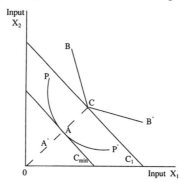

along C_1 are greater than the minimal costs associated with the true (and feasible) Pareto technology. In principle, the true efficiency score is $0A/0C < 1$. This implies that a DEA target overstates efficiency and obscures some fraction of the savings which could accrue from Pareto efficient production at A. Note that production at $0A'$ is infeasible by definition. Consequently, the savings defined by DEA can never be *over*-estimates but may *under*-estimate the potential gains from production for as long as there is a discrepancy between the true and estimated boundaries. The scale of this under-estimate is generally unclear because, as some research now recognises (Seiford and Thrall (1990)), the location of the true production frontier is unknown.

Allocative efficiency

Only where the true production technology overlaps the piecewise DEA estimate can the technical efficiency ratio predict an analytically accurate reduction in costs. Even in this unlikely case, technical efficiency *per se* could not be taken to imply full cost minimisation. This can be discussed in terms of Figure 6.3.2 (below) where the cost-minimising input choice is defined from C. At this point, Pareto efficiency (*PE*) can be dichotomised into technical (*TE*) and allocative (*AE*) components according to Farrell's original (1957) multiplicative efficiency identity:

(6.3.1) $PE = TE.AE$

Technical efficiency is the radial distance of the LEA from the estimated isoquant. For LEA_1 this distance is zero and it is said to be best-practice with:

(6.3.2) $TE = 0B/0B = 1$

Allocative efficiency, on the other hand, is the radial distance between the isocost line and the LEA. This defines:

(6.3.3) $AE = 0A/0B < 1$

for LEA_1 which is judged not to be allocatively efficient. Thus for LEA_1 Pareto efficiency (*PE*) is less than unity. It follows that where the best-practice estimate overlaps the true technology, a technical-efficiency score of unity cannot be taken to guarantee a cost minimum. This is because the technical-efficiency score is defined independent of the factor prices. It follows that whilst production at B is best-practice with *TE* equal to unity, costs remain greater than minimum costs. A further reduction in costs accounting for allocative inefficiences would be required to establish full cost efficiency (as at C).

In Figure 6.3.2 there is a non-zero opportunity cost in production at B measured by $(C_1 - C_{min})$. This implies that welfare gains are still possible through the reallocation of some fraction of the resources used by LEA_1 because it is allocatively inefficient. It is inaccurate and misleading therefore to label a position of technical efficiency as Pareto efficient, as is the tendency in DEA literature, because of the strong probability that $AE < 1$. Pareto efficiency requires the much stronger and more discriminating condition that opportunity costs are minimised and hence that $AE = TE = 1.0$; i.e., that production is both technically *and* allocatively efficient. This more demanding

Figure 6.3.2

Overlapping reference technologies

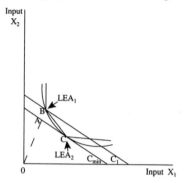

criterion will generally increase the numbers of DMUs identified inefficient since allocatively inefficient units will drop out of best practice.   Morey, Fine and Loree (1990) have recently found empirical support for this effect in a study of hospital performance which adjusts for input prices.

The implications of allocative efficiency are far reaching.   Conventional target-setting, for example, suggests that inputs at inefficient DMUs should be reduced equi-proportionately along a radial contraction path.   This assumes there are no trade offs between inputs and is counter intuitive.   Price information would generally indicate that the opportunity costs of consumption of one input over another are not the same (Morey *et al* (1990)).   Consequently it might be optimal to reduce inputs in non-equal proportions reflecting their differing opportunity costs.   Targeting then involves the adjustment of the ratios of inputs as well as their levels. In Figure 6.2.1 DMU F would wish to lower the ratio of X_2 to X_1 moving down a non-radial contraction path to a point of allocative efficiency at G.

Public sector measurement problems

Note in passing that the isocost line in Figure 6.3.2 is defined by the *LEA* cost function with input prices conventionally given in competitive factor markets.   It is of the form $\Sigma W_k X_k$ and indicates for a given level of cost the various feasible input combinations. As a matter of fact, however, the position of the isocost line may not be known or is at least ambiguous in many contexts because of pricing problems in the public sector (Sexton, Silkman and Hogan (1986)).   True resource costs (relative prices) may be unknown and notional prices must be imputed on the basis of an accounting convention.   Alternatively, linear programs may be used to generate shadow prices on inputs and outputs.[1] Perrakis (1980) and Stewart (1978) have demonstrated a further source of ambiguity in markets where there is input price uncertainty.   In these (plausible) circumstances, management can be expected to use relatively more of lower risk and less of higher risk inputs as compared to the cost-minimising outcome under certainty.   This effect persists even for a risk-neutral manager and is reinforced

(1)   Margolis (1971) discusses the nature and role of shadow prices for incorrect or non-existent market values. Sen (1975b) Chapter 11 is also a useful discussion.

under risk-averse behaviour.   Under these difficulties, true relative prices may remain unknown—even *ex post*.   It follows that whilst a Pareto efficient choice of resources is technically feasible, it may never be identified.   As hinted by Sen (1975a,b) the concept of Pareto efficiency is unobservable.   Its use as a decision criterion for DMU evaluation is therefore fallacious for practical purposes.

The importance of allocative efficiency
The importance of the allocative dimension to the Pareto Criterion has been explicitly overlooked in the DEA literature.   Charnes, Cooper and Rhodes (1981) for example have maintained that: "DEA approaches and efficiency concepts are at their best when applied to situations in which there is an agreed upon set of objectives and in which resource diversions to other programs are not at issue . . . How any of the conserved amounts [from realised DEA targets] might best be redistributed to other activities, e.g., to activities of a non-education variety, involves issues of pricing and weighting that are not addressed in our formulations." In a neoclassical full-employment economy, poorly combined, unemployed or under-used inputs imply a non-zero opportunity cost in terms of output foregone.   To ignore these allocative considerations amounts to a presumption that unemployed resources have no output potential elsewhere in the economy or that the allocative dimension is unnecessary to support the use of the Pareto Criterion.   Neither of these presumptions   can be maintained as may now be demonstrated.

Consider a hypothetical 2x2 economy which produces education and "other goods" using two inputs, X_1 and X_2 Production of the education good by the *LEA* sector is defined from the origin 0_Y and analogously for the production of "other goods" from 0_Q in the Edgeworth Box in Figure 6.3.3.   The lengths of the X_1 and X_2 axes represent the amount of these two factor services available to the economy and all points within

Figure 6.3.3
Education in a 2x2 economy

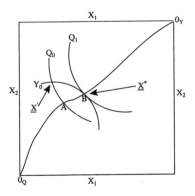

the box represent feasible allocations of X_1 and X_2 between the two sectors. Isoquants representing the output of education (Y) are drawn relative to the origin 0_Y and those representing the output of other goods (Q) relative to 0_Q. 0_Q0_Y is a production contract curve—that is the locus of points where the ratio of input prices is equal to the ratio of the marginal products of the inputs—and the economy will be in equilibrium somewhere along it on the assumption that output is produced under competitive conditions. Allocations on the contract curve between and including A and B are Pareto Superior to points elsewhere like $\underline{X}'$.

Although at $\underline{X}'$ the *LEA* sector is technically efficient it is allocatively inefficient and restraining the output of other goods by $(Q_1 - Q_0)$. By altering its input mix to $\underline{X}^*$ with output given at Y_0 educational costs are minimised and resources are released and may be diverted into the production of other goods to make up the output deficit $(Q_1 - Q_0)$. $\underline{X}^*$ minimises opportunity costs in the economy and dominates vectors such as $\underline{X}'$ on utility grounds. Net utilities at $\underline{X}^*$ have risen (indeed are maximised) *vis-à-vis* $\underline{X}'$ because education costs are lower and the output of "other goods" is higher.

6.4. A new utility basis for DEA efficiency

Section 6.3 has distinguished between Pareto efficiency and DEA efficiency. It has been shown that the requirements for Pareto efficiency are much stronger than the literature has acknowledged. This undermines the conventional justification for setting best-practice targets. Section 6.4 develops a more appropriate basis for targeting by formalising the utility implications of best-practice. This makes it possible to re-justify the DEA target in a manner which does not invoke Pareto efficiency.

Dominance concepts for efficiency measurement

Debreu (1951) characterised efficiency through its implications for utility in the economy. Thus preferred states of the world are those production plans which yield greater utility. These plans (or choices) are said to be "dominant". That is, on some appropriate criterion like costs or utilities, one state of the world can be ranked against another (see e.g. Sen (1975a)).

All concepts of efficiency can be expressed in terms of a relation of dominance and this is a useful way to rank best-practice production against Pareto efficiency. Performance comparisons using dominance concepts have a substantial history. The concept of a dominant reference group was first introduced by Hyman (1942) and then Merton (1957) and applied to goal formation and attainment in productive organisations by March and Simon (1963). The concept is also discussed in Sen (1975a) and Johnson and Lewin (1984). An appropriate economic criterion on which to examine dominance is utility. In Figure 6.3.3 the Pareto input mix $\underline{X}^*$ was chosen by excluding feasible but allocatively inefficient choices. Formally, this optimal vector may be said to dominate these sub-optimal choices if, by choosing $\underline{X}^*$ instead of some other, $\underline{X}$, none of the utility functions in the economy decrease and at least one of them effectively increases. More generally, in a full-employment economy, resources released from inefficient production will be diverted into new production elsewhere. This permits welfare enhancing trades which are precluded so long as inefficient consumption of resources persists. Following Frisch (1966) this suggests the following definition of Pareto-efficient choices:

DEFINITION: Pareto efficiency

A vector $\underline{X}^* = (X_1^*, \ldots, X_m^*)$ is said to be Pareto efficient when—within the limits of the feasible production set $\underline{P}$—there exists no vector $\underline{X} = (X_1, \ldots, X_m)$ which would have the property that on passing from $\underline{X}^*$ to $\underline{X}$ the utility functions in the economy, $U_1, \ldots, U_k$, do not decrease and at least one of them effectively increases.

Section 6.2 discussed the limitations of best-practice as an indicator of efficiency. These limitations suggest that best-practice production would be dominated in utility terms by a production plan satisfying the definition of Pareto efficiency. This is illustrated in Figure 6.4.1.

Assume that production is taking place using inputs X'' with costs C_2. This is clearly inefficient *vis-à-vis* best-practice at $\underline{X}'$ where costs are only C_1. However $\underline{X}'$ is itself dominated by the Pareto input bundle X^* where costs are minimised. In utility terms $\underline{X}'$ yields greater utility than $\underline{X}''$ since best-practice production releases resources $(C_2 - C_1)$ which can be diverted into greater production elsewhere in the economy.

Figure 6.4.1

A DEA-dominant target, $\underline{X}'$

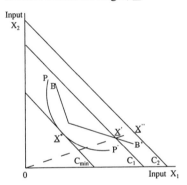

However the greatest utility would accrue where the opportunity costs are minimised, as at $\underline{X}^*$. It follows that the technically inefficient $(\underline{X}'')$ and the DEA-efficient $(\underline{X}')$ choices are dominated by the Pareto production plan in utility terms, *viz.* :

(6.4.1) $U(\underline{X}^*) \geq U(\underline{X}') \geq U(\underline{X}'')$

where $U(.)$ is the net total utility in the economy resulting from a given selection of the choice variables. Specifically, the Pareto plan dominates the DEA-efficient plan which is itself preferred to the non-boundary allocation, $\underline{X}''$. In terms of the formalised definition of Pareto efficiency above this means that on moving from a technically inefficient vector $\underline{X}''$ to its best-practice counterpart $\underline{X}'$, at least one of the utility functions in the economy effectively increases and so $\underline{X}'$ is preferred to $\underline{X}''$.

Assuming then the backcloth of a full-employment, neoclassical economy, the release of resources from inefficient production raises output and utility in other sectors of the economy. On this basis a production plan $\underline{X}'$ in Figure 6.4.1 can be termed *DEA-Dominant* over another plan $\underline{X}''$ which consumes more resources. It is clear however that a further input bundle $\underline{X}^*$ dominates the best-practice alternative. $\underline{X}^*$ is therefore *Pareto-Dominant*.

6.5. The DEA target as a Pareto Improvement

The main normative aspect of DEA is the recommendation of a best-practice target. If the target is not Pareto efficient but "DEA-dominant", this suggests the target requires an alternative justification.   This can be provided using the utility interpretation of efficiency developed in section 6.4.

Underlying targeted reductions (increases) in costs (outputs) derived from DEA-efficiency scores is a value judgement on utility formation; that is, *ceteris paribus*, reductions (increases) in costs (outputs) are desirable in the presence of inefficiency.   If this is the case, targets remain justifiable but on the basis of the new DEA-Dominance Criterion.   Targets set on this basis, e.g. at X' in Figure 6.4.1, are not Pareto efficient but will bring DEA-inefficient performance up to the utility standards attainable by best-practice DMUs.   The best-practice target OX' defined on the reference technology BB' dominates the technically inefficient vector $\underline{X}''$ in utility terms with costs $C_1 < C_2$. $\underline{X}'$ is itself dominated by $\underline{X}^*$, defined on the true Pareto technology PP'.   The Pareto allocation $\underline{X}^*$ minimises opportunity costs yielding maximal utility for the economy.   Nonetheless any reduction in costs below C_2 frees resources which can be diverted into the production of output elsewhere.   Thereby an attainable, "second-best" DEA target lowering costs by $(C_2 - C_1)$ and/or raising output remains worthwhile in utility terms *vis-à-vis* the status quo at $\underline{X}''$: For as Sen (1975a) argued "a production plan which is inefficient will yield less social value of output than some other [less inefficient] alternative".   The DEA target therefore has the status of a Pareto Improvement and does not (in general) confer full Pareto efficiency.

A fortiori the DEA target is observable and may be elucidated in quantitative terms. The Pareto technology, while feasible, exists only qualitatively from the operational point of view because of price uncertainty and definitional problems in the public sector.   Definitional and measurement problems imply a non-full information set on prices and quantities which creates a sub-optimal decision environment for the DMU manager.   In these conditions Tinbergen (1985) has argued that a first best, full information outcome is unattainable.   It follows that only second-best policies, such as the DEA target are feasible.   Indeed that the best-practice technology is observed is evidence that DEA-Dominant targets may be attainable and tractable to operational definition.

Utility and efficiency measurement

Before moving onto fresh arguments in section 6.6 it is worth emphasising the significance of utility to efficiency measurement.   In his first published paper, Nobel laureate Gerard Debreu (1951) defined a "coefficient of resource utilisation" which is comparable in intention to the DEA-efficiency score.   Debreu's coefficient was derived in the context of the two fundamental theorems of Paretian welfare theory. Very briefly, his measure of inefficiency in an economy is a measure of deadweight loss—the quantity of resources which could be saved in inefficient production, holding existing utility levels constant.   Debreu's coefficient, ρ, indicates the monetary value of this deadweight loss where $0 \le \rho \le 1$. $\rho = 1$ implies there is no deadweight loss in the economy and the associated monetary value of excess use of commodities is zero.   In this situation allocations are Pareto optimal.   Analogously, *mutatis mutandis*, for $\rho < 1$.

That Debreu (1951) explicitly defined the welfare implications of his resource-utilisation measure, contrasts sharply with the development of DEA efficiency. Much of the work on DEA is to be found in the case-oriented operations research literature wherein scant attention has been given to its implications for economic theory. This is a serious oversight. DEA is essentially an empirical calculus for which there is clearly a necessity to provide analytical foundations. In this regard, Fare, Grosskopf and Lovell (1985) initiated research into the implications of inefficiency for production theory. Specific utility implications, however, have been overlooked in the modern literature. As a consequence, this Chapter has suggested a utility dimension to the DEA target—that a DEA target remains justified if it leads to a net improvement in welfare.

6.6. Some remaining difficulties with the DEA target

(1) The DEA target and noise in production

Debreu's suggestive (1951) term deadweight loss contains ruminations of a logical difficulty in the definition of a DEA target. The target is derived from an efficiency score based on an *historical* cross section at time t. But the associated target is set for period $t + 1$. Clearly it has to be asked in what sense the efficiency information relevant to period t can be carried forward to $t + 1$? The excess-spend in a budget in t is historical and it follows trivially that it is impossible to set a target in $t + 1$ for a budget already spent. The only feasible target is for a future budget, as yet unspent. To set a target for this future budget on the basis of current efficiency information implicitly assumes that efficiency is stable over time; that is, that the efficiency score can be given an interpretation similar to a structural, time invariant-parameter estimated in an econometric model.

A priori it is not clear that this interpretation is acceptable since the DEA frontier is estimated deterministically from a single cross section of data. In this context apparent variations in performance may be no more than once-off, random events. Nonetheless, the problem of stochastic behaviour affects all areas of applied economic analysis and has not restrained the development of alternative deterministic methodologies. A well-known example occurs in the estimation of the technological coefficients underlying input-output models. Ever since the pioneering work of Leontief,[1] mainstream input-output analysis has largely ignored the implications of stochastic data. It is notable that this has not halted the rise of input-output analysis in applied economics.

Like input-output analysis, and despite some recent innovations, DEA is essentially a deterministic methodology which generally makes no explicit assumptions about the distribution of noise. If noise is present in an observation on the interior of the possibility set, the consequences are limited to that DMU: Its efficiency score will be biased towards or away from the frontier depending on the nature of the aberrance. Data errors or random outcomes in frontier DMUs are more serious since these will shift the location of at least one facet. In principle, this could alter the efficiency

---

(1)   See W. Leontief (1951) *The Structure of American Economy* 1919–1939. Second edition. Fair Lawn, NJ: Oxford University Press.

score of every observation in the data set.   In a trial run by Silkman *et al* (1986), a data error on one variable at one DMU reduced the average efficiency of the whole cross section by 12%.   Seven DMUs, formerly efficient on the correct data, achieved non-unit efficiency scores in the error-ridden data set.

In some studies, *ad hoc* procedures have been implemented to limit the impact of noise on estimated levels of efficiency.   These have focused around the pooling of cross section data over several years to create panel data sets.   A more stable picture of performance can be extracted from these by performing separate envelopments on successive cross sections and deriving the mean efficiency score of a DMU over time. This was the approach taken by Fare, Grosskopf and Logan (1987).   Thomas, Greffe and Grant (1988) have also worked with a panel of data on electricity utilities in Texas between 1979 and 1984.   It was argued that noise in outcomes might be identified in unexpected or abrupt change in the efficiency ranking of utilities year-on-year. Spearman's rank correlation coefficient was used in order to establish whether the rankings changed significantly.   A high value of the coefficient was taken to represent stable efficiency scores which reflect underlying levels of performance.   Stable estimates of efficiency are then the basis of acceptable targets.

Charnes, Clark, Cooper and Golany (1985) have also used a panel data set on US Air Force tactical-fighter wings to improve efficiency measurement.   Their procedure, which they call "window analysis", involves pooling successive cross sections of data and enveloping the whole of the resulting data simultaneously.   If there are *n* cross sections in a panel, each unit is represented *n* times in the estimated possibility space. A unit may appear both on the frontier and within according to changes in its performance year by year.   The resulting composite frontier gives less weight to unusual observations and is therefore more robust to stochastic events.

As a rule of thumb, then, the collection of panel data sets is probably to be recommended to replace efficiency estimates from single cross sections.

An older suggestion is in Timmer (1971).   Timmer argued that a Farrell boundary can be constructed iteratively.   That is, by successively eliminating outlying data points and re-estimating the frontier until the resulting efficiency estimates stabilise.   This is possible in larger data sets, although it means that excluded units will have no efficiency score in the final iteration.   The Timmer adjustment is arbitrary to the extent that it is not clear *a priori* precisely when the efficiency scores have stablised to a sufficient degree to accept that random outcomes have been eliminated.   Indeed there is nothing to say that underlying and sustainable levels of performance have not been excluded.   Recent developments of the Timmer approach can be found in Sengupta (1988, 1987b,c, 1982), Sengupta and Sfeir (1988) and Banker (1988).

On a tentative basis it has been suggested in the literature that costs (or inputs) are generally more predictable than outputs, giving cost targets a greater credibility than those for outputs.   Sengupta (1987, page 2,290) has argued that: ". . .data variations may arise in practical situations . . . when the output measures have large and uncertain measurement errors which are much more significant than in the input measures.   For example in school efficiency studies, the input costs, such as teachers' salaries, administrative expenses, etc., may have low measurement errors whereas the performance test scores of students may contain large errors of measurement of true student quality." This argument is most compelling where measurement errors are large relative to true random fluctuations in the production process.

In summary then, to carry the target forward depends on the stability of the efficiency score. This itself turns on the correct specification of the model and the limitation of the effects of noise. If adequate adjustment for noise is not possible the resulting efficiency scores may be unstable over time. This must cast serious doubt on the credibility of DEA targets which are carried forward when there is little guarantee of similarity in next period's performance. In general the practitioner is forced to make the implicit assumption that variations around the frontier are largely due to differences in technical efficiency, there being only trivial amounts of noise.

The policy-maker disbursing new, target budgets may also wish to make adjustment for exogenous price inflation in the coming year. Without inflation-adjustment of the target, the DMU may be unfairly penalised for pressures on costs beyond its own control. Of course inflation-adjustment must be based on current *expectations* of price changes in the forthcoming financial year. Where these expectations are not realised, the DMU may, in the event, have been over- or under-compensated for inflation. The interplay of efficiency- and inflation-related adjustments is likely to complicate the budget setting-process from year to year.

Further aspects of the target, such as the quality dimension also deserve attention. Research in the wider performance literature shows there to be a close link between quality and productivity (see Mefford (1991)). Moreover Thor (1991) has argued that it is quality of service, rather than cost containment *per se*, which is of interest to the consumer. The price, or cost of production of a service, are generally poor quality signals (Hjorth-Andersen (1991)). Supplementary quality data, in addition to that already available on productivity, will generally have to be provided to fulfil the requirements of customers.

Lastly, public sector production has a normative and merit-derived significance which may still prohibit the straightforward application of a target. For example there are large areas of public sector production which have lower limits on levels of service which are imposed by humanitarian and legal constraints. These important practical difficulties cannot be overlooked in the implementation of targets.

(2) Ambiguities in relative efficiency measures

The conceptual difficulties in measuring service sector productivity were being debated more than a generation ago by Hall and Winsten (1957) and are not resolved in modern writing on the subject, e.g. Kendrick (1987), Aanestad (1987). The existence of *degrees* of dominance, *viz.* Pareto Dominance and DEA Dominance, is indicative of ambiguities which call into question the meaningfulness of relative efficiency measures.

Koutsoyiannis (1979) for example has noted that in the private sector firms often consider operations at 80% of capacity as an acceptable utilisation of inputs. Clearly public sector producers which operate in controllable environments are likely to have comparable notions of normal utilisation of capacity and differences in these across DMUs may be confused with differences in efficiency by DEA. That is, DMUs with lower utilisation rates may be identified as inefficient *vis-à-vis* others with higher rates when the latter themselves are using capacity at less than 100%. Given that surplus capacity is inconsistent with the extreme optimising behaviour necessary for Pareto production, this reinforces the need for a decomposition of efficiency which identifies a separate (notional) frontier consistent with Pareto optimal production and a best-practice "frontier" composed of best-practice DMUs operating less efficiently with surplus capacity.

The best-practice "frontier" is constructed on the basis that the cross section is of a homogeneous set of DMUs using the same (presumably the latest) vintage of technology. *A priori* it is not clear if all DMUs will utilise the same technology—but clearly it is possible they will not (see Gregory and James (1973)). DEA efficiency becomes ambiguous in this case: A relatively inefficient DMU could be utilising a technology with maximal results but be constrained by the possibilities inherent in this technology such that it cannot perform as efficiently as some other DMU or linear combination of DMUs which are using a later, improved technology. This sort of efficiency ambiguity requires careful scrutiny to restrict a data set to a comparable set of DMUs so subsequent DEA comparisons are equitable and meaningful.

It should be noted that the problems of capacity utilisation and of technology vintage are essentially problems of comparing like-with-like. All relative effficiency measures (not merely DEA) should be used in a way which ensures legitimate comparisons of organisations.

6.7. Conclusion

This Chapter has examined some difficulties in the interpretation of DEA efficiency. This has become necessary owing to the uncritical manner in which DEA has often been used. Silkman (ed.) (1986) made a comparison between the high hopes for DEA in the 1980s and the optimism surrounding use of regression analysis in the early 1960s.

The main normative aspect of DEA is the recommendation of a target where technical inefficiency is identified. This target has been justified by the use of the Pareto Criterion. The main theme of this Chapter has been that there is a wealth of empirical and analytical evidence which suggests that in general best-practice is not Pareto efficient. Indeed, even if it were, this could not be observed as such.

Section 6.2 discussed the definition of best-practice in the literature. It argued that the many sources of inefficiency which may exist in real production environments are likely to compromise best-practice. There is nothing in DEA to suggest that best-practice performance is satisfactory in an absolute sense. Studies of efficiency have often shown that even the "best" in certain circumstances can improve (see Prison Department and PA Management Consultants (1986) on the state of operations in the prison service prior to the introduction of the Fresh Start scheme). Measures of technical efficiency derived in DEA should therefore be thought of as *approximate* guides to performance.

Additional "fuzziness" in empirical efficiency measures is caused by the definitional problems associated with public sector production. It is only for narrowly defined engineering systems (like a robot-based production line) for which the maximal performance of the technology can be unambiguously defined. In other processes like incarceration and education it is more difficult to define the relevant inputs and outputs. Public sector processes are often highly dependent upon labour inputs. As Leibenstein pointed out, labour effort is variable and delivered voluntarily. Consequently it is difficult to define best-practice since it is hard to specify at what point greater work intensity leads to a fall-off in quality. Hence Mayston and Smith (1987, page 183) argued that: "In general, there is no way of knowing whether the empirical measure of efficiency . . . gives rise to . . . the true technical efficiency of an organisation; that is the measure of efficiency we would obtain if the true production frontier (rather than the linear approximation) were known."

Lubulwa and Oczkowski (1987) suggested that "as the sample size increases, the best-practice converges to the absolute frontier". It is true that the addition of DMUs cannot worsen best-practice performance. But presumably the location of the technology can only improve on the addition of *better* performance. If incentives and motivation to inputs are low throughout an "industry" or programme then full convergence to the notional frontier could be by no means assured.

Section 6.3 examined the definition of Pareto efficiency. It was shown that best-practice is a form of technical efficiency defined independent of the factor prices. Pareto efficiency has a broader "welfare" dimension which also accounts for the allocative efficiency of production. Consequently best-practice performance is too narrowly defined to be consistent with full Pareto efficiency. It must be stressed that this conclusion is not an intrinsic rejection of the Pareto Criterion as such or of best-practice DEA targets. There is already a well-known spectrum of objections to Pareto welfare arguments ranging from the radical Marxist (Drago (1987)) to the "Welfarist" critique of Sen (1987, 1979) and more traditional objections regarding efficiency and distribution (Little (1957)). These are not the concern of Chapter 6 which examines the *relevance* of the Pareto Criterion and its congruence with DEA efficiency.

It is paradoxical that the DEA literature has set out to identify the sources and magnitude of inefficiency but should incorporate a neoclassical performance standard —that of Pareto efficiency—which actually rules this out. To quote Fare, Grosskopf and Lovell (1985, page 5): "Traditional neoclassical production theory assumes away the problems of information and uncertainty so the producer successfully allocates resources in an efficient manner: Efficient relative to the constraints imposed by the structure of production technology and by the structure of input and output markets, and relative to whatever behavioural goal, e.g. cost minimisation, is attributable to the producer. The technology constraint in the producer's behavioural optimisation problem is binding, eliminating technical efficiency. Satisfaction of the first-order conditions necessary for optimisation eliminates allocative inefficiency." Thus FGL conclude that "Testable hypotheses about producer behaviour then refer to the behaviour of efficient producers only" and advocate the development of a modern theory of producer behaviour which explicitly acknowledges inefficient production.

In this respect, sections 6.4 and 6.5 developed a more appropriate interpretation of DEA efficiency.   This involved the definition of efficiency in utility terms. Specifically, a DEA target (which in general is not Pareto efficient) can still be regarded as a Pareto Improvement *vis-à-vis* technically inefficient production within an estimated boundary.   The DEA target does not confer the full utility gain that could accrue from Pareto production.   It nevertheless remains worthwhile in yielding a net utility gain over existing inefficient production plans.

Finally, section 6.6 discussed some additional difficulties in the interpretation and implementation of DEA.   These included the problems of noise, inflation and quality adjustment. The existence of noise, for example, may undermine the ability of DEA to identify a meaningful target for period $t + 1$ on the basis of data in period t. Various procedures have been suggested in the literature to control for noise.   They are essentially *ad hoc* and involve averaging of efficiency scores or the pooling of data.   Since no well-developed formal treatment of noise exists in DEA, future research on efficiency will probably benefit most from the use of panel data rather than the use of isolated cross sections.   This applies particularly to the use of DEA in real policy environments.   Adjustments in funding based on DEA targets should be made only where there is evidence that the efficiency measure reflects underlying levels of performance.   If measured efficiency is the result of once-off difficulties then the application of the targeting formula to cut resources may worsen future performance.

CHAPTER 7

ASPECTS OF THE DISCRIMINATING POWER OF DATA ENVELOPMENT ANALYSIS

7.1. Introduction

Chapter 6 examined some important difficulties of interpretation in DEA methodology. This Chapter undertakes empirical work in an attempt to illustrate some of these problems using data from a real production environment. In doing so it is able to examine the sensitivity and discriminating power of DEA.

Unlike most conventional econometric procedures Data Envelopment Analysis is not endowed with any formal system of hypothesis testing (Seiford and Thrall (1990)). This is because DEA is a non-statistical technique which makes no explicit assumptions on the distribution of the residuals. This, and other problems, have left DEA open to criticism. For example, the selection of input-output variables is essentially *ad hoc*. In recognition of these difficulties Charnes, Cooper, Lewin, Morey and Rousseau (1985) initiated work on a DEA-sensitivity analysis. This involved an examination of the effects on the efficiency score of deleting variables. Subsequently research has begun to focus increasingly on sensitivity issues (Epstein and Henderson (1989)). Ahn and Seiford (1990) found that the omission of key variables had a significant impact on recorded efficiencies in public and private universities. More generally this research points to a link between the number of variables and the (average) efficiency of DMUs. In particular, as the size of the variable set increases—for given DMUs—the discriminating power of DEA declines with increasing numbers of DMUs attaining best practice (Seiford and Thrall (1990)). This outcome is not so much a flaw in DEA, as a direct result of the dimensionality of the input-output space rising relative to the number of DMUs—an analogy may be drawn with the dimensionality constraints imposed by "degrees of freedom" considerations in econometrics. The dimensionality problem may nevertheless curtail the managerial policy relevance of DEA. In particular, real applications are constrained by the need to limit the numbers of DMUs labelled best practice.

In this vein, Chapter 7 investigates the sensitivity of DEA-efficiency, but with respect to changes in the size of the cross section rather than in the number of variables. It uses the local education authority data set familiar from Chapter 3 and examines the effects on targets and peer groups of changes in the size of the LEA comparisons. This involves grouping LEAs into recognised administrative clusters and re-estimating frontier performance for each cluster. This is equivalent to varying the number of constraints in the fractional DEA program (recall the model 2.4.2 in Chapter 2). There is some precedent for data clustering in the literature. In a study of performance in Californian hospitals, Grosskopf and Valdmanis (1987) cluster their sample into two parts (one publicly-owned and the other privately-owned) to assess the effect of ownership on efficiency status. Similarly, Golany and Roll (1989) and Sexton, Silkman and Hogan (1986) have advocated the clustering of large cross sections in order to ensure that *relative* efficiency comparisons are of like-with-like. Without this pre-DEA filtering, DMUs with widely differing characteristics and dissimilar technologies may be built into the same frontier invalidating the efficiency comparison.

As should become clear, the clustered results are broadly consistent with the arguments in Chapter 6 that best-practice is ambiguous in some cases and cannot be interpreted as a firm indicator of Pareto efficiency. In addition, the greater preponderance of best-practice found in the results provokes a discussion of the ability of DEA to identify a complete efficiency ordering together with a meaningful target and peer group.

In outline, Chapter 7 develops as follows. Section 7.2 discusses the rationale for clustering and outlines the criteria used to partition the LEA data set. The broader empirical effects of clustering are examined in section 7.3. Section 7.4 explores the impact of clustering on the rank of the efficiency ordering, the stability of the peer group and the existence of targets. The main conclusions are drawn together in section 7.5.

7.2.   The need for clustering of LEA performance

Recall from Table 3.3.2 in Chapter 3 that DEA chooses a peer group of best-practice LEAs which, in principle, the inefficient LEA uses as a managerial blueprint to improve performance (Charnes *et al* (1990) and Smith and Mayston (1987)). It is important to decision-makers, however, that the peer group is drawn from a comparable set of LEAs because demographic, occupational and social conditions affecting performance vary markedly over the whole cross section of LEAs. In the peer groups for inefficient London boroughs in Table 3.3.2 one or more peer LEAs are drawn from outside of the London area. This Chapter examines the effects of excluding these "non-indigenous" LEAs from the performance comparison. That is, the 96 LEAs in England have been grouped into 3 recognised administrative clusters:

(1) 21 Inner and Outer London boroughs;
(2) 36 Metropolitan boroughs;
(3) 39 English counties.

A DEA boundary has been estimated for each of these smaller cross sections using the same varying returns to scale and strong disposability assumptions adopted in Chapter 3. The advantage of such an analysis is, in principle, that it enforces the choice of peer LEAs to come from the same "home" cluster as that of the inefficient LEA.

There is some precedent for the clustering of performance in the literature. In a study of Californian education, Sengupta and Sfeir (1986) split high-school districts into rural and urban classes; similar adjustments were made by Grosskopf and Valdmanis (1987) in an evaluation of hospital performance. These clustered analyses of performance are based on a "rule of thumb" suggested in Golany and Roll (1989, page 239) that in general "the larger the number of units in the analysed set, the lower the homogeneity within the set". Thus Golany and Roll have argued that: "another direction in the analysis of efficiency outcomes is partitioning the group of DMUs into categories, according to some characteristic which was not entered into the model as a factor determining input-output relationships. The purpose of such categorisation is twofold: One is to gain a better relative assessment of efficiency, by comparing performance within sub-groups of units operating under similar conditions (e.g. the same geographical region). The other is a comparison between categories, such as in the case where a category signifies a programme which a sub-group of DMUs operates" (*ibid.*).

Two possible objections could be raised to these criteria for the clustering of performance. In the first place there may be difficulties in the definition of the cluster. Generally speaking, empirical clustering criteria have been rather crude and cannot exclude the possibility that a peer drawn from the *same* cluster may nevertheless be quite unlike the inefficient DMU for which it has been chosen. This will always be true in a trivial sense because every DMU is likely to have some unique characteristic, *viz.* location. In the context of LEA performance there appears to be some genuinely different spending patterns in rural as against urban (i.e. London and the Metropolitan) authorities—see Table 7.4.2 (below). This is borne out in other studies of educational costs. Kenny (1982), for example, found sizable differences between schooling costs in rural and urban areas in California.

A second potential objection to clustering focuses on the inclusion in the model of background variables (to reflect for example parental occupation) which are already designed to capture the impact of differences in LEA catchment area. Although the inclusion of background variables is widely recognised in educational efficiency studies (Mayston and Smith (1987)) there remains some dispute in the literature as to the effects of noncontrollable variables on efficiency and precisely how these should be incorporated into empirical DEA models (see e.g. Golany (1988a), Ray (1988) and Banker and Morey (1986a,b)). If the inclusion of background variables is not sufficient to allow for the differences in LEAs across the country, then the clustering of LEAs may still be required to make the performance comparison equitable. Notwithstanding these problems, the effects of clustering on efficiency remain valuable in clarifying the discriminating power of DEA in terms of its ability to identify meaningful targets and peer groups.

In response to these potential criticisms, it is worth noting that more rigorous procedures for clustering have begun to emerge. Banker (1989) develops an F-statistic which allows a test of the internal homogeneity of the cross section. The test is implemented on a sample of 111 government supported hospitals in North Carolina in Banker, Das and Datar (1989). Their results suggested the data set could be partitioned into two sub-groups based on the hospitals' client base. One of the sub-groups served a large number of older, Medicare/Medicaid patients requiring cost intensive care. The composition of the client base therefore constrained the ability of some hospitals to attain best practice. Others, without the demands of treatment of the elderly, possessed a statistically significant advantage and could be separated into a higher-performing group.

Banker *et al* (1989) argue that clustering embodies attainable targets. More demanding "tight" targets can be given for the higher-performing group. For the other group, "looser" targets may be set at, say, 90% of best-practice attainments. This procedure, in making targets more equitable, should go some way to increasing the acceptability of DEA assessment.

In this Chapter formal clustering criteria such as developed in Banker (1989) have been eschewed. The chosen clusters are based on recognised administrative groups of LEAs which make the key distinction between rural and urban schooling. Results on this basis are examined below in sections 7.3 and 7.4.

7.3. Results on LEA efficiency after clustering

In Chapter 3 around 55% of LEAs were input inefficient to varying degrees and hence less than half the education authorities in England were identified as best-practice. This result was based on a frontier comparison of 96 LEAs. Table 7.3.1 contains a summary of the numbers of LEAs identified as inefficient in the 3 separate administrative analyses of performance undertaken for this Chapter. It is immediately clear that far fewer LEAs are identified as inefficient in the smaller administrative clusters. The most notable change is for the London boroughs where only 6 out of 21 LEAs have non-unit efficiencies. By contrast the results in Chapter 3 suggested 13 of the London authorities were inefficient.

Table 7.3.1
Comparison of clustered and non-clustered results: Numbers of inefficient LEAs

	London boroughs %	Metropolitan boroughs %	English counties %	All areas combined %
Separate clusters	28.6	33.3	41.0	35.4
Non-clustered (Chapter 3)	61.9	52.8	51.3	54.2

Notes:
(1) The Table shows the ratio of inefficient to best-practice LEAs.
(2) The efficiency scores underlying this Table can be found below in Table 7.4.1.
(3) The number of best-practice LEAs is simply 100 minus the percentage of inefficient LEAs. In the London cluster for example, (100 - 28.6) = 71.4%; that is, over two-thirds of the London cluster is best-practice in the new results.
Source: Authors' calculations.

This changes the interpretation of the results regarding efficiency in the London boroughs.   In particular it suggests that there is a greater preponderance of best-practice education in London than has hitherto been identified. A similar, but less marked, change can also be recognised in authorities outside London.   In the Metropolitan boroughs the number of best-practice LEAs has risen from 17 to 24; and in the counties from 19 to 23. Across all three clusters, this adds an additional 18 best-practice authorities making a total of 62.

This apparent improvement in LEA performance is reflected in a small gain in the mean inefficiency score of the London boroughs and the counties. However the mean performance of the Metropolitan authorities has fallen slightly to an average of 0.916 (see Table 7.3.2).

Table 7.3.2
Comparison of clustered and non-clustered results: Mean inefficiency scores

	London boroughs %	Metropolitan boroughs %	English counties %	All areas combined %
Separate clusters	0.935	0.916	0.961	0.941
Non-clustered (Chapter 3)	0.925	0.921	0.958	0.936

Notes:
The Table shows the mean efficiency of LEAs with non-unity efficiency scores.
Source: Authors' calculations.

The *prima facie* substance of these results belies the strength of the comparisons being made in the LEA clusters. In particular, it is probably the case that London performance improves dramatically because the comparison of London boroughs with themselves alone is less exacting. The same is true for the Metropolitan LEAs and the counties whose performance also improves in the smaller clustered analyses (cf Table 7.3.1). Hence it would probably be inaccurate to conclude that the preponderance of best-practice performance is more widespread among LEAs than was suggested in Chapter 3.

7.4. Aspects of the discriminating power of DEA

Section 7.4 is divided into 3 parts, each of which explores an aspect of the discriminating power of Data Envelopment Analysis. Part 1 examines the ability of DEA to identify *untied* efficiency scores to reveal finer variations in performance. The efficiency ordering resulting from the clustering of LEA performance is compared with that derived from the whole-sample comparison in Chapter 3. The second part of section 7.4 looks at the effects of clustering on the peer group. Part 3 then examines the stability of targets for the adjustment of performance at inefficient operations.

(1) Best-practice and the efficiency ordering in LEA clusters

Before proceeding, it is important to define precisely what is meant by "the discriminating power of DEA". When DEA compares the performance of organisations, it divides them into two groups: The first is best-practice with unit-efficiency scores; the second, dominated by the first, is relatively inefficient. It is not possible on the basis of efficiency scores alone to distinguish between best-practice performers because best-practice efficiencies are tied. Without additional criteria best-practice performance cannot be ranked and by implication is equally satisfactory at all branches. Generally speaking, however, the performance of *inefficient* producers can be ordered completely (although there may sometimes be a small number of ties).

The discriminating power of DEA therefore refers to the ability of the technique to identify untied efficiency scores. Clearly this largely depends on the numbers of best-practice. Tied-efficiency scores indicate that a full ranking of performance in the sample as a whole is not possible. In other words, the efficiency ordering is incomplete.[1] Note that an untied efficiency ordering rests on the notion of efficiency dominance; that is, untied efficiency scores imply that the performance of one LEA is better than that of another in that, *ceteris paribus*, it uses less inputs or produces more output. However discrimination between LEAs might also be achieved on the basis of the shadow prices. Zero shadow prices could be interpreted as indicators of inadequate performance in certain key variables. Thus DMUs with larger (absolute) shadow prices would be ranked above those performing with lower shadow prices. Acknowledging this possibility, Chapter 7 nonetheless concentrates on the efficiency score as a basis for ranking performance and leaves discrimination on the basis of shadow prices to future research.

The results which have been obtained from the clustering of LEAs into smaller cross sections call into question the ability of DEA to identify untied efficiency scores. The London cluster contains 21 LEAs and found the highest proportion of best practice (cf Table 7.3.1). Compared with the London cluster, *relatively* fewer best-practice LEAs were found in the larger clusters. In the 36 Metropolitan boroughs, 67% of LEAs were best practice as against 71% in London. The largest cluster, the 39 English counties, had the lowest proportion of best-practice at 59%. Larger cross sections, therefore, appear to be associated with relatively smaller numbers of best practice. As would be expected *a priori*, more discriminating comparisons (yielding fewer best-practice efficiencies) necessitate enlarging the feasible number of candidates in the cross section. From a computational point of view, enlarging the number of LEA comparisons in the determination of the efficiency score amounts to increasing the number of constraints in the (fractional) DEA program.

The number of best-practice authorities identified by the program is an important indicator of the discriminating power of DEA. For the higher are the numbers of best-practice the lower are the numbers of authorities with a unique, untied efficiency status. Given the widely differing conditions in which LEAs operate, it may be unrealistic to label large numbers of them as uniformly best-practice. For this implies that all authorities are operating equally satisfactorily on all target variables. It is unlikely that this is the case so that, in principle, a ranking of performance exists among best-practice LEAs.

In Chapter 3, 44 out of 96 LEAs were given identical unit-efficiency scores. The clustered analysis in this Chapter has added a further 18 LEAs with unit-efficiency scores giving 62 best-practice authorities in total. As far as active decision-making is concerned, DEA is only capable of suggesting adjustments to performance in relatively inefficient LEAs. Consequently, nothing can be said about performance at around two thirds of the LEAs after clustering—other than the implicit presumption that, in attaining best-practice, their performance is satisfactory and "equivalent". Since best-practice is not necessarily adequate in any absolute sense, it would be useful for the decision-maker to have more guidance on the quality of best-practice performance. This is an important point, for as the discriminating power of the technique falls, the coarser is the summary picture of performance yielded by DEA. In

---

(1)   The concept of a complete ordering over states of the world is discussed at greater length in Sen (1973), Chapter 1.

situations where *programme* performance is under scrutiny (as in Chapter 5), the more ambiguous the picture for a single organisation, the greater is the error which is likely to be built into the aggregate performance picture.

Improving discriminating power

The clustering of LEA performance suggests that the discriminating power of DEA falls in smaller cross sections. It is important in practical applications to know how discriminating power might be improved to give a finer breakdown of variations in performance.

That the discriminating power of DEA is limited by the identification of best-practice broaches a more general problem of the relative merits of the CRS and the VRS linear programs. In particular, the number of best-practice will vary with the technology assumption. Chapter 5 compared the CRS and VRS efficiency of local prisons and remand centres. The results suggested that a CRS assumption identifies fewer best-practice. It was demonstrated that this is an intuitive result given the nesting of empirical technologies. Clearly the technology assumption has implications for the ordering of efficiencies which can now be developed.

The CRS and VRS efficiency ordering

Both the VRS and CRS efficiency results on prison and LEA efficiency in Chapters 3, 4 and 5 suggest best-practice units may account for a large share of the sample under investigation. This means that the efficiency ordering is incomplete in the sense that all establishments do not have an *untied* efficiency rating.

It is clearly desirable from first principles to maximise discriminating power so that finer variations in performance can be identified. The *maximum* theoretical discriminating power in a cross section of n units would define a distinct technical-efficiency score (TE) for each LEA in the sample. That is:

$$(7.4.1) \qquad 1 = TE_1 > TE_2 > \ldots > TE_n > 0$$

where the subscript denotes rank. (7.4.1) is a complete ranking of efficiencies (without ties) of order n.

Practical applications of DEA are unlikely to yield a complete efficiency ordering unless the comparison is based on a single variable. Indeed even this unlikely circumstance could not guarantee the identification of a single best-practice establishment since two or more could dominate (i.e., tie) on the variable in question. In a sample size of n units, the ordering resulting from a VRS technology assumption could be of the form:

$$(7.4.2) \qquad 1 = TE_1 = \ldots = TE_1 > TE_2 > \ldots > TE_{j+1} > 0,$$

and $j + 1 \leq n$. Assuming that non-unit efficiencies are untied, the ranking is of order $j + 1$, where j is the number of inefficient units. The ordering is incomplete in that $j + 1$ is less than the feasible number of untied efficiencies, i.e., $j + 1 \leq n$. Notice that if efficiency is defined in relative terms, j *must* be less than n to permit the definition of at least one best-practice unit, i.e. $j \leq (n - 1)$. Hence, $(n - j)$ is the number of best-practice.

In (7.4.2) $(n - j)$ best-practice organisations have a homogeneous efficiency status. However it is possible to increase the rank of the efficiency ordering under an alternative technology. In general a CRS technology yields fewer best-practice than VRS (see Chapter 5 or Grosskopf and Njinkeu (1988) and Grosskopf (1986)). The corresponding constant returns ordering is:

$$(7.4.3) \qquad\qquad 1 = TE_1 = \ldots = TE_1 > TE_2 > \ldots > TE_{k+1} > 0,$$

and $k + 1 \leq n$ and $k > j$ in (7.4.2). Assuming that non-unit efficiencies are untied, the CRS ranking is of order $k + 1$, where k is the number of inefficient units. The order of (7.4.3), $k + 1$, is greater than that in (7.4.2), $j + 1$, because the CRS program identifies relatively more inefficient units: i.e., $k > j$ and so $k + 1 > j + 1$. Equally, the number of best-practice under CRS, $(n - k)$, is less than under VRS, $(n - j)$. As a consequence, there are arguments for preferring the CRS assumption because it yields a finer (though still not complete) ordering of performance. That is, a CRS assumption generates fewer best-practice ties and hence has a greater discriminating power than a VRS technology.

Ties in non-unit efficiency scores
The ranking of efficiencies according to the underlying technology in (7.4.2) and (7.4.3) made the assumption that there are only ties in best-practice efficiencies. However, inspection of Table 7.4.1 (below) suggests that this may not be the case. In the clustered results there is one tie within the counties, between Avon and Hertford where $TE = 0.922$ in both cases (see Table 7.4.1 (c), below). There is also a small number of ties across (rather than within) clusters between Oldham and Northants $(TE = 0.986)$, Leeds and Kent $(TE = 0.994)$ and between Redbridge and Hampshire $(TE = 0.963)$. However all of these ties are due to rounding in Table 7.4.1. If the efficiency score is reported to 4 decimal places all of these ties can be broken so that the rank of the efficiency ordering is not compromised. On this basis, for example, Avon has $TE = 0.9221$ and Hertfordshire $TE = 0.9215$.

In the non-clustered results in Table 3.3.2 of Chapter 3 there are 9 apparent ties in non-unit efficiency scores. All but one of these is due to rounding—at 4 decimal places only Northamptonshire remains indistinguishable from Hereford with $TE = 0.9726$. Clearly this tie can be broken by reporting the efficiency score to a greater number of decimal places. However the extra digits rapidly cease to have any meaning. Nevertheless the tie compromises the definition of the rank of the efficiency ordering. Recall that for a cross section of size n and a VRS technology assumption the efficiency ordering is:

$$(7.4.2) \qquad\qquad 1 = TE_1 = TE_1 = \ldots = TE_1 > TE_2 > \ldots > TE_{j+1} > 0,$$

and $j + 1 \leq n$. If j is the number of inefficient branches then the rank of the efficiency ordering is $j + 1$. However this definition assumes that there are no tied *non-unit* efficiencies. Since these are possible, the ordering has rank:

(7.4.2*) $1 = TE_1 = TE_1 = \ldots = TE_1 > TE_2 > \ldots > TE_{j+1-x} > 0,$

where j is the number of inefficient branches, and x is the number of tied non-unit efficiency scores. That is, adjusting for ties at inefficient organisations lowers the rank of the efficiency ordering to $j + 1 - x$.

In principle, the adjustment (x) for ties in non-unit efficiencies could alter the relationship between a comparable CRS and VRS ranking. In (7.4.2) the rank of the VRS technology was given as $j + 1$; and in (7.4.3) the CRS rank is $k + 1$ where in general $(j + 1) < (k + 1)$ because CRS will identify fewer best-practice efficiencies. However if the number of tied non-best-practice efficiencies were sufficiently large under CRS then $(j + 1 - x_{vrs}) > (k + 1 - x_{crs})$ is feasible. I.e., the rank of the VRS technology could be greater than under CRS if the number of additional non-unit ties under CRS (x_{crs}) is sufficiently large. It has to be said however that this is unlikely. In many applications the number of ties in non-unit efficiencies under both CRS or VRS is relatively small.

In the VRS results in Chapter 3 $j = 52$ with 1 tie (between Northamptonshire and Hereford, $TE = 0.9726$). Hence the efficiency ordering has rank $j + 1 - x = 52$. Taking the clustered results as a whole there are 62 best-practice LEAs under VRS leaving $j = 34$ non-unit efficiencies. A small number of the latter are tied; however, at 4 decimal places all inefficient scores were distinct and $x = 0$. Hence the rank of the efficiency ordering, $j + 1 - x$, is 35.

It is clear that the clustered results taken as a whole yield a far less distinct picture of performance. Numbers of best-practice were significantly lower in Chapter 3 (44 as against 62 in this Chapter) such that finer variations in performance in efficiency were identified. This suggests that the discriminating power of Data Envelopment Analysis improves with the size of the cross section. That is, the rank of the efficiency ordering, $j + 1 - x$, rises with n, the size of the cross section. Note however that in very large cross sections the ranking would be unlikely to be completed. A complete efficiency ordering with no ties would require the existence of a single best-practice DMU and no ties in non-unit efficiencies.

Parkan (1987) has suggested that a further improvement in discriminating power may lie in the iterative use of the DEA program under either CRS or VRS technologies. The program may be computed initially over all n establishments which are thereby separated into relatively efficient and inefficient subsets. The program may then be re-computed on the efficient subset only. This will break down the units originally identified as best-practice into two smaller groups. One of these will still have unit-efficiency scores, but the second group (best-practice in the initial run of the program) will now be relatively inefficient. Subsequent re-computations of the program may then be undertaken on the remaining best-practice units. At each run the number of best-practice units remaining will fall, gradually extending the efficiency ordering. It is unlikely however that this iterative procedure would complete the efficiency ordering. A comparison of the London, Metropolitan and county clusters of LEAs suggested that smaller cross sections are less discriminating than larger ones.

Hence the addition to the ordering at each subsequent iteration of the program would probably fall until a "core" of best-practice units is reached.

The discriminating power of DEA will also be affected by the size of variable set, in addition to the effects of alternative scale assumptions. Following Nunamaker (1985), Tomkins and Green (1988) suggested that because dominance on merely a single variable is sufficient to yield an efficiency score of unity, the probability of best-practice rises with the size of the variable set. Accordingly, it is possible to enhance the efficiency status of organisations by the inclusion of additional variables in the model. In some circumstances this could take the form of a policy of extreme specialisation, wherein a particular organisation becomes dominant simply because no other units have a presence in the chosen area of specialisation. This aspect of the problem of discrimination may be limited by the use of variable sets based on core activities alone. *Ceteris paribus*, to obtain the maximum distinction among efficiencies requires the use of a smaller number of input and output variables to describe the production process (Seiford and Thrall (1990)).

Discriminating power could be increased still further by the introduction of a more exacting dominance criterion. Conventionally, dominance in only a single variable is sufficient for best-practice. A stronger criterion would be dominance on *all* variables. This would generally produce a much smaller number of best-practice. However this criterion may be so exacting in some circumstances as to reduce the number of best-practice to zero, i.e., no units in the sample might be dominant in all dimensions. In the absence of best-practice the *relative* efficiency measure is undefined and the performance comparison breaks down. In many practical applications, therefore, this criterion may be too demanding.

At this point it is possible to summarise the main influences on discriminating power and the efficiency ordering: (1) the size of the cross section; (2) the size of the variable set; and (3) the scale assumption. To maximise the discriminating power of DEA on all 3 criteria suggests the use of the largest feasible cross section (to make the comparison on each variable more exacting); the use of the smallest realistic variable set (to exclude dominance on obscure aspects of production) and a strongly disposable CRS technology (which dominates all empirical alternatives, *viz.*, varying returns and non-increasing returns to scale). Each of these stategies will tend to limit the identification of best-practice and thereby increase the discriminating power of DEA.

(2) The choice of a peer group

An important additional aspect of the discriminating power of DEA is its ability to choose a meaningful group of peer LEAs which have similar characteristics to those of an inefficient LEA.[1] In Chapter 3 the peer LEAs chosen were often counter-intuitive. For example, West Sussex and Wiltshire are contained in the peer groups for the London LEAs Bromley, Havering and Richmond. In as far as these LEAs bear little resemblance to the inefficient LEA, this would seem to undermine the regular recommendation in the literature that the attainment of targets is assisted by appeal to

---

(1)   Formal aspects of the definition of the peer group are discussed in Fare and Hunsaker (1986) and Fare, Lovell and Zieschang (1983).

the peer group (see Charnes *et al* (1990), Bowlin (1987, 1986) and the discussion in Chapter 4). The potential dissimilarity of peer LEAs is an important justification of the clustering of LEAs into administrative groupings prior to computation since the peer groups then chosen by DEA can only be drawn from the appropriate "home" cluster.

Table 7.4.1 (a)
DEA discriminating power and peer group comparisons in the London boroughs

LEA	Efficiency clustered	Efficiency all LEAs	Peer group clustered	Peer group all LEAs
1. Barking	1.000	0.961	1	25,44
3. Bexley	1.000	0.971	3	50,59,86,95
5. Bromley	1.000	0.911	5	48,78,95
6. Croydon	0.962	0.939	7,8,12,15,19	2,15,50,59
8. Enfield	1.000	0.997	8	2,7,15,50,59
9. Haringey	0.992	0.992	4,7,16	4,16,48
11. Havering	1.000	0.891	11	10,26,82,86,96
13. Hounslow	1.000	0.961	13	2,7,22,50
14. Kingston	0.980	0.965	2,12,15,19	2,19,48
17. Redbridge	0.963	0.940	7,8,12,15,19	2,7,50,59
18. Richmond	0.907	0.853	2,3,7,12,15,19	2,15,19,48,95
20. Waltham	1.000	0.853	20	7,16,22,48
21. ILEA	0.805	0.788	7,15,16	4,16,48

Number best-practice
London :   15   8

Notes: See Table 7.4.1 (c)
Source: Authors' calculations.

Table 7.4.1 (b)
DEA discriminating power and peer group comparisons in the Metropolitan boroughs

LEA	Efficiency clustered	Efficiency all LEAs	Peer group clustered	Peer group all LEAs
24. Dudley	1.000	0.979	24	19,23,50,64,86
27. Walsall	0.902	0.895	28,30,46,48,50	28,46,48,50
31. St Helens	1.000	0.929	31	46,50,64
32. Sefton	1.000	0.953	32	19,50,64,86
33. Wirral	1.000	0.934	33	19,50,64,86
34. Bolton	0.926	0.910	28,50	48,50,78,95
35. Bury	0.945	0.904	26,32,40,50	19,50,95
36. Manchester	0.874	0.872	23,25,30,46	25,30,44,64
37. Oldham	0.986	0.986	44,48	44,48
38. Rochdale	0.856	0.834	37,50	44,48,78
39. Salford	0.881	0.881	44,46,48	44,46,48
40. Stockport	1.000	0.951	40	48,78,95
41. Tameside	0.952	0.952	46,48,50	46,48,50
42. Trafford	1.000	0.933	42	50,78,86,95
43. Wigan	1.000	0.901	43	46,50,64,86
47. Sheffield	0.933	0.909	26,28,46,50,55	26,28,46,50,59
51. Leeds	0.944	0.987	48,50	48,50,78,95
53. Gateshead	0.935 ·	0.935	46,48,52	46,48,52
54. Newcastle	0.804	0.856	26,46,50	22,78,86

Number best-practice
Metropolitan :   24   17

Notes: See Table 7.4.1 (c)
Source: Authors' calculations.

Table 7.4.1 (c)
DEA discriminating power and peer group comparisons in the English counties

LEAs	Efficiency clustered	Efficiency all LEAs	Peer group clustered	Peer group all LEAs
58. Avon	0.922	0.922	59,78,86,95	59,78,86,95
63. Cheshire	0.942	0.925	78,80,86,95	48,78,86,95
67. Derbyshire	1.000	0.994	67	45,46,50,82,86
68. Devon	0.961	0.958	67,70,78,86,92,96	48,86,92,96
69. Dorset	0.984	0.985	78,50,95,96	50,59,86,95
70. Durham	1.000	0.982	70	28,44,48,86
71. E Sussex	0.983	0.958	78,80,95	48,78,86,95
72. Essex	0.966	0.963	59,78,95	48,78,95
73. Gloucester	0.969	0.969	61,81,86,95,96	61,81,86,95,96
74. Hampshire	0.963	0.963	78,95,96	50,59,86,95
75. Hereford	0.977	0.973	59,78,81,86,90	48,78,86,90,95
76. Hertford	0.922	0.903	59,61,95	2,19,48,95
79. Kent	0.994	0.969	67,78,80,81,86,95	50,78,86,95
80. Lancashire	1.000	0.992	80	65,82
83. Norfolk	0.954	0.947	77,81,86,90	48,86
85. Northampton	0.986	0.973	64,78,81,86,96	48,86,90,96
87. Nottingham	0.973	0.937	64,67,70,77,81	44,46,48,86,96
88. Oxfordshire	1.000	0.999	88	86,88,95,96
89. Shropshire	0.929	0.929	81,86,90,96	81,86,90,96
91. Stafford	0.957	0.926	67,78,80	44,48,78,86

Number best-practice
Counties: 23   19

Numbers best-practice
All clusters: 62   44   (Tables 7.4.1 (a), (b) & (c))

(1) Column 1 contains efficiency scores based on the three separate administrative clusters of LEAs.
(2) Column 2 contains the efficiency scores from Chapter 3 based on a single frontier for all 96 LEAs.
(3) The peer groups in column 3 originated in the clustered analyses of performance and those in column 4 in the whole-sample evaluation undertaken in Chapter 3.

Source: Authors' calculations.

The difference in peer groups in the clustered and non-clustered results can be seen in Tables 7.4.1 (a), (b) and (c). It is apparent that the peer LEAs have changed substantially using the smaller clustered cross sections. In the London boroughs none of the peer groups are identical with the results reported in Chapter 3. In the Metropolitan authorities only four peer groups have not changed (those for Oldham, Salford, Tameside and Gateshead) and in the counties only three are identical (for Avon, Gloucestershire and Shropshire). Often, however, the difference in peer groups is small (perhaps one LEA has been removed or added, as in the case of Haringey).

Although most of the peer groups are different in the clustered analysis, this is to be expected in some measure after the cross section has been re-defined. Indeed one of the main arguments for clustering was that the selection of peers should be adjusted such that they are drawn only from a comparable group of LEAs. Consequently, Newcastle-upon-Tyne for example, is now compared with its Metropolitan counterparts Solihull, Rotherham and Kirklees. In the non-clustered analysis the peer group included the seemingly dissimilar authorities in the Isle of Wight and

Northumberland in addition to a more intuitive comparison with Birmingham (see Table 7.4.1 (b)). This example apparently lends some support to the argument in Chapter 4 that there is no clear, formal link between the peer group and less efficient production. In particular the larger, "indiscriminant" comparison of all 96 LEAs in Chapter 3 appears to have led to the selection of counter-intuitive peers in many cases. Restricting the comparison to a smaller group of more comparable authorities seems to have defined more acceptable peers for inefficient authorities. In this case the widespread recommendation in the literature of the peer group as a blueprint for improving inefficient performance is more plausible. Equally, for as long as there is evidence that the performance comparison is too broad, the peer group loses much of its managerial significance.

(3) The existence of targets

A third element in discriminating power is the ability of DEA to identify an accurate target. A clear definition of the target is crucial for the adjustment of performance at the inefficient LEA. The possibility that target performance may have changed with the choice of the cross section is explored in Table 7.4.2 (a) and (b) which compares the input targets for teaching expenditure per pupil in the clustered and non-clustered DEA results. Note that Table 7.4.2 includes only those LEAs with non-unit efficiency scores in *both* sets of results to reduce its size to more tractable proportions.

In both the counties and the urban authorities, the non-clustered results from Chapter 3 suggest the greater adjustments in teaching expenditure. The average adjustment to spending in the counties is 5% in the non-clustered context and 3.7% in the clustered results (Table 7.4.2 (b)). Similarly, the average non-clustered target for the urban authorities suggests a larger adjustment of 9.2% in teaching expenditure, as against an average of 8.1% in the separate clusters (Table 7.4.2 (a)). It is notable that in either set of results the urban authorities have the larger potential savings. Indeed, the average *target* for the urban authorities on a clustered basis (= £622) is very close to the *actual* average spend in the counties.

The efficiency status of some individual LEAs has changed dramatically after clustering. Havering, for example, had one of the ten lowest efficiencies (*TE* = 0.89) in the non-clustered DEA run, on which basis it could be recommended to make an 11% cut in teaching spend per pupil. Yet the DEA results estimated on the London LEAs alone suggested that Havering is best-practice such that no resource reductions could be recommended. (As already indicated, Table 7.4.2 includes only those LEAs with non-unit efficiency scores in both clustered and non-clustered results. Hence Havering is excluded from Table 7.4.2 (a) but can alternatively be found in Table 7.4.1 (a).)

Large changes in the target spend are also apparent at other authorities—for example Richmond, Bury, Nottinghamshire and Staffordshire. In most cases efficiency status has improved such that their potential savings in the clustered DEA runs are smaller. However, two of the rural LEAs, Dorset and Norfolk, together with the Metropolitan borough of Newcastle are *less* efficient on the clustered basis. A few other authorities (Oldham, Salford, Gateshead, Avon, Gloucestershire and Shropshire) have a consistent efficiency evaluation irrespective of the cross section in which their efficiencies have been evaluated. It will also be noted that these LEAs have identical peer groups in the clustered and the whole-sample evaluation. In this small kernal of inefficient authorities, the DEA efficiency ratings would appear to be unequivocal. With stable peer groups there is, in principle, clearer information to improve productive performance.

Yet for the 18 authorities like Havering newly rated best-practice in the clustered runs, there remains considerable ambiguity over their performance. The efficiency of Waltham Forest and Havering, for example, has risen dramatically: From, respectively, 0.85 and 0.89 to unity using the clustered cross sections.

Table 7.4.2 (a)
The target level of teaching expenditure per pupil before and after clustering in London and the Metropolitan boroughs

LEA	Actual	Target clustered	Target all LEAs	Saving clustered	Saving all LEAs
	£	£	£	%	%
London Boroughs					
6. Croydon	664	638	623	3.9	6.2
9. Haringey	761	755	755	0.8	0.8
14. Kingston	644	631	621	2.0	3.6
17. Redbridge	668	643	628	3.7	6.0
18. Richmond	707	641	603	9.3	14.7
21. ILEA	883	671	657	24.0	25.6
Metropolitan Boroughs					
27. Walsall	667	602	597	9.7	10.5
34. Bolton	641	590	582	8.0	9.2
35. Bury	652	616	589	5.5	9.7
36. Manchester	749	654	653	12.7	12.8
37. Oldham	589	581	581	1.4	1.4
38. Rochdale	686	587	572	14.4	16.6
39. Salford	684	603	603	11.8	11.8
41. Tameside	620	590	589	4.8	5.0
47. Sheffield	669	624	608	6.7	9.1
51. Leeds	588	585	580	0.5	1.4
53. Gateshead	638	593	593	7.1	7.1
54. Newcastle	739	594	634	19.6	14.2
Average (London and Metropolitan)					
	681	622	615	8.1	9.2

Notes: See Table 7.4.2 (b)

Source: Authors' calculations.

Some variation in targets is to be expected in a smaller cross section because best-practice will have changed. However it is not encouraging that efficiency status has changed dramatically in some individual cases. This has two important implications. In the first instance it suggests the target may be subject to significant and unpredictable change. The scale of adjustments required to improve inefficient organisational performance have become unclear with substantially different implications for future funding. Secondly, it undermines the Pareto interpretation of the target which is widely found in the literature. For example in the clustered results

Waltham Forest is best-practice and by convention Pareto efficient. However the broader comparison in Chapter 3 found it had a non-unit efficiency of 0.85 and so, by the same convention, it cannot be Pareto efficient.

Table 7.4.2 (b)
The target level of teaching expenditure per pupil before and after clustering in the English countries

LEA	Actual	Target clustered	Target all LEAs	Savings clustered	Savings all LEAs
	£	£	£	%	%
58. Avon	638	588	588	7.8	7.8
63. Cheshire	632	595	584	5.9	7.6
68. Devon	616	592	585	3.9	5.0
69. Dorset	604	589	595	2.5	1.5
71. E Sussex	617	607	591	1.6	4.2
72. Essex	602	582	579	3.3	3.8
73. Gloucester	622	603	603	3.1	3.1
74. Hampshire	618	616	595	0.3	3.7
75. Hereford	602	588	586	0.7	3.1
76. Hertford	664	612	599	7.8	9.8
79. Kent	605	601	586	0.7	3.1
83. Norfolk	623	594	601	4.7	3.5
85. Northampton	609	601	592	1.3	2.8
87. Nottingham	637	620	597	2.7	6.3
89. Shropshire	639	594	594	7.0	7.0
91. Stafford	635	608	588	4.3	7.4
Average:	623	599	591	3.7	5.0

Notes: The target in column 3 and the savings in column 5 originate in the non-clustered analysis in Chapter 3.
Source: Authors' calculations.

This difficulty with targets goes back to a general problem in *relative* efficiency measurement of comparing like-with-like. (The discussion in section 6.6 of Chapter 6 gives further examples of problems in defining efficiency in relative terms.) There may be grounds in some cases for a smaller comparison to exclude non-comparable organisations. The LEA data set was grouped into 3 smaller clusters in an attempt to improve the peer group comparison. It was argued that the peer might be more appropriately defined in terms of LEAs operating in similar conditions.

It is perhaps not unreasonable to suggest that local authority management would argue that membership of the cross section should be restricted. London boroughs for example may feel that the inclusion of rural authorities in the comparison unfairly depresses their efficiency score.

Nunamaker (1985) argued that organisations have incentives to manipulate their efficiency score through expansion of the input-ouput variable set. This increases the probability that an organisation will dominate in at least one dimension. With equal effect organisations can protect future funding by arguing for smaller comparisons and hence, in effect, higher efficiency scores.

Clearly there are several reasons for varying the size of the cross section used in evaluation. Some of these—for example the manipulation of efficiency scores—are less compelling. In other circumstances, however, restricting membership may be more appropriate. The clustering approach in this Chapter was an attempt to add meaning to the peer group comparison, so that inner city boroughs would not be compared with prosperous rural authorities facing quite different problems.

However there should be limits to the extent to which the performance comparison is curtailed. All authorities can presumably point to some unique feature in their catchment area. To attempt to take account of all such factors would have high costs and ultimately make relative efficiency measurement meaningless.

To bring section 7.4 to a close the following conclusions can be noted. It is apparent that several aspects of DEA are not invariant to the size of the cross section used to explore performance. The replication of the LEA results on a clustered basis has shown that the efficiency score and its associated target, together with the peer group are susceptible to substantial (and largely unpredictable) change as the size of the cross section is altered. Accordingly, as smaller numbers of LEAs were compared, the DEA-efficiency scores tended to rise (Table 7.4.1) and the implied resource reductions (in general) fell (Table 7.4.2), and the peer groups for inefficient LEAs were reselected (Table 7.4.1). Combining the results from the three clusters yielded 18 additional best-practice LEAs; these significantly reduced the rank of the efficiency ordering *vis-à-vis* the broader comparison in Chapter 3.

The ambiguity of best-practice performance in the results calls into question the pervasive Pareto interpretation of DEA-efficiency in the literature (e.g. in Charnes and Cooper (1985)). The results in this section are therefore consistent with the *a priori* arguments in Chapter 6 on the distinct definitions of Pareto and DEA- efficiency.

7.5.   Conclusion

This Chapter has investigated aspects of the discriminating power of Data Envelopment Analysis. This was achieved via an examination of frontier efficiency in administrative clusters of LEAs. The clustering procedure was prompted by a desire to ensure that the performance comparison was of "like-with-like". On this basis three separate (and smaller) frontier comparisons were undertaken—of London boroughs, of Metropolitan boroughs and of the English counties. In principle, each of these clusters has greater internal homogeneity than the whole-sample comparison of rural and urban LEAs; and in principle the peer may not be drawn from among authorities to which the inefficient LEA bears less resemblance.

The clustering procedure constitutes a form of sensitivity analysis. Earlier work (e.g. Ahn and Seiford (1990), Charnes *et al* (1985), Nunamaker (1985)) concentrated on the effects of adding or deleting variables from the model. Clustering, by contrast, examines the effects of altering the size of the comparison for a given number of variables.

The clustered results provide evidence that three aspects of DEA are not invariant to the size of the cross section used to evaluate performance. These are (1) the number of untied efficiency scores; (2) the choice of peer group; and (3) the existence of targets. Each of these is important in the identification and (where necessary) adjustment of operations for improved performance. For example, the ranking of outcomes (however derived) has been widely undertaken in the literature on educational evaluation—see the league tables constructed by Gray and Jesson (1987) on the basis of exam pass rates. The definition of a peer group, meanwhile, broaches the general problem of comparabilty in relative efficiency measures; it suggests a requirement for some form of (pre-) DEA filtering to eliminate non-comparable DMUs from the performance comparison.

In the clustered performance, relatively larger numbers of best-practice were identified in each cluster. The most marked change occurred in London where 13 authorities achieved best-practice as against only 6 in Chapter 3. Similar changes were noted in the other clusters.

The increase in best-practice decreased the rank of the efficiency ordering. In Chapter 3, 51 authorities had untied non-unit efficiencies giving the input-efficiency ordering rank 52; the clustered results identified an additional 18 best-practice authorities and so the rank of the efficiency ordering of the whole cross section (summing across clusters) is reduced to 35. The ability of DEA to identify finer variations in performance therefore appears to be limited by the size of the cross section. Hence a smaller number of comparisons will in general lead to more tied efficiency scores as the number of best-practice rises.

The definition of a meaningful peer group touches on the problem of comparing like-with-like in relative efficiency measures. "Non-comparable" units should be excluded in the selection of the peer group. This implies restricting membership of the cross section such that peers can only be drawn from the same family of organisations. The clustering which this suggests may lead to the selection of a more intuitive peer group. For example, in the non-clustered analysis the peer group for the urban authority Newcastle-upon-Tyne included the rural Isle of Wight and Northumberland. After clustering, the peer group included only Solihull, Rotherham and Kirklees. Likewise all other peer groups were selected only from the appropriate "home" cluster of authorities. This meant that in nearly all cases the peer group changed *vis-à-vis* that selected in Chapter 3. Nonetheless at some inefficient authorities the peer group was identical in both the clustered and non-clustered results (i.e. at Oldham, Salford, Tameside, Gateshead, Avon, Gloucestershire and Shropshire). The stability of these peer groups suggests that they are robust to changes in the breadth of the comparison and that they are drawn from the appropriate LEA family. In these circumstances the peer group comparison is a much more plausible indicator of what (and how) the inefficient authority may be able to achieve. Equally, the revised peer groups are more intuitive than their predecessors and may come closer to fulfilling the role of operational blueprints for improved performance. Unless the peer group fulfils this role, its identification in DEA is of little practical purpose and in this sense the discriminating power of DEA is curtailed. Clearly the definition of a meaningful peer group is an area for future research.

The new targets identified from the clustered results were less satisfactory than the new peer group comparisons.   In some individual cases (e.g. Waltham Forest, Havering and Wigan) efficiency has changed dramatically leading to the complete elimination of the target.   Efficiency scores on the whole were higher, reducing the potential savings from targets.   The average target in the urban authorities suggested potential savings of around 8.1%, falling from 9.2% in the non-clustered analysis (Table 7.4.2 (a)); in the counties the average savings fell from 5% to just 3.7% (Table 7.4.2 (b)) suggesting that rural performance is relatively better than in the urban authorities—irrespective of the breadth of the comparison underlying the efficiency scores.

The marked changes in efficiency after clustering, especially the increasing preponderance of best-practice calls into question the pervasive Pareto interpretation of DEA-efficiency in the literature.   For example, can an LEA like Waltham Forest with an efficiency score of 0.85 be credibly considered best-practice after clustering? The large change in the efficiency status of LEAs like Waltham Forest is due to the less exacting nature of the performance comparison in the smaller clusters, which significantly raises an authority's probability of dominance on at least one variable (see Table 7.3.1).   Since in some circumstances the appropriate size of the performance comparison may be disputed (because of problems in confronting like-with-like) it may not be possible to pin down an unambiguous set of best-practice. Other things equal, the probablity of dominance in LEAs will vary according to the choice of cross section.   This undermines the credibility of DEA-dominance as an evaluation criterion since it does not define clearly those levels of performance which might, in principle, be attainable.   In this sense, the clustered results are consistent with the arguments in Chapter 6 on the distinct definitions of Pareto and DEA-efficiency—in particular that DEA best-practice may be a welfare inferior definition of dominance.

Finally, it was noted that the proportion of best-practice was relatively higher in the smaller, clustered cross sections.   The smaller of the LEA groups, the 21 London boroughs, had the largest proportion of best-practice; similarly, the largest of the clusters, the 39 counties, had the lowest proportion of best-practice.   This suggested that the discriminating power of DEA can be increased by broadening the evaluation cross section to include more DMUs.

Various other strategies were also identified in order to reduce the sensitivity of DEA to the size of the cross section.   For a fixed number of DMUs, a CRS technology will dominate VRS or NIRS (non-increasing returns) alternatives so that in general the numbers of best-practice will be lower under constant returns.   Second, a smaller number of variables is likely to reduce the set of dominant units (Seiford and Thrall (1990)).   Tied unit-efficiencies can therefore be limited by restricting the variable set to "core" activities alone.   Parkan (1987) also suggested the iterative use of DEA to break best-practice ties.

CHAPTER 8

A CONCLUSION AND APPRAISAL

This Chapter examines some of the broader conclusions which have arisen during the course of the book and adds some suggestions for future research. The core problem throughout has been the development of a methodology appropriate to the unusual evaluation difficulties of the public sector. A range of considerations suggest that Data Envelopment Analysis (DEA) goes some way towards overcoming these difficulties and is superior to traditional alternatives such as single-factor ratios. Section 8.1 summarises the principal advantages of DEA to public-sector applications. The main results of the empirical work are recapitulated in section 8.2 and some suggestions for future research are noted in section 8.3.

8.1. The public sector and DEA

In the public sector a large public-spending programme will typically produce multiple outputs. Very often these will be qualitative in nature and will not accrue in discrete, countable units. Historically, these output measurement difficulties have been sidestepped by national accounts statisticians who have opted for the use of input measures. Where output measures can be found, these will most probably be denominated in non-homogeneous units, owing to the diversity of public-sector activity. Traditional single-factor ratios may be used in these circumstances to produce a set of *ad hoc* productivity measures. Yet there is no reason *a priori* why a collection of single-factor ratios should yield a consistent summary view of organisational (or programme) performance.

A summary, total-factor measure of performance avoids the ambiguity of single-factor ratios, but requires the aggregation of inputs and outputs. DEA embodies a total-factor view of efficiency and in addition produces the weights necessary for aggregation. Naturally, private-sector organisations are able to use weights based on market prices. But in the absence of market prices, non-traded production requires an alternative valuation system, such as DEA is able to provide. The existence of a set of non-subjective weights endogenously generated by DEA is of particular significance for merit outputs such as education where policy-makers' priorities may be in dispute.

Several other considerations motivate the use of DEA, particularly *vis-à-vis* an econometric approach. In the past, productive performance has often been couched in terms of the *average* standard embodied in least squares cost and production functions. This is unsatisfactory in as far as a performance norm based on average practice may allow the persistence of inefficiency. The *full* gains from improved productivity are only available on the boundary of the production set. Any less demanding norm will tend to legitimise some degree of inefficiency and is inconsistent with the economic theory of production. Based on observed best practice, DEA is, in principle, consistent with the more demanding—not to say more appropriate—standards set by boundary production.

Of course a frontier *per se* can be estimated either econometrically or through DEA. Early DEA applications were applicable to only a limited range of technologies, namely those exhibiting constant returns to scale and strong disposability. This initially discouraged use of DEA. However, as a wider range of reference technologies have become available, the comparative advantage of DEA has increased.

This advantage is enhanced by the weaker information requirements of DEA which impose only limited assumptions on the shape of the possibility set. An econometric boundary necessarily imposes a functional form (Cobb-Douglas, C.E.S., translog, etc.) on the data. In the absence of intimate knowledge of the underlying production process, the resulting technology may be a good "fit", but otherwise quite arbitrary. An interesting paper by Banker, Conrad and Strauss (1986) confronted DEA and translog estimates of a hospital production function. Their translog results suggest a constant returns technology, while the DEA procedure indicates the presence of both increasing and decreasing returns. The translog estimate is based on a single optimisation over the whole data set. The fitted technology that results is an "average" or sample-wide estimate, which may not replicate scale behaviour at individual DMUs. In employing a series of optimisations, one for each DMU, DEA provides a better fit to each observation and a better approximation to the scale properties of individual DMUs. As a consequence the revealed technology is a closer estimate of the true, unknown technology underlying the data. Moreover an empirical procedure requiring independent optimisation for each DMU is consistent with the maximisation postulate embedded in mainstream neoclassical economics.

8.2. Overview of the empirical results

This book has taken advantage of the revised VRS program of Banker to estimate the efficiency of production in two areas of the British public sector. The first case study, reported in Chapters 3 and 7, examined data on the performance of local authority production of education; and the second, in Chapters 4 and 5, the incarceration of inmates in a group of 33 prisons with a high remand population. The choice of these two activities is designed to be illustrative of the many potential applications elsewhere in the public sector. Any department or programme with a branch structure may be a candidate. The level of aggregation is variable, ranging from larger decision-making units like local authorities to smaller point-of-delivery units like schools, hospitals, post offices and job centres.

Existing sources of performance indicator, such as the supplementary volumes of the UK public expenditure White Paper, contain a confusing range of measures in these areas. The use of DEA offers an alternative source of performance "statistic" yielding a more consistent overview of operations than is possible with traditional measures. In the analysis of local education authority (LEA) spending, the performance of all 96 English LEAs is reduced to a simple scalar reflecting their total-factor productivity. Prison performance is simplified in an analogous manner.

Educational efficiency

The results in Chapter 3 are based on an eight variable model of educational production.   The selection of the variables is inevitably *ad hoc* but is nevertheless broadly representative of educational activities and influences.   Three intermediate outputs—exam pass rates—are included to cover the full range of educational attainment.   Five inputs are incorporated into the model.   Only one of these— secondary school teaching expenditure per pupil—is controllable.   The other inputs are non-controllable background variables incorporating the educational impact of family income, occupational status and ethnic origin.   Although social non-controllables have no value in alternative uses, their inclusion is essential in assessing performance on the target variable, teaching expenditure per pupil.

Of the 96 LEAs in the cross section, 44 obtain a score of unity and thus are *relatively* efficient in their management of teaching expenditure.   The remainder, 52 in all, are relatively input inefficient to varying degrees, attaining an efficiency score less than unity.   The results suggest the total potential reduction in spending per pupil across all LEAs averages close to 3½%.   Excluding best practice, the average targeted reduction in spending rises to around 6½%.   These savings are not evenly distributed across LEAs.   The lowest efficiency scores are recorded among the London and Metropolitan authorities.   The rural authorities appeared to perform rather better.   It is possible that exam pass rates are not covering the full range of activities (outputs) provided by the higher spending urban authorities.   In this sense the comparison may have been discriminating unfairly, especially against the former Inner London Education Authority (ILEA), which in terms of student numbers and spending is almost in a league of its own.   Future research would benefit from access to a broader range of standardised output measures which, where possible, are defined as net rather than gross outputs.

In addition to the efficiency implications for LEAs, Chapter 3 examined the information contents of the reference or peer group.   In the setting of targets, the literature regularly appeals to the peer group as providing the foundations of a blueprint for improvement.   How far this recommendation is acceptable is probably only determinable on a case by case basis.   In the limit, it may be reasonable to argue that "peers" are no more than an artefact of the linear program with no genuine operational significance.   It is not clear that the number of citations a peer receives is evidence of its efficiency in any absolute sense.   A high number of citations denotes only comparability of the DMU and conveys nothing in-and-of-itself on the quality of best practice.

The robustness of DEA efficiency to noise, alternative model specifications, etc. deserves more attention than it has received.   Early sensitivity analyses have focused on the addition or deletion of variables.   Holding the number of variables constant, Chapter 7 examines the sensitivity of educational efficiency to the size of the cross section.   LEAs were grouped into three recognised administrative clusters and frontier performance re-estimated for each cluster.   There is some precedent for clustering since it is now recognised that in general the larger the number of DMUs, the lower the internal homogeneity of the the data set.   Without clustering, DMUs with widely differing characteristics and dissimilar technologies may be built into the same frontier, invalidating the efficiency comparison. Banker (1989) has gone so far as to develop a formal statistical test for partitioning large cross sections into sub-groups of closer internal homogeneity. The clustering criterion adopted in Chapter 7 is *ad hoc*, but captures the key distinction of rural *vs.* urban education. Similar criteria were brought to bear upon the prison case study in Chapters 4 and 5. Of over 100 penal institutions in the UK, only those 33 with a significant remand content were included in the efficiency comparison. Since remand inmates are generally more costly to keep, it would be inappropriate to include lower cost, non-remand institutions.

The clustered results in Chapter 7 provide evidence that several aspects of DEA are not invariant to the size of the cross section used to evaluate performance. In nearly all cases the peer group changed *vis-à-vis* those originally selected in Chapter 3. For example, in the non-clustered analysis the peer group for the urban authority Newcastle included the rural Isle of Wight and Northumberland. After clustering, the peer group included only Solihull, Rotherham and Kirklees. Being drawn from the appropriate home cluster, the new peer groups are more intuitive than their predecessors and perhaps come closer to fulfilling their widely advocated role of operational blueprints for improved performance.

In the smaller cross sections the numbers of best-practice LEAs rose steeply, reducing the overall level of discrimination between DMUs. The reduced rank of the efficiency ordering is a cause for concern since poorer performance appears to be absorbed into best practice. Various strategies can be suggested to reduce the sensitivity of DEA to the size of the cross section. For a given number of DMUs, a CRS technology (with strong disposability) will dominate VRS or NIRS alternatives so that in general the numbers of best practice will be lower under constant returns. *Ceteris paribus,* restricting the variable set to core activities alone lowers the probability of a particular DMU becoming dominant.

Some variation in targets is to be expected in a smaller cross section, owing to the less exacting nature of the comparison. Yet the variation in efficiency scores at some LEAs creates considerable ambiguity as to their underlying performance. At Waltham Forest and Havering for example efficiency rose dramatically in the clustered runs to unity from, respectively, 0.85 and 0.89. Difficulties in identifying underlying performance will complicate future budget allocations which, in these circumstances, may be more firmly based on non-DEA criteria.

The nature of efficiency

That the number of best-practice LEAs, targets and peer groups varies unpredictably in Chapter 7 suggests there is some ambiguity in the concept of DEA efficiency. The literature has generally equated the best-practice technology with Pareto efficiency. Chapter 6 argues this must be inappropriate in as far as a neoclassical view of the world actually rules out the possibility of inefficient decisions. If there is a welfare justification for DEA targets, it is not that of Pareto efficiency.

A host of arguments suggest that the best-practice technology may represent more modest achievement. The public sector is non-profit-making with non-financial merit objectives, limiting the attainment of full cost efficiency. In addition, arguments for the presence of X-efficiency suggest that principals and agents satisfice rather than obey the strict maximisation postulate.

Despite some recent innovations, the key allocative dimension to efficiency has been overlooked, so that in many applications best practice has included allocatively inefficient DMUs. Of course this partly reflects definitional problems in the public sector. Nevertheless the full welfare implications of production are unclear so long as efficiency ignores relative prices. Where price information is available, this will reveal the relative opportunity cost of consuming one input over another. Targeting for cost minimisation may then involve adjustment of the ratios of inputs in addition to the conventional radial contraction advocated in the literature.

Since best practice may represent only modest achievement, it is useful to distinguish between DEA Dominance and a notional Pareto Dominance. A Pareto allocation would then yield the full maximal improvement over a position of inefficiency. A DEA target, while inferior to the Pareto outcome, remains credible if it nonetheless yields a net improvement in welfare *vis-à-vis* the initial inefficient allocation. That is, DEA targeting offers the possibility of a Pareto Improvement releasing limited resources to allow welfare-enhancing trades elsewhere in the economy.

Efficiency and incarceration

It is perhaps fair to say that the economics of crime and justice have joined the mainstream literature since the seminal developments of the 1960s. Nonetheless, with the exception of Ganley and Cubbin (1987), frontier estimates of prison efficiency are unavailable, despite the attention prisons have received in the wider management literature (e.g. Morgan (1992)). In response, Chapters 4 and 5 have developed a model of incarceration based on data published by the UK prison department. Like the LEA model, activity is couched in terms of intermediate rather than final outputs. Four input variables are included and these, like the outcome variables, are disaggregated where possible to reflect the important distinction between remand and non-remand prisoners. The resulting DEA revealed that, relative to a VRS technology, 13 establishments were operating below best-practice. Among these, some particularly poor performance was evident with potential cost savings of between 20% and 30%. Over the cross section as a whole, prisons appeared to be operating with costs of around 4 ½% greater than projected on the frontier.

It appears that for both prisons and LEAs the average reduction in costs through the whole cross section is fairly limited under VRS—in each case less than 5%. Much of the value of the technique in these applications has been to identify those units whose performance is clearly well out of line with the bulk of the sample. For example prisons at Leicester and Bedford achieved technical efficiencies of, respectively, 0.78 and 0.71 while the ILEA scored 0.79 in the education comparison.

Close scrutiny of a representative peer group at Canterbury indicated that there were few clear lessons to be drawn from best practice. Certainly the raw input-output data at peer establishments offered little in the way of guidance as to how far—or even in which direction—an inefficient prison should alter its target variables. The mapping from inefficient to best-practice performance being unclear, inefficiency may persist.

Future research would do well to assemble post-DEA criteria to guide attainment of targets.

It is difficult to over-stress the problems involved in reaching targets. There is little in the way of post-DEA guidance as to their implementation. Moreover there are arguments to suggest that targets may be at least partially unattainable in the short run. These rigidities in performance reflect a range of factors—some of which were developed in Chapter 4 drawing on the work of Leibenstein. In as far as their priorities differ from those of the organisation as a whole, employees choose effort levels inconsistent with the target. These effort levels will maximise their individual utilities, and as such, will not be increased voluntarily. If employees can be bribed into increased effort—through better work conditions and pay for example—it may be possible to share the resulting gains between organisation and worker. Although the *full* target remains unattainable in these circumstances, the impact of inefficiency is at least curtailed. It follows that it may be necessary to accept a second-best, or intermediate, target in the short run. This is consistent with Banker's arguments for loose targets which would bring performance towards, but not on to, the efficient frontier.

Programme efficiency

Allocation of broader public-sector budgets is not generally feasible on the basis of DMU-level efficiency scores—these will generally embody more detail than is practical for central (as distinct from line) decision-makers. This prompts a need for aggregation of DMU performance in programmes with a branch structure. Aggregate efficiency scores may then be used to allocate funds in favour of more efficient programmes. Currently, programme performance, like line performance, is generally evaluated using a range of *ad hoc* criteria. Various alternative possibilities exist which allow aggregation of DMU efficiency. For example, the total of individual DEA efficiency scores provides at least an ordinal indication of the success of programmes. More useful for budgetary purposes is the summation of actual and target levels of spending. These totals can be used to define aggregate efficiency scores which feed into the annual budgeting process. Subject to exogenous constraints (such as relevant legislation), it is possible to target whole programmes, redirecting spending into more productive areas. As at the micro-level, the programme efficiency score is based on a total-factor view of performance.

Taking this approach, Chapter 5 examines performance of the prison spending programme under alternative CRS and VRS technology assumptions. The more discriminating CRS approach identified 11 best-practice institutions, compared to 20 under VRS. This was reflected in programme efficiency which under VRS suggested potential savings in total costs of 4½% rising to just over 13% with CRS. The increase in excess costs under the constant returns technology reflects the inclusion of divergences from scale efficiency. Taking account of the scale of operations dramatically affected the performance of certain institutions. Brixton is a case in point. Under VRS it obtained a unity efficiency ratio whilst under CRS its efficiency score fell to almost one half (0.53). Other establishments, Bedford, Oxford and Wormwood Scrubs for example, also experienced a marked fall in efficiency under constant returns. Using the Banker (1984) scale indicator it was possible to identify whether the scale problem was one of increasing or decreasing returns. Thus Brixton appeared to have very strong decreasing returns whilst others like Latchmere House had increasing returns. In the sample as a whole 17 prisons had IRS and 5 DRS, suggesting that there may be scope for a policy of reallocation of inmates from DRS to IRS institutions.

The analysis of scale has recently been qualified by the contribution of Banker and Thrall (1989). This suggests there may not be a unique point of maximum average productivity in the estimated frontier, but rather an infinity of such points along a particular facet. The Banker and Thrall solution to this problem involves identification of the bounds on slopes of facets in the frontier to reveal the returns to scale. This approach appears to be intractable to conventional L.P.s and may be of limited practical value. An alternative procedure of our own is to calculate the maximum and minimum values of the original Banker (1984) scale indicator. Results based on this criterion appeared to confirm at least the possibility of a non-unique maximum average productivity.

8.3. Directions for future research

Although DEA has several advantages over other methodologies for performance evaluation, it nonetheless suffers from a variety of weaknesses which should be the subject of future research. This final section outlines some of these future possibilities. The order in which these topics is presented should not be taken as denoting their relative importance.

Treatment of noise

The deviation of observed performance from frontier performance is attributed *entirely* to DMU inefficiency in standard DEA models. This clearly ignores the implications of measurement error in extreme observations. Banker, Gadh and Gorr (1989), for example, have performed an extensive Monte Carlo simulation which suggests that the reliability of DEA results deteriorates considerably *vis-à-vis* an econometric approach when measurement errors become large. Traditional DEA also assumes, implausibly, that the input-output data are not subject to a stochastic generating mechanism. Future progress would seem to require that DEA make explicit recognition of noise in frontier outcomes, as in econometric frontier applications.

Some valuable progress has already been made in this direction, notably by Charnes *et al* (1991), Sengupta (1990 a,b) and Banker, Das and Datar (1989) who have examined methods for identifying "gross data errors" and regions of data stability. However these developments remain in their infancy and feel rather *ad hoc*. The ultimate research objective probably lies in some form of marriage of parametric and non-parametric techniques. This would circumvent one of the principal difficulties currently inherent in a non-parametric frontier approach.

Variable selection criteria

In standard econometric model-building, the preferred functional form is usually derived through "testing down" from a general to a more specific equation. Variables are eliminated by conventional hypothesis tests. Formal selection criteria are unavailable in DEA, the input-output variables in a "model" usually being based on intuitive or pragmatic considerations—the literature recommends they be "broadly representative" or "proto-typical" (Haag, Jaska and Semple (1992)). One of the few studies to examine the problem carefully—Roll, Golany and Seroussy (1989)—used a selection of arbitrary statistical criteria (e.g. simple correlation analysis) in an attempt to pin down the appropriate variable set.

This is clearly unsatisfactory in introducing an undesirable subjective factor into the analysis which creates considerable scope for dispute. DMUs can argue for alternative input-output sets which maximise their efficiency score. Indeed the literature now recognises the possibility of games between DMUs and the central evaluator, the former trying to maximise, the latter to minimise, the efficiency score in each play of the game (i.e., in each application of DEA). Empirically there is so far little support for the accumulation of inefficiency as a deliberate strategy (Banker, Charnes, Cooper and Clarke (1989) and Charnes, Clarke and Cooper (1989)). But the possibility of manipulation of the efficiency score remains. Formal variable selection procedures implemented prior to the DEA would help to establish a core data set which is not open to question, thereby undermining the game. One potentially fruitful avenue for selection criteria may come through the development of a system of hypothesis testing such as is already fundamental to econometric modelling.

Dynamic considerations

The standard DEA model is a static, one-period evaluation. This heightens the problem of noise and makes once-off performance assessment highly tentative. In response, panel data and window analyses have been adopted to minimise the distortions in isolated cross sections. The resulting efficiency scores are thought to give a better assessment of "underlying" performance. However the repeated application of DEA through a panel data set produces little more than a continuum of "static" results, when a static perspective may be inappropriate. In reality the behaviour underlying the production process is likely to be dynamic because DMUs may take more than one time period to adjust their choice variables to desired levels. Furthermore capital inputs have a multi-period dimension since they generate outputs in future periods. Yet models in the applied literature are based almost exclusively on current inputs, biasing efficiency comparisons against capital intensive processes (Sengupta (1992) is an exception). It would clearly be appropriate to move towards some more general dynamic DEA modelling. This would have to deal with the problems of trended data in growing organisations and inflationary environments (see Perman (1991)). In addition it would need to provide an explicit partial adjustment mechanism, which should include appropriately discounted capital inputs. Without inclusion of the full range of inputs, it is difficult to accept DEA as a true total-factor measure—one of the prime justifications for use of DEA.

Use of peer groups and targets

The principal normative implications of DEA are couched in terms of the peer group and the target. Throughout this book concern has been expressed as to the adequacy of these concepts for actual implementation of DEA results. Although these are really "post-DEA" problems they are crucial nonetheless. For example, Charnes, Huang, Semple, Song and Thomas (1990) recommend that the number of citations in peer groups can be read as indicating the robustness of best practice. However several key problems undermine this interpretation. It requires a fair like-with-like comparison, without which a peer's dominance may be artificial. Moreover the number of citations is in reality little more than a measure of a peer's comparability (in terms of factor proportions) with the rest of the data set. It reveals nothing on a DMU's efficiency in an absolute sense.

The peer comparison may be ambiguous, since the peer can be "dominant" on a single variable. Consequently an inefficient DMU may dominate its peer(s) on some of the target variables. This was shown to be the case for Canterbury prison in Chapter 4. This suggests the need for stronger criteria for the selection of peers, e.g. dominance on all variables. This would be consistent with a "robust efficiency," although it is likely that this particular criterion would be so demanding in practice as to yield no peers at all!

In conclusion, without further research, an appropriate—if conservative—starting assumption should be that the peer has minimal information content. Further research is needed to show how far at the operational level the peer can be used to facilitate improvements in performance. Similar comments apply to the DEA target. The problem of noise may overstate the necessary change in performance while rigidities in labour supply and organisational structures may make the full target unobtainable in the short run. The setting of targets also needs to recognise the exogenous constraints on outcomes (legislation, convention, etc.) which should be built explicitly into the L.P. —see the work undertaken by Charnes, Cooper, Huang and Sun (1990), Beasley and Wong (1989) and Dyson and Thanassoulis (1988). Finally, targets should not be perceived as a punitive weapon (Schuller (1989)). Thus if a DMU is rated efficient with IRS, then a budget *increase* may be in order to exploit the benefits of increasing returns.

More generally, and beyond the scope of Data Envelopment Analysis entirely, there is a need for research on the definition of public outputs and relative prices. Attitudes have changed in recent years and less use is being made of input measures as crude proxies for outcomes. Nevertheless a great deal remains to be done in the definition and classification of public-sector production.

REFERENCES

Aanestad, J (1987) "Measurement problems in the service economy", *Business Economics*, 22, 32-37.

Achabal, D, Heineke, J and McIntyre, S (1985) "Productivity measurement and the output of retailing", *Journal of Retailing*, 61, 83-88.

Afriat, S (1972) "Efficiency estimation of production functions", *International Economic Review*, 13, 568-598.

Ahn, T, Arnold, V, Charnes, A and Cooper, W (1989) "DEA and ratio efficiency analyses for public institutions of higher learning in Texas", *Research in Governmental and Nonprofit Accounting*, 5, 165-185.

Ahn, T and Seiford, L (1990) "Sensitivity of DEA to models and variable sets in a hypothesis-test setting: The efficiency of university operations", in Y Ijiri (ed.) *Creative and Innovative Approaches to the Science of Management*.

Aigner, D, Amemiya, T and Poirier, D (1976) "On the estimation of production frontiers: Maximum Likelihood estimation of the parameters of a discontinuous density function", *International Economic Review*, 17, 377-396.

Aigner, D and Chu, S (1968) "On estimating the industry production function", *American Economic Review*, 58, 826-839.

Aigner, D, Lovell, C and Schmidt, P (1977) "Formulation and estimation of stochastic frontier production functions", *Journal of Econometrics*, 5, 21-38.

Alessi, L (1983) "Property rights, transactions costs and X-efficiency: An essay in economic theory", *American Economic Review*, 73, 64-81.

Aly, Y, Grabowski, R, Pasurka, C and Rangan, N (1990) "Technical, scale and allocative efficiencies in US banking: An empirical investigation", *Review of Economics and Statistics*, 72, 211-218.

Armitage, J and Sabot, R (1987) "Socio-economic background and the returns to schooling in two low-income economies", *Economica*, 54, 103-108.

Aschauer, D (1989) "Is public expenditure productive?", *Journal of Monetary Economics*, 23, 177-200.

Audit Commission (1986a) *Towards better management of secondary education*. London: HMSO.

Audit Commission (1986b) *Performance review in local government education*. London: HMSO.

Bagi, F and Huang, C (1983) "Estimating production technical efficiency for individual farms in Tennessee", *Canadian Journal of Agricultural Economics*, 31, 249-256.

Balachandran, K and Steuer, R (1982) "An interactive model for the CPA firm-audit staff problem with multiple objectives", *The Accounting Review*, January, 125-140.

Banker, R (1989) "Econometric estimation and Data Envelopment Analysis", *Research in Governmental and Nonprofit Accounting*, 5, 231-243.

Banker, R (1988) "Stochastic Data Envelopment Analysis", mimeo, *Carnegie Mellon University, School of Urban and Public Affairs*, revised September 26.

Banker, R (1984) "Estimating the most productive scale size using Data Envelopment Analysis", *European Journal of Operational Research*, 17, 35-44.

Banker, R, Charnes, A and Cooper, W (1984) "Some models for estimating technical and scale inefficiencies in Data Envelopment Analysis", *Management Science*, 30, 1078-1092.

Banker, R, Charnes, A, Cooper, W and Clarke, R (1989) "Constrained game formulations and interpretations for Data Envelopment Analysis", *European Journal of Operational Research*, 40, 299-308.

Banker, R, Charnes, A, Cooper, W and Schinnar, A (1981) "A bi-extremal principle for frontier estimation and efficiency evaluations", *Management Science*, 27, 1370-1382.

Banker, R, Charnes, A, Cooper, W, Swarts, J and Thomas, D (1990) "An introduction to Data Envelopment Analysis with some of its models and their uses", *Research in Governmental and Nonprofit Accounting*, 5, 125-163.

Banker, R, Conrad, R and Strauss, R (1986) "A comparative application of Data Envelopment Analysis and translog methods: An illustrative study of hospital production", *Management Science*, 32, 30-44.

Banker, R, Das, S and Datar, S (1989) "Analysis of cost variances for management control in hospitals", *Research in Governmental and Nonprofit Accounting*, 5, 269-291.

Banker, R, Gadh, V and Goor, W (1989) "A Monte Carlo Comparison of efficiency estimation methods", *Carnegie Mellon University, Working Paper*.

Banker, R and Maindiratta, A (1988) "Nonparametric analysis of technical and allocative efficiencies in production", *Econometrica*, 56, 1315-1332.

Banker, R and Maindiratta, A (1986) "Piecewise loglinear estimation of efficient production surfaces", *Management Science*, 32, 126-135.

Banker, R and Morey, R (1989) "Incorporating value judgements in efficiency analysis", *Research in Governmental and Nonprofit Accounting*, 5, 245-267.

Banker, R and Morey R (1986a) "The use of categorical variables in Data Envelopment Analysis", *Management Science*, 32, 1613-1627.

Banker, R and Morey R (1986b) "Efficiency analysis for exogenously fixed inputs and outputs", *Operations Research*, 34, 513-521.

Banker, R and Thrall, R (1989) "Estimation of returns to scale using Data Envelopment Analysis", mimeo, *Carnegie Mellon University, School of Urban and Public Affairs*, June.

Bauer, P (1990) "Recent developments in the econometric estimation of frontiers", *Journal of Econometrics*, 46, 39-56.

Beasley, J (1988) "Comparing university departments", mimeo, *Imperial College, London, The Management School*, January, revised June.

Beasley, J and Wong, Y (1988) "Restricting weight flexibility in Data Envelopment Analysis", mimeo, *Imperial College, London, The Management School*, revised February.

Becker, G (1968) "Crime and punishment: An economic approach", *Journal of Political Economy*, March-April, 169-217.

Beeton, D (1988) "Performance measurement: The state of the art", *Public Money and Management*, 8, 93-103.

Berger, A and Humphrey, D (1990) "The dominance of inefficiencies over scale and product mix economies in banking", *Board of Governors of the Federal Reserve System, Finance and Economics Discussion Series*, no. 107.

Berndt, E and Khaled, M (1979) "Parametric productivity measurement and choice among flexible functional forms", *Journal of Political Economy*, 87, 1220-1245.

Besley, J (1989) "Ex ante evaluation of health states and the provision for ill-health", *Economic Journal*, 99, 132-146.

Bessent, A and Bessent, W (1980) "Determining the comparative efficiency of schools through Data Envelopment Analysis", *Educational Administration Quarterly*, 16, 57-75.

Bessent, A, Bessent, E, Charnes, A, Cooper, W and Thorogood, N (1983) "Evaluation of educational program proposals by means of DEA", *Educational Administration Quarterly*, 19, 82-107.

Bessent, A, Bessent, W, Elam, J and Clark, T (1988) "Efficiency frontier determination by constrained facet analysis", *Operations Research*, 36, 785-796.

Bessent, A, Bessent, W, Elam, J and Long, D (1984) "Educational productivity council employs management science methods to improve educational quality", *Interfaces*, 14, 1-8.

Bessent, A, Bessent, W, Kennington, J and Reagan, B (1982) "An application of mathematical programming to assess productivity in the Houston independent school district", *Management Science*, 28, 1355-1367.

Bjurek, H, Forsund, F and Hjalmarsson, L (1986) "Productivity change and productive efficiency in Swedish social welfare offices", mimeo, March.

Bjurek, H, Hjalmarsson, L and Forsund, F (1990) "Deterministic parametric and non-parametric estimation of efficiency in service production: A comparison", *Journal of Econometrics*, 46, 213-228.

Blaug, M (1980) *The methodology of economics*. Cambridge: Cambridge University Press.

Bol, G (1986) "On technical efficiency measures: A remark", *Journal of Economic Theory*, 38, 380-385.

Bös, D and Peters, W (1991) "When employees free ride: A theory of inefficiency", *University of Bonn, Department of Economics, Discussion Paper*, no. A-327.

Boussofiane, A, Thanassoulis, E and Dyson, R (1991) "Using Data Envelopment Analysis to assess the efficiency of perinatal care provision in England", *Warwick Business School Research Papers*, no. 5.

Bovaird, T (1981) "Recent developments in output measurement in local government", *Local Government Studies*, September-October, 35-53.

Bowlin, W (1987) "Evaluating the efficiency of US Air Force real-property maintenence activities", *Journal of the Operational Research Society*, 38, 127-135.

Bowlin, W (1986) "Evaluating performance in governmental organizations", *The Government Accountants' Journal*, 35, 50-57.

Bowlin, W and White, J (1988) "Program auditing in Federal operations", mimeo, submitted to *Auditing : A Journal of Practice and Theory*.

Boyd, G and Fare, R (1984) "Measuring the efficiency of decision-making units: A comment", *European Journal of Operational Research*, 15, 331-332.

Burley, H (1980) "Productive efficiency in US manufacturing: A linear programming approach", *Review of Economics and Statistics*, 62, 619-622.

Button, K (1985) "Potential differences in the degree of X-inefficiency between industrial sectors in the United Kingdom", *Quarterly Review of Economics and Business,* 25, 85-95.

Carley, M (1980) *Rational techniques in policy analysis*. London: Heinemann Educational Books Ltd.

Carr-Hill, R and Stern, N (1979) *Crime, the police and criminal statistics*. London: Academic Press.

Charnes, A, Clarke, R and Cooper, W (1989) "An approach to testing for organisational slack via Banker's game theoretic DEA formulations", *Research in Governmental and Nonprofit Accounting*, 5, 211-229.

Charnes, A, Clarke, C, Cooper, W and Golany, B (1985) "A developmental study of Data Envelopment Analysis in measuring the efficiency of maintenence units in the US Air Force", *Annals of Operations Research*, 2, 95-112.

Charnes, A and Cooper, W (1985) "Preface to topics in Data Envelopment Analysis", *Annals of Operations Research*, 2, 59-94.

Charnes, A and Cooper, W (1984) "The non-Archimedean CCR ratio for efficiency analysis: A rejoinder to Boyd and Fare", *European Journal of Operational Research*, 15, 333-334.

Charnes, A and Cooper, W (1980a) "Auditing and accounting for program efficiency and management efficiency in not-for-profit entities" *Accounting, Organisations and Society*, 5, 87-107.

Charnes, A and Cooper, W (1980b) "Management science relations for evaluation and management accountability", *Journal of Enterprise Management*, 2, 143-162.

Charnes, A and Cooper, W (1973) "An explicit general solution in linear fractional programming", *Naval Research Logistics Quarterly*, 20.

Charnes, A and Cooper, W (1962) "Programming with linear fractional functionals", *Naval Research Logistics Quarterly*, 9, 181-185.

Charnes, A, Cooper, W, Divine, D, Ruefli, T and Thomas, D (1989) "Comparisons of DEA and existing ratio and regression systems for effecting efficiency evaluations of regulated electric co-operative in Texas", *Research in Governmental and Nonprofit Accounting*, 5, 187-210.

Charnes, A, Cooper, W, Golany, B, Seiford, L and Stutz, J (1985) "Foundations of Data Envelopment Analysis for Pareto-Koopmans efficient empirical production functions", *Journal of Econometrics*, 30, 91-107.

Charnes, A, Cooper, W, Huang, Z, Sun, D (1990) "Polyhedral cone-ratio DEA models with an illustrative application to large commercial banks", *Journal of Econometrics*, 46, 73-91.

Charnes, A, Cooper, W, Lewin, A, Morey, R and Rosseau, J (1985) "Sensitivity and stability analysis in DEA", *Annals of Operations Research*, 2, 139-156.

Charnes, A, Cooper, W and Rhodes, E (1981) "Evaluating program and managerial efficiency: An application of Data Envelopment Analysis to Program Follow Through", *Management Science*, 27, 668-697.

Charnes, A, Cooper, W and Rhodes, E (1979) "Measuring the efficiency of Decision-Making Units", *European Journal of Operational Research*, 3, 339.

Charnes, A, Cooper, W and Rhodes, E (1978) "Measuring the efficiency of Decision-Making Units", *European Journal of Operational Research*, 2, 429-444.

Charnes, A, Haag, S, Jaska, P and Semple, J (1991) "Stability analysis for the additive model in Data Envelopment Analysis", *International Journal of Systems Science*, forthcoming, 1992.

Charnes, A, Huang, Z, Semple, J, Song, T and Thomas, D (1990) "Origins and research in Data Envelopment Analysis", *The Arabian Journal of Science and Engineering*, 15, 617-625.

Cowing, T and Stevenson, R (1984) *Productivity measurement in regulated industries.* Academic Press.

Craig, C and Harris, R (1973) "Total productivity measurement at the firm level", *Sloan Management Review*, spring, 13-29.

Danilin, V, Materov, I, Rosefielde, S and Lovell, C (1985) "Measuring enterprise efficiency in the Soviet Union: A stochastic frontier analysis", *Economica*, 52, 225-233.

Dawson, P (1987) "Technical efficiency relative to a stochastic cost frontier for the England and Wales dairy sector", *Oxford Agrarian Studies*, 16, 45-55.

Dawson, P and Lingard, J (1988) "Comparative efficiency of rice farms in central Luzon, the Philippines", *University of Newcastle upon Tyne, Department of Agricultural Economics and Food Marketing, Discussion Paper*, no. 6/88.

Debreu, G (1959) *Theory of value. An axiomatic analysis of economic equilibrium.* Cowles Foundation Monograph 17. London: Yale University Press.

Debreu, G (1951) "The coefficient of resource allocation", *Econometrica*, 19, 273-292.

Department of Education and Science (1984) "School standards and spending: Statistical analysis. A further appreciation", *Statistical Bulletin*, no. 13/84.

Department of Education and Science (1983) "School standards and spending: Statistical analysis", *Statistical Bulletin*, no. 16/83.

Department of Health and Social Security (1985) *Performance indicators for the NHS: Guidance for users.* London: DHSS.

Department of Health and Social Security (1983) *Performance indicators: National summary for 1981*. London: DHSS.

Dessent, G (1987) "Prison perimeter cost-effectiveness", *Journal of the Operational Research Society*, 38, 975-980.

Diewert, W and Parkan, C (1983) "Linear programming tests of regularity conditions for production functions", in *Quantitative studies on production and prices*. Edited by Eichhorn, W, Henn, R, Neumann, K, and Shephard, R. Vienna: Physica-Verlag.

Dmitruk, A and Koshevoy, G (1991) "On the existence of a technical efficiency criterion", *Journal of Economic Theory*, 55, 121-144.

Duncan, O, Featherman, D and Duncan, B (1972) *Socioeconomic background and achievement*. New York: Seminar Press.

Dunlop, W (1985) "The elusive concept, efficiency: A survey of the conceptual and measurement issues", *University of Newcastle, N.S.W., Australia, Department of Economics, Occasional Paper*, no. 109.

Dyson, R and Thanassoulis, E (1988) "Reducing weight flexibility in Data Envelopment Analysis", *Journal of the Operational Research Society*, 39, 563-576.

Epstein, M and Henderson, J (1989) "Data Envelopment Analysis for managerial control and diagnostics", *Decision Sciences Journal*, 20, 90-119.

Fare, R and Grosskopf, S (1990) "A distance function approach to price efficiency", *Journal of Public Economics*, 43, 123-126.

Fare, R and Grosskopf, S (1983a) "Measuring congestion in production", *Zeitschrift für Nationalokonomie*, 43, 257-271.

Fare, R and Grosskopf, S (1983b) "Measuring output efficiency", *European Journal of Operational Research*, 13, 173-179.

Fare, R, Grosskopf, S, Li, S, Wang, Z and and Yaisawarng, S (1990) "Productivity growth in Illinois electric utilities", *Resources and Energy*, 12, 383-398.

Fare, R, Grosskopf, S and Logan, J (1987) "The comparative efficiency of Western coal-fired steam-electric generating plants: 1977-1979", *Engineering Costs and Production Economics*, 11, 21-30.

Fare, R, Grosskopf, S and Logan, J (1985) "The relative performance of publicly-owned and privately-owned electric utilities", *Journal of Public Economics*, 26, 89-106.

Fare, R, Grosskopf, S and Lovell, C (1988) "An indirect approach to the evaluation of producer performance", *Journal of Public Economics*, 37, 71-89.

Fare, R, Grosskopf, S and Lovell, C (1987) "Non-parametric disposability tests", *Zeitschrift für Nationalokonomie*, 47, 77-85.

Fare, R, Grosskopf, S and Lovell, C (1985) *The measurement of efficiency of production*. Boston: Kluwer-Nijhoff.

Fare, R, Grosskopf, S and Lovell, C (1983) "The structure of technical efficiency", *Scandinavian Journal of Economics*, 85, 181-190.

Fare, R, Grosskopf, S and Njinkeu, D (1988) "On piecewise reference technologies", *Management Science*, 34, 1507-1511.

Fare, R and Hunsaker, W (1986) "Notions of efficiency and their reference sets", *Management Science*, 32, 237-243.

Fare, R and Lovell, C (1981) "Measuring the technical efficiency of production: Reply", *Journal of Economic Theory*, 453-454.

Fare, R and Lovell, C (1978) "Measuring the technical efficiency of production", *Journal of Economic Theory*, 19, 150-162.

Fare, R, Lovell, C and Zieschang, K (1983) "Measuring the technical efficiency of multiple output production technologies", in *Quantitative studies on production and prices*. Edited by Eichhorn, W, Henn, R, Neumann, K and Shepherd, R. Vienna: Physica-Verlag.

Farrell, M (1957) "The measurement of productive efficiency", *Journal of the Royal Statistical Society*, Series A (General), 120, 253-281.

Farrell, M and Fieldhouse, M (1962) "Estimating efficient production functions under increasing returns to scale", *Journal of the Royal Statistical Society*, Series A (General), 2, 252-267.

Ferrier, G and Lovell, C (1990) "Measuring cost efficiency in banking: Econometric and linear programming evidence", *Journal of Econometrics*, 46, 229-245.

Field, K (1990) "Production efficiency of British building societies", *Applied Economics*, 22, 415-426.

Fisk, D (1984) "Public sector productivity and relative efficiency: The state of the art in the United States", in Haveman, R (ed.) (1984) *Public finance and the quest for efficiency*. Proceedings of the 38th Congress of the International Institute of Public Finance. Detroit: Wayne State University Press.

Ford, R and Poret, P (1991) "Infrastructure and private-sector productivity", *OECD Department of Economics and Statistics, Working Paper*, no. 91.

Forsund, F and Hjalmarsson, L (1979) "Generalised Farrell measures of efficiency: An application to milk processing in Swedish dairy plants", *Economic Journal*, 89, 294-315.

Forsund, F and Jansen, E (1977) "On estimating average and best practice homothetic production functions via cost function", *International Economic Review*, 18, 463-476.

Forsund, F, Lovell, C and Schmidt, P (1980) "A survey of frontier production functions and of their relationship to efficiency measurement", *Journal of Econometrics*, 13, 5-25.

Foucault, M (1977) *Discipline and punish: The birth of the prison* (trans.). New York: Pantheon.

Frain, J (1990) "Efficiency in commercial banking", *Central Bank of Ireland, Research Department, Technical Paper*, no. 4/RT/90.

Frantz, R (1988) *X-efficiency: Theory, Evidence and Applications.* Norwell, MA: Kluwer Academic Press.

Frisch, R, in collaboration with **Nataf, A** (1966) *Maxima and minima: Theory and economic applications.* Dordrecht, Holland: Reidel Publishing.

Gadrey, J (1988) "Rethinking output in services", *Service Industries Journal*, 8, 67-76.

Ganley, J (1989) "Relative efficiency measurement in the public sector with Data Envelopment Analysis", Ph.D. thesis, *University of London, Queen Mary College*.

Ganley, J and Cubbin, J (1987) "Performance indicators for prisons", *Public Money*, 7, 57-59.

Ganley, J and Grahl, J (1988) "Competition and efficiency in refuse collection: A critical comment", *Fiscal Studies*, 9, 80-85.

Garland, D (1985) *Punishment and welfare. A history of penal strategies.* Aldershot: Gower Publishers.

Goetz, S and Debertin, D (1991) "A caution about measuring school outputs in educational production functions", *Atlantic Economic Journal*, 19, 62.

Golany, B, (1988) "An interactive MOLP procedure for the extension of DEA to effectiveness analysis", *Journal of the Operational Research Society*, 39, 725-734.

Golany, B, (1988a) "A note on including ordinal relations among multipliers in Data Envelopment Analysis", *Management Science*, 34, 1029-1033.

Golany, B and Roll, Y (1989) "An application procedure for DEA", *Omega: The International Journal of Management Science*, 17, 237-250.

Grabowski, R, Kraft, S, Pasurka, C and Aly, H (1990) "A ray-homothetic production frontier and efficiency: grain farms in Southern Illinois", *European Review of Agricultural Economics*, 17, 435-448.

Gray, J and Jesson, D (1987) "Exam results and local authority league tables", in *Education and training UK 1987*. Edited by Harrison, A and Gretton, J. Newbury: Policy Journals.

Greenberg, R and Nunamaker, T (1987) "A generalized multiple criteria model for control and evaluation of nonprofit organizations", *Financial Accountability and Management*, 3, 331-342.

Gregory, R and James, D (1973) "Do new factories embody best practice technology?", *Economic Journal*, 83, 1133-1155.

Grosskopf, S (1986) "The role of the reference technology in measuring productive efficiency", *Economic Journal*, 96, 499-513.

Grosskopf, S and Valdmanis, V (1987) "Measuring hospital performance. A non-parametric approach", *Journal of Health Economics*, 6, 89-107.

Haag, S, Jaska, P and Semple, J (1992) "Assessing the relative efficiency of agricultural production units in the Blackland Prairie, Texas", *Applied Economics*, 24, 559-565.

Hahn, F (1973) *On the notion of equilibrium in economics: An inaugural lecture*. Cambridge: Cambridge University Press.

Hall, M and Winsten, C (1957) "The ambiguous notion of efficiency", *Economic Journal*, 69, 71-86.

Hammond, C (1986) "Estimating the statistical cost curve: An application of the stochastic frontier technique", *Applied Economics*, 18, 971-984.

Hammond, P (1987) "Review of *Production, income and welfare* by Jan Tinbergen", *Journal of Economic Literature*, 25, 1316-1317.

Hammond, P (1981) "Ex ante and ex post welfare optimality under uncertainty", *Economica*, 48, 235-250.

Hanoch, G and Rothschild, M (1972) "Testing the assumptions of production theory: A nonparametric approach", *Journal of Political Economy*, 80, 256-275.

Hanusch, H (1982) "Determinants of public productivity" in Haveman, R (ed.) (1982) *Public finance and public employment*. Proceedings of the 36th Congress of the International Institute of Public Finance. Detroit: Wayne State University Press.

Hanushek, E (1986) "The economics of schooling: Production and efficiency in public schools", *Journal of Econometrics*, 19, 319-331.

Haveman, R (ed.) (1984) *Public finance and the quest for efficiency*. Proceedings of the 38th Congress of the International Institute of Public Finance. Detroit: Wayne State University Press.

Haveman, R (ed.) (1982) *Public finance and public employment*. Proceedings of the 36th Congress of the International Institute of Public Finance. Detroit: Wayne State University Press.

Hjerppe, R (1982) "Measurement of the role of the public sector in the Finnish economy", *Review of Income and Wealth*, 28, 449-456.

Hjerppe, R (1980) "The measurement of real output of public sector services", *Review of Income and Wealth*, 26, 237-250.

Hjorth-Andersen, C (1991) "Quality indicators: In theory and fact", *European Economic Review*, 35, 1491-1505.

Hollas, D, and Stansell, S (1988) "Regulation, interfirm rivalry and the economic efficiency of natural gas distribution facilities", *Quarterly Review of Economics and Business*, 28, 21-37.

Huang, C and Bagi, F (1984) "Technical efficiency on individual farms in northwest India", *Southern Economic Journal*, 51, 108-115.

Hughes, M (1988) "A stochastic frontier cost function for residential child care provision", *Journal of Applied Econometrics*, 3, 203-214.

Hyman, H (1942) "The psychology of status", *Archives of Psychology*, no. 269.

Jackson, P (1987) "Performance measurement and value for money in the public sector: The issues", in *Research in action—performance measurement*. Edited by Cook, P. London: CIPFA.

Jarrat, Sir Alex (1985) *Report of the Steering Committee for efficiency studies in universities*. London: Committee of Vice-Chancellors and Principals.

Jesson, D and Mayston, D (1989) "Measuring performance in local authorities and schools", in *Education and training UK 1989*. Edited by Harrison, A and Gretton, J. Newbury: Policy Journals.

Johnson, R and Lewin, A (1984) "Management and accountability models of public sector performance", in *Public sector performance: A conceptual turning point*. Edited by Miller, T. London: John Hopkins Press.

Johnston, J (1960) *Statistical cost analysis*. New York: McGraw-Hill.

Jondrow, J, Lovell, C, Materov, I and Schmidt, P (1982) "On the estimation of technical inefficiency in the stochastic frontier production function model", *Journal of Econometrics*, 19, 233-238.

Kendrick, J (1987) "Service sector productivity", *Business Economics*, 22, 18-24.

Kenny, L (1982) "Economies of scale in schooling", *Economics of Education Review*, 2, 1-24.

Kleinsorge, I and Karney, D (1992) "Management of nursing homes using Data Envelopment Analysis", *Socio-economic Planning Sciences*, 26, 57-71.

Koopmans, T (ed.) (1951) *Activity analysis of production and allocation*. New York: John Wiley.

Kopp, R (1981) "The measurement of productive efficiency: A reconsideration", *Quarterly Journal of Economics*, 96, 477-503.

Kopp, R and Diewert, E (1982) "The decomposition of frontier cost function deviations into measures of technical and allocative efficiency", *Journal of Econometrics*, 19, 319-331.

Koutsoyiannis, A (1979) *Modern microeconomics*. Second edition. London: Macmillan.

Kumbhakar, S (1988) "Estimation of input-specific technical and allocative inefficiency in stochastic frontier models", *Oxford Economic Papers*, 40, 535-549.

Lee, L and Tyler, W (1978) "The stochastic frontier production function and average efficiency: An empirical analysis", *Journal of Econometrics*, 7, 385-390.

Leibenstein, H (1987) *Inside the firm: The inefficiencies of hierarchy*. London: Harvard University Press.

Leibenstein, H (1980) *Beyond economic man. A new foundation for microeconomics*. London: Harvard University Press.

Leibenstein, H (1979) "X-efficiency: From concept to theory", *Challenge*, 22, 13-22.

Leibenstein, H (1978) "On the basic proposition of X-efficiency theory", *American Economic Review*, 68, 328-332.

Leibenstein, H (1975) "Aspects of the X-efficiency theory of the firm", *Bell Journal of Economics*, 6, 580-606.

Leibenstein, H (1969) "Organisational or frictional equilibria, X-efficiency and the rate of innovation", *Quarterly Journal of Economics*, 83, 600-623.

Leibenstein, H (1966) "Allocative vs. "X-efficiency", *American Economic Review*, 56, 392-415.

Leibenstein, H and Maital, S (1992) "Empirical estimates and partitioning of X-inefficiency: A Data-Envelopment approach", *American Economic Review (Papers and Proceedings)*, 82, 428-433.

Levitt, M and Joyce, M (1987) *The growth and efficiency of public spending.* Cambridge: Cambridge University Press.

Levitt, M and Joyce, M (1986) "Government output in the National Accounts", *National Institute Economic Review*, no. 115, 48-51.

Lewin, A and Morey, R (1981) "Measuring the relative efficiency and output potential of public sector organisations: An application of Data Envelopment Analysis", *International Journal of Policy Analysis and Information Systems*, 5, 267-285.

Lewin, A, Morey, R and Cook, T (1982) "Evaluating the administrative efficiency of courts", *Omega: The International Journal of Management Science*, 10, 401-411.

Lewis, D (1987) "The economics of crime: A survey", *Economic Analysis and Policy*, 17, 195-220.

Lewis, S (ed.) (1986) "Output and performance measurement in central government: Progress in Departments", *H.M. Treasury, Working Paper*, no. 38.

Lovell, C and Schmidt, P (1988) "A comparison of alternative approaches to measurement of productive efficiency", in *Applications of modern productivity theory: Efficiency and productivity.* Edited by Dogramaci, A and Fare, R. Boston: Kluwer Academic Publishers.

Lovell, C and Wood, L (1992) "Monitoring the performance of Soviet cotton-refining enterprises: Sensitivity of findings to estimation techniques", *Atlantic Economic Journal*, 20, 25-31.

Lubulwa, A and Oczkowski, E (1987) "Technical efficiency: An interstate comparison of railways in Australia", *Australian Transport Research Forum*, 1, 173-198.

McAleer, M and Veall, M (1987) "How fragile are fragile inferences? A re-evaluation of the deterrent effect of capital punishment", *Australian National University, Department of Economics, Working Paper*, no. 152.

McGuire, A (1987) "The measurement of hospital efficiency", *Social Science and Medicine*, 24, 719-724.

MacRae, D (1985) *Policy Indicators.* North Carolina: University of North Carolina Press.

Maindiratta, A (1990) "Largest size-efficient scale and size efficiencies of decision-making units in Data Envelopment Analysis", *Journal of Econometrics*, 46, 57-72.

Maltz, M (1984) *Recidivism*. Orlando, Florida: Academic Press.

March, J and Simon, H (1963) *Organisations*. New York: John Wiley.

Margolis, J (1971) "Shadow prices for incorrect or nonexistent market values", in *Public expenditures and policy analysis*. Edited by Haveman, R, and Margolis, J. New York: Markham Publishing Company.

Marris, R (1985) "The paradox of services", *Political Quarterly*, November, 242-252.

Marshall, A (1920) *Principles of economics*. 8th edition. London: MacMillan.

Matthews, R (1981) "Morality, competition and efficiency", *Manchester School of Economics and Social Studies*, 49, 289-309.

Meeusen, W and Broek, J (1977) "Efficiency estimation from Cobb-Douglas production functions with composed error", *International Economic Review*, 18, 435-444.

Mefford, R (1991) "Quality and productivity: The linkage", *International Journal of Production Economics*, 24, 137-145.

Mellander, E and Ysander, B (1987) "What can input tell about output?", *Uppsala University, Department of Economics, Discussion Paper*, no. 1987:3.

Mersha, T (1989) "Output and performance measurement in out-patient care", *Omega: The International Journal of Management Science*, 17, 159-167.

Merton, R (1957) "The role-set: Problems in sociological theory", *British Journal of Sociology*, 8, 74-89.

Miller, S (1987) "The value for money audit", *Management Accounting*, April, 37.

Morey, R, Fine, D and Loree, S (1990) "Comparing the allocative efficiencies of hospitals", *Omega: The International Journal of Management Science*, 18, 71-83.

Morgan, R (1992) "Prisons: Managing for change", *Public Money and Management*, 12, 17-22.

Morgan, R and King, R (1987) "Profiting from prison", *New Society*, 23 October, 21-22.

Mortimore, P and team (1985) "The ILEA junior school study: An introduction", Chapter 8 in *Studying school effectiveness*. Edited by Reynolds, D. Lewes: The Falmer Press.

National Audit Office (1986) *Financial reporting to Parliament*. London: HMSO.

Nelson, R (1981) "Research on productivity growth and productivity differences: Dead ends and new departures", *Journal of Economic Literature*, 19, 1029-1064.

Nunamaker, T (1985) "Using Data Envelopment Analysis to measure the efficiency of non-profit organisations: A critical evaluation", *Managerial and Decision Economics*, 6, 50-58.

Packer, M (1983) "Measuring the intangible in productivity", *Technology Review*, 48-57.

Parkan, C (1987) "Measuring the efficiency of service operations: An application to bank branches", *Engineering Costs and Production Economics*, 12, 237-242.

Perl, L (1973) "Family background, secondary school expenditure and student ability", *Journal of Human Resources*, 8, 156-180.

Perman, R (1991) "Cointegration: An introduction to the literature", *Journal of Economic Studies*, 18, 3-30.

Perrakis, S (1980) "Factor-price uncertainty with variable proportions: Note", *American Economic Review*, 70, 1038-1088.

Peston, M (1980) "Accountability in education: Some economic aspects", *Education Policy Bulletin*, 8, 115-126.

Petersen, N (1990) "Data Envelopment Analysis on a relaxed set of assumptions", *Management Science*, 36, 305-314.

Phillips, D, Ravindran, A and Solberg, J (1976) *Operations research: Principles and practice*. New York: Wiley.

Pickering, J (1983) "Efficiency in a departmental store group", *Omega: The International Journal of Management Science*, 11, 231-237.

Pliatzky, L (1986) "Can government be efficient?", *Lloyds Bank Review*, no. 159, 22-32.

Popper, K (1976) *Unended quest: An intellectual autobiography*. London: Fontana.

Prison Department and PA Management Consultants (1986) *Study of prison officers' complementing and shift systems*, vols 1 (Report) and 2 (Appendices). London: Home Office Prison Department.

Pyle, D (1983) *The Economics of Crime and Law Enforcement*. London: MacMillan.

Rangan, N, Grabowski, R, Aly, H and Pasurka, C (1988) "The technical efficiency of US banks", *Economic Letters*, 28, 169-176.

Rawlins, G (1985) "Measuring the impact of IRDP II upon the technical efficiency level of Jaimacan peasant farmers", *Social and Economic Studies*, 34, 71-96.

Ray, S (1988) "Data Envelopment Analysis, nondiscretionary inputs and efficiency: An alternative interpretation", *Socio-economic Planning Sciences*, 22, 167-176.

Rees, R (1985) "The theory of principal and agent", Part One and Part Two, *Bulletin of Economic Research*, 37, nos. 1 and 2.

Reifschneider, D and Stevenson, R (1991) "Systematic departures from the frontier: A framework for the analysis of firm inefficiency", *International Economic Review*, 32, 715-724.

Richardson, P and Gordon, J (1980) "Measuring total manufacturing performance", *Sloan Management Review*, winter, 47-48.

Richmond, J (1974) "Estimating the efficiency of production", *International Economic Review*, 15, 515-521.

Roll, Y, Golany, B and Seroussy, D (1989), "Measuring the efficiency of maintenance units in the Israeli Air Force", *European Journal of Operational Research*, 43, 136-142.

Ruchlin, H (1977) "Problems in measuring institutional productivity", *Topics in Health Care Financing*, 4, 13-27.

Russell, R (1989) "Continuity measures of technical efficiency", *University of California, Riverside, Graduate School of Management, Working Paper in Economics*, no. 90-6.

Saraydar, E (1991) "Productivity and X-efficiency: A reply to Singh and Frantz", *Economics and Philosophy*, 7, 91-92.

Saraydar, E (1989) "The conflation of productivity and efficiency in economics and economic history", *Economics and Philosophy*, 7, 55-67.

Schmidt, P (1986) "Frontier production functions", *Econometric Reviews*, 4, 289-328.

Schmidt, P and Lin, Tsai-Fen (1984) "Simple tests of alternative specifications in stochastic frontier models", *Journal of Econometrics*, 24, 349-361.

Schmidt, P and Lovell, C (1979) "Estimating technical and allocative inefficiency relative to stochastic production and cost frontiers", *Journal of Econometrics*, 9, 343-366.

Schmidt, P and Witte, A (1988) *Predicting recidivism using survival models.* New York: Springer-Verlag.

Schroeder, R, Anderson, J and Scudder, G (1986) "White collar productivity measurement", *Management Decision*, 24, 3-7.

Schuller, T (1989) "Performance indicators and their ambiguities", *Higher Education Quarterly*, 43, 192-194.

Seiford, L and Thrall, R (1990) "Recent developments in DEA: The mathematical approach to frontier analysis", *Journal of Econometrics*, 46, 7-38.

Seitz, W (1971) "Productive efficiency in the steam-electric generating industry", *Journal of Political Economy*, 79, 876-886.

Seitz, W (1970) "The measurement of efficiency relative to a frontier production function", *American Journal of Agricultural Economics*, 52, 505-511.

Sen, A (1975a) "The concept of efficiency" in Parkin, M and Nobay, A (eds.) *Contemporary issues in economics*, proceedings of the AUTE Conference, Warwick, 1973. Manchester: Manchester University Press.

Sen, A (1975b) *Employment, technology and development*. Oxford: Basil Blackwell.

Sen, A (1973) *On economic inequality*. Oxford: Clarendon Press.

Sengupta, J (1992) "Non-parametric approach to dynamic efficiency: A non-parametric application of cointegration to production frontiers", *Applied Economics*, 24, 153-159.

Sengupta, J (1990a) "Transformations in stochastic DEA models", *Journal of Econometrics*, 46, 109-124.

Sengupta, J (1990b) "Testing Farrell efficiency by stochastic dominance", *Economic Notes*, 3, 429-440.

Sengupta, J (1988) "A robust approach to the measurement of Farrell efficiency", *Applied Economics*, 20, 273-283.

Sengupta, J (1987a) "Efficiency measurement in non-market systems through Data Envelopment Analysis", *International Journal of Systems Science*, 18, 2279-2304.

Sengupta, J (1987b) "Production frontier estimation to measure efficiency: A critical evaluation in light of Data Envelopment Analysis", *Managerial and Decision Economics*, 8, 93-99.

Sengupta, J (1987c) "Data Envelopment Analysis for efficiency measurement in the stochastic case", *Computers and Operations Research*, 13, 117-129.

Sengupta, J (1982) "Efficiency measurement in stochastic input output systems", *International Journal of Systems Science*, 13, 273-287.

Sengupta, J and Sfeir, R (1988) "Efficiency measurement by Data Envelopment Analysis with econometric applications", *Applied Economics*, 20, 285-293.

Sengupta, J and Sfeir, R (1986) "Production frontier estimates of scale in public schools in California", *Economics of Education Review*, 5, 297-307.

Sexton, T, Silkman, R and Hogan, A (1986) "Data Envelopment Analysis: Critique and extensions" in Silkman, R (ed.) (1986) *Measuring efficiency: An assessment of Data Envelopment Analysis*. New directions for program evaluation, no. 32. London: Jossey-Bass Publishers.

Shaw, S (1984) "Why prisons have become a growth industry", *Public Money*, 4, 37-40.

Shephard, R (1974) *Indirect production functions*. Mathematical systems in economics, no. 10. Meisenheim Am Glad: Verlag Anton Hain.

Shephard, R (1970) *Theory of cost and production functions*. Princeton: Princeton University Press.

Shephard, R (1953) *Cost and production functions*. Princeton: Princeton University Press.

Sherman, H (1984a) "Data Envelopment Analysis as a new managerial audit methodology—Test and valuation", *Auditing: A Journal of Practice and Theory*, 4, 35-53.

Sherman, H (1984b) "Hospital efficiency measurement and evaluation. Empirical test of a new technique", *Medical Care*, 22, 922-938.

Sherman, H and Gold, F (1985) "Bank branch operating efficiency: Evaluation with Data Envelopment Analysis", *Journal of Banking and Finance*, 9, 297-315.

Silkman, R (ed.) (1986) *Measuring efficiency: An assessment of Data Envelopment Analysis*. New directions for program evaluation, no. 32. London: Jossey-Bass Publishers.

Singh, H and Frantz, R (1991) "The conflation of productivity and efficiency in economics and economic history", *Economics and Philosophy*, 7, 87-89.

Smith, P (1990) "Data Envelopment Analysis applied to financial statements", *Omega: The International Journal of Management Science*, 18, 131-138.

Smith, P (1988) "Assessing competition among local authorities in England and Wales", *Financial Accountability and Management*, 4, 235-251.

Smith, P and Mayston, D (1987) "Measuring efficiency in the public sector", *Omega: The International Journal of Management Science*, 15, 181-189.

Smith, V, Palmquist, R and Jakus, P (1991) "Combining Farrell frontier and hedonic travel cost models for valuing estuarine quality", *Review of Economics and Statistics*, 73, 694-699.

Sobel, J (1992) "How to count to one thousand", *Economic Journal*, 102, 1-8.

Stern, V (1987) "Our political prisons", *New Society*, 24 April, 11-13.

Stevenson, R (1983) "X-efficiency and interfirm rivalry: Evidence from the electric utility industry", *Land Economics*, 58, 52-66.

Stewart, M (1978) "Factor-price uncertainty with variable proportions", *American Economic Review*, 68, 468-473.

Talley, W (1988) "Optimum throughput and performance evaluation of marine terminals", *Maritime Policy and Management*, 15, 327-331.

Thanassoulis, E, Dyson, R and Foster, M (1987) "Relative efficiency assessments using Data Envelopment Analysis: An application to data on rates departments", *Journal of the Operational Research Society*, 38, 397-412.

Thomas, D, Greffe, R and Grant, K (1988) "Application of Data Envelopment Analysis to management audits of electric distribution utilities", mimeo, *Public Utility Commission of Texas, Austin, Texas*.

Thompson, R, Langemeier, L, Lee, C, Lee, E and Thrall, R (1990) "The role of multiplier bounds in efficiency analysis with application to Kansas farming", *Journal of Econometrics*, 46, 93-108.

Thor, C (1991) "A guide to organisational productivity and quality improvement", *Business Economics*, October, 32-39.

Thrall, R (1985) "A taxonomy for decision models", *Annals of Operations Research*, 2, 23-27.

Timmer, C (1971) "Using a probabilistic frontier production function to measure technical efficiency", *Journal of Political Economy*, 79, 776-794.

Tinbergen, J (1985) *Production, income and welfare: The search for an optimal social order*. Brighton: Harvester Press.

Todd, D (1985) "Productive performance in West German manufacturing industry 1970-1980: A Farrell frontier characterisation", *Journal of Industrial Economics*, 33, 295-316.

Tomkins, C and Green, R (1988) "An experiment in the use of Data Envelopment Analysis for evaluating the efficiency of UK university departments of accounting", *Financial Accountability and Management*, 4, 147-164.

Tulkens, H (1990) "Non-parametric efficiency analyses in four service activites: Retail banking, municipalities, courts and urban transit", *Universite Catholique de Louvain, CORE Discussion Paper*, no. 9050.

Tyler, W and Lee, L (1979) "On estimating stochastic frontier production functions and average efficiency: An empirical analysis with Columbian micro data", *Review of Economics and Statistics*, 61, 436-438.

Varian, H (1990) "Goodness-of-fit in optimizing models", *Journal of Econometrics*, 46, 125-140.

Varian, H (1985) "Non-parametric analysis of optimizing behavior with measurement error", *Journal of Econometrics*, 30, 445-458.

Varian, H (1984) "The non-parametric approach to production analysis", *Econometrica*, 52, 579-597.

Varian, H (1978) *Microeconomic analysis*. London: Norton and Co.

Vassiloglou, M and Giokas, D (1990) "A study of the relative efficiency of bank branches: An application of Data Envelopment Analysis", *Journal of the Operational Research Society*, 41, 591-597.

Wilson, J and Hernstein, R (1985) *Crime and human nature*. New York: Simon and Schuster.

Zeleny, M (1974) *Linear multiobjective programming*. Vienna: Springer-Verlag.

Zieschang, K (1984) "An extended Farrell technical efficiency measure", *Journal of Economic Theory*, 33, 387-396.